LOVE
BUSTERS

John A Kaiser

LOVE BUSTERS

Overcoming Habits
That Destroy Romantic Love

REVISED EDITION

WILLARD F. HARLEY, JR.

Fleming H. Revell
A Division of Baker Book House Co
Grand Rapids, Michigan 49516

Copyright © 1992, 1997, 2002 by Willard F. Harley, Jr.
Published by Fleming H. Revell
a division of Baker Publishing Group
P.O. Box 6287, Grand Rapids, MI 49516-6287

Sixth printing, April 2006

Printed in the United States of America

Some of the material in this book and its basic principles previously appeared in *Marriage Insurance* and *Give and Take* by Willard F. Harley, Jr.

Library of Congress Cataloging-in-Publication Data
Harley, Willard F.
    Love busters : overcoming the habits that destroy romantic love / Willard F. Harley Jr.—rev. ed.
       p.   cm.
    ISBN 10: 0-8007-1807-0
    ISBN 978-0-8007-1807-7
    1. Marriage. 2. Communication in marriage. 3. Man-woman relationships. I. Title.
HQ734.H284   2002
646.7p8—dc21   2001048933

ISBN 0-8007-5890-0 (intl. pbk.)

CONTENTS

INTRODUCTION

Has a friend ever asked for your advice about his (or her) marriage? Where do you begin? How would you help him so that his marriage could be fulfilling instead of disappointing?

In describing the problem, your friend would probably tell you what his wife was **doing** that made him so unhappy. And then he would tell you what his wife was **not doing** that caused him to feel particularly unfulfilled in his marriage.

But if you talked to your friend long enough, you would probably discover that his problems go beyond what his wife was or was not doing. You would discover what I have discovered in the majority of couples I've counseled—your friend has fallen out of love with his wife. Whatever feeling of love he once felt for her is now gone.

How would you help your friend?

When it comes to solving marital problems sometimes it's easier to see the solution when it turns out to be somebody else's problem. In your friend's case it might be clear to you that if his wife would stop doing the things that upset him and start doing things that would make him feel more fulfilled, his feeling of love for her might return. So you might begin by going to his wife with his complaints, and by trying to encourage her to make a few changes in her behavior.

But if his wife were like most of the wives (and husbands) I've counseled, you wouldn't get very far in describing those complaints. Assuming that she would even hear you out, after you had uttered your last word you'd be hearing her litany of complaints about your friend—how he's been doing all sorts of outrageous things to upset her and how he's failed miserably in making her feel fulfilled in their marriage. And if she were honest with you about her deepest feelings, you might also discover that she doesn't feel any more love for him than he does for her.

It wouldn't take long for you to discover that each of them understood the other person's problems, but not their own. And you would also discover that they did not understand how their mistakes contributed to their loss of love for each other.

Just about everything you and your spouse do affects the feeling of love you have for each other.

When a couple first comes to my office, I do not talk to them together. That's because they are likely to spend the first session criticizing each other the whole time. If I would let them talk to me together, they would leave my office in worse shape than when they arrived. Instead, I talk to them one at a time to gain insight into how they affect each other—how they make each other miserable and how they have failed to make each other happy. I also try to estimate how much love they have lost for each other.

During their very first counseling session, I make a very important point. It's a point I want you to fully understand: Just about everything that you and your spouse do affects the feeling of love you have for each other. What you do either builds your love for each other, or it destroys that love.

How spouses affect each other has a tremendous bearing on the success and failure of marriage. If your friend's wife would simply stop doing the things that upset him and start doing the things that make him feel terrific, your friend's complaining would be over, and something else would happen, too. Your friend would once again be in love.

Of course, your friend would also have to make some changes. He would need to take his wife's complaints to heart and accommodate her feelings. Then she would be in love with him, too. But whatever it would take to restore their love would be worth doing because it would create something that they both want very badly—a fulfilling marriage.

A Fulfilling Marriage Requires Passion

Marriage is like an aircraft with exceptional performance—when it flies fast. But when it flies slowly, it cannot stay aloft—it stalls and crashes. When a husband and wife are in love with each other, they are happier, healthier, wiser, and more productive than ever. But when love fades, they lose everything that made them better people. What once seemed almost effortless becomes awkward and very difficult. Instincts that work *for* a couple who are in love work **against** them when they lose their love for each other. And in most cases, the relationship eventually becomes so bad that couples try to escape each other through divorce or permanent separation.

Take my word for it because it's based on years of experience: If you want a marriage that satisfies both you and your spouse, you must have a passionate marriage. (I will be using the phrase, *feeling of love,* and the word, *passion,* interchangeably.)

That's because a mediocre marriage lacking passion will not remain mediocre very long. Once you lose the feeling of love in your marriage, it's a slippery slope all the way down to disliking, or even hating, each other. Instead of bringing out the best in each other, you will find yourselves bringing out the worst.

When a man and woman get married, they think their feelings of love will last a lifetime. The vows and commitments they make depend on that assumption.

But their passion for each other is usually short-lived. Some couples sustain it for just a few months or years after the wedding. For others, it's only days. And when passion goes, the commitments of marriage usually go with it.

Some marriage counselors advise couples to accept the inevitable: Enjoy it while it lasts but don't expect it to continue forever. Some recommend rising to a higher form of passionless love, while others suggest divorce.

But I believe that couples don't have to accept the loss of love as inevitable. Instead, they can *restore* the love they once had for each other. And once it's back, all thoughts of divorce or passionless love vanish.

> **When a husband and wife are in love with each other, they are happier, healthier, wiser, and more productive than ever.**

Impossible, you may say. And it may certainly seem that way. When you're in love, it seems impossible that you will ever lose that feeling; and when you're "out of love," it seems impossible to get it back. Most couples I counsel don't believe they will ever feel that love for each other again. But my methods for restoring passion do not require faith—they require action! When a couple follows my instructions, their love usually returns, ending the threat of divorce.

This book and its companion, *His Needs, Her Needs,* work together in helping couples build and sustain the feeling of love. While *His Needs, Her Needs* will help you *build* love by teaching you how to meet each other's most important emotional needs, *Love Busters* will help you avoid *losing* love.

During courtship, a man and woman create the feeling of love for each other by meeting each other's most important emotional needs. But after they get married, they usually develop habits that destroy their love for each other. I call those destructive habits Love Busters. And as long as Love Busters are tolerated, love doesn't have a chance.

> **Place great value on the passion you share for each other.**

The lessons of this book will teach you how to throw those rascals out. I'll identify the six most common Love Busters and explain how couples have learned to overcome them. Once they're gone, romantic love has free rein in marriage.

The assignments suggested in this book require the use of questionnaires, inventories, worksheets, and other forms. But due to space and size limitations, I've had many requests to print them in a larger and more convenient form. In response to these requests, they're now available in *Five Steps to Romantic Love: A Workbook for Readers of* Love Busters *and* His Needs, Her Needs. I recommend it to you as a supplement to this book.

I encourage you and your spouse to place great value on the passion you share for each other. The strength of your marriage depends on it. If you have lost it, don't despair. It can be restored to your marriage if you follow my advice. And once it is restored, you'll agree that it is too valuable to ever lose again.

part one

SETTING THE STAGE

chapter one

HOW LOVE BUSTERS CAN WRECK A MARRIAGE

Karen couldn't even remember what it was like being in love with Jim. Whenever he was home, her stomach knotted up and she often felt sick. When they talked, which wasn't very often, she was usually defensive. Vacationing together was unthinkable—if she wanted to relax, he had to be far away. Could she survive this marriage long enough for her children to grow up? It was looking increasingly hopeless to her.

When I talked with Karen for the first time, she wanted a separation from Jim, one that would help her survive a few more years of their marriage. Their youngest daughter, Lisa, was thirteen. For Lisa's sake, Karen wanted to wait five or six years before divorcing Jim.

You may not be feeling as desperate as Karen felt that day but perhaps you know what she was going through—the fighting, the sarcasm, the disrespect, and . . . the loneliness. But marriage is supposed to be different, isn't it? It should be a caring relationship, where a husband and wife treat each other with kindness and consideration, not with rudeness and anger.

Karen had expected her marriage to be that way—caring and thoughtful. And while she was dating Jim, she had no reason to expect anything else. He talked to her almost every day, focusing his attention on what he could do to help her, and he eagerly helped her whenever she had a problem; he changed his plans whenever they conflicted with hers; and he was rarely argumentative, usually willing to see things from her perspective. Again and again Jim proved to Karen that caring for her was his highest priority—and that made her feel very secure.

Jim had never known a woman as attractive to him as Karen, and—miracle of miracles—she *liked* him! She was not only beautiful, but she also showered him with affection and admiration. This was the woman he wanted for life; she seemed perfect in every way. Within a year they were married.

Jim's Neglect

It wasn't long after the wedding that Jim felt the financial pressure of becoming a family man. Karen was pregnant and wanted to work fewer hours after their child arrived. Jim figured his income had to increase to make up the difference, so he decided to work longer hours.

With more of his time and energy spent at work, Jim's ability to meet Karen's emotional needs eroded. During her pregnancy, when she needed his emotional support more than ever, he now expected her to work things out on her own. Instead of factoring her needs into his plans, he seemed to cut her adrift. At least that's how Karen felt about the way he neglected her.

But from Jim's perspective, his thoughtlessness made sense. *After all,* he thought, *we're both intelligent adults. She can take the car to the garage just as easily as I can. Why should she expect me to drop everything at work to do something she can do for herself? Am I her slave? Is she a princess?*

At first, Karen was deeply troubled by his change of attitude, though she tried not to show it. She made a valiant effort to accommodate his new approach to their relationship, troubleshooting around the home, rearranging her schedule to fit his, but when she was alone, she cried. *Why had he changed so much? Is it because I'm pregnant? Does he find me unattractive?*

14

By the time little Andrea arrived, Karen's conviction that Jim cared for her had been seriously damaged. He had not only failed to support her during pregnancy, but he made matters worse by having little to do with Andrea after her birth. He was so focused on becoming a success at work that he had become a failure at home. Karen felt utterly abandoned. *Maybe,* she thought, *he no longer loves me.*

As the chemistry of their relationship deteriorated, her care for him deteriorated with it. In response to Jim's neglect of her, Karen began to neglect him. She no longer asked him how his day went. She did not show him much affection or admiration anymore. And she wasn't very enthusiastic about making love either.

Karen's Loss of Sexual Interest

Jim didn't pay much attention to the fact that Karen had stopped being affectionate or that she wasn't as admiring. But he sure noticed her loss of sexual interest. When they were first married, she had looked forward to making love to Jim, but now it was something she tried to avoid. Whenever they made love, she felt used.

One day Jim got up the courage to ask her what was going on. "Karen, what's happening to you? Why aren't you interested in making love anymore?"

"I'm sorry, Jim," she replied. "I just haven't been in the mood lately. I don't know why."

There were a host of common excuses that she could have used. After a child's birth the mother is usually exhausted much of the time, and sex requires energy. She could have used that as an excuse. Or, she could have focused attention on the fact that Andrea took away their privacy. But deep down, she knew that her loss of sexual interest had something to do with her feeling of being neglected by Jim. But she didn't think there would be any point in discussing it. He was excited about his career, they needed his financial support, and he kept telling her that he was giving her as much of his time as he could afford. What was there to discuss? Why even mention his neglect?

"What do you think it would take to get you in the mood?" It was difficult for Jim to raise the subject. He felt like he was begging.

But Karen wasn't making it easy for him, either. "I don't know," she answered. "I've never given it much thought."

The truth was that Jim had stopped doing the things that made Karen fall in love with him. He was not as supportive, not as accommodating, and worst of all, he spent very little time alone with her. Her emotional needs were not being met anymore. Consequently, she was not as motivated to meet any of his needs. Sex, it turned out, was something she felt like doing only when she knew that Jim loved and cared for her. Now she was feeling emotionally neglected, so what had formerly been effortless became very difficult.

While Jim and Karen were dating, they often expressed their feeling of love for each other. That's because those feelings were so strong, they could hardly avoid mentioning it. But when Karen's passion for Jim began to erode, she did not warn him. In fact, she kept telling him she loved him, when deep down she knew her feelings were changing. Her married friends told her that loss of passion in marriage was something she had to expect. After all, they said, passion was for newlyweds, not for couples who become parents. So Karen focused her attention away from Jim and toward Andrea. Her daughter became her highest priority in life.

From the beginning of their marriage, Jim and Karen had rarely discussed problems with their relationship. When one offended the other, it was usually shrugged off. But now they had a problem they could not shrug off so easily—or at least Jim could not shrug off. He didn't want to go through life with a sexually reluctant wife and he didn't know how to fix the problem.

If Jim had understood what was bothering Karen, he could have solved their problem rather easily. He had simply failed to meet her emotional needs and that had taken its toll on his sexual attractiveness. His career had become his highest priority instead of Karen. If he had gone back to doing what had drawn her to him in the beginning, cheerfully helping her whenever she had a problem, accommodating her in his schedule, and now that

Andrea had joined them, taking an active role in the care of their new daughter, *presto,* the sexual problem would be solved! (See chapters 16 and 17 for that solution to Jim's problem.)

But Jim didn't understand how important it was to make Karen his highest priority. And his frustration introduced a new and destructive chapter in their marriage. He had a choice. He could solve his sexual problem with care and understanding or he could try to force the issue. Regretfully, he chose the latter.

The Road to Marital Disaster

One night, after Jim and Karen had gone to bed, he reached over to kiss her goodnight. Thinking he was trying to initiate love making, she pushed him away. Jim's feelings of resentment had been building for some time and her rejection pushed him over the edge. He was furious. Throwing her out of bed, he called her names and lectured her for half an hour about her bad attitude. All his resentment poured out in a moment of unrestrained rage.

Karen huddled in a corner, afraid he would hit her. She didn't dare say a word. Eventually he settled down.

When it was over, Jim felt much better. He had finally said what he had felt for such a long time. But Karen was a basket case. He started to apologize for losing his temper but then stopped himself. *I'm glad I had the courage to say what I felt,* he thought. *Now we're getting somewhere!*

They were getting somewhere all right but not where Jim thought. They were now on the road to marital disaster.

Jim put his arm around Karen, telling her how much he loved her. Still in the corner, she didn't dare push him away now. All she could do was cry. As he became more amorous, she let him do anything he wanted—eventually they made love. Jim felt it was one of their best sexual experiences ever. Karen felt raped.

Many women would have gone straight to an attorney the next day to end the marriage, but Karen believed she had married Jim for life. So after she had time to reflect on the nightmare she had experienced, she made some decisions that she thought would help her survive.

First, she would never be found cowering in a corner again. Next time he lost his temper, she would fight fire with fire—let him know what a creep she thought he had become.

Second, because Jim got what he wanted by forcing his will on her, she would get what she wanted by forcing her will on him. In the past, when she needed something from him and he refused, she would do it herself. Now she would not accept no for an answer. She would *demand* what she wanted.

Third, she would learn to emotionally distance herself from Jim. He did not hit her that fateful night but he hurt her deeply—emotionally. She would remain married to him but never again become so emotionally vulnerable. She had already been doing almost everything without him, but she had remained emotionally bonded to him in the hope that some day they would return to the passion they once had for each other. But now she was convinced that her only hope for survival was to create a life of her own that was completely separate from his, physically and emotionally.

Karen made one huge concession, however. What made him so angry was his unmet need for sex, so anytime he wanted sex, she would oblige him. She felt it was her duty as long as they were married. She would even try to enjoy it but she knew she would never again feel sexually attracted to Jim. So she would pretend he was a fantasy lover.

At first, Jim thought his prayers had been answered. Whenever he wanted sex, he got it. And Karen seemed more passionate. For the first week they made love every night.

But the rest of their relationship was going downhill fast. Whenever Karen demanded help from Jim, even when he did what she wanted, it didn't really meet her emotional needs because she gave him no credit. He didn't help her because he cared for her, she reasoned. He helped her because she made him do it. Besides, she didn't even want him to do anything that would meet her most important emotional needs, because that would make her too emotionally vulnerable.

Instead, Karen began to demand that Jim give her more freedom to do whatever she pleased. She demanded more money to spend on herself and she spent almost all of her leisure time with her friends. Andrea was still Karen's highest priority, but she began to think that she had forgotten to care for herself all these years. So her own personal interests came in a very close second to those of Andrea. Jim's interests, of course, were near the bottom of the list.

Karen developed a weekly schedule that did not include Jim. She encouraged him to leave for work early and come home late. If he planned to be home for the weekend, she would plan to do something with her friends. She did not even deposit her own check into their joint account. The money she earned went into her own separate account and she made Jim pay as many of the bills as she could.

Despite all this distancing behavior, she stayed true to her decision to give Jim the sex he wanted—at least at first.

Though Jim now had no sexual complaints, he was still frustrated much of the time. He was particularly upset with Karen's failure to let him know where she was going or what she had been doing. Whenever he asked, she told him it was none of his business. When he argued with her about her secrecy, she would scream at him to leave her alone. Then she would threaten to leave him. That was usually effective in backing him off.

Jim might have been willing to suffer through the bad marriage for the rest of his life if Karen had made love to him every night, but, as it turns out, her commitment didn't last very long. At first, she allowed herself to say no once in a while, but within a few months she was saying no almost all the time.

Actually, her commitment was poorly conceived. None of us can force ourselves to do something that's unpleasant indefinitely. Sooner or later we all find excuses to avoid it. There's hardly a woman anywhere who can consistently make love to a husband she dislikes. And Karen was getting to hate hers. Eventually, Karen couldn't force herself to make love to Jim at all. Her stomach knotted up at the very thought of it.

The brief reprieve that had been brought on by frequent lovemaking came to an end. Jim and Karen were left with their independent lifestyles, demands, anger, disrespect, and dishonesty. No marriage can last very long with those weights dragging it down.

By the time they made their first appointment with me, they were not meeting any of each other's emotional needs. But what's worse, they were deliberately hurting each other. They could hardly remember what it was like being in love.

Stop the Train! Let Me Off!

Jim and Karen's experience is all too common in today's marriages. What starts out as a caring and thoughtful relationship often disintegrates into thoughtlessness. As a husband and wife stop meeting each other's needs and start hurting each other, their love turns into hate.

Some couples try to suffer through it for the sake of their children or their religious convictions. But most often, they decide that they are on the wrong train and they must get off—they file for divorce. Unfortunately, the train of their marriage doesn't stop to let them off. It's rushing forward at a high speed, and all exits lead to disaster for the couple and their family.

Since so much personal and familial happiness depends on the success of marriage, you'd think that couples would approach it with a careful plan to insure success. But sadly, most don't give their marriages much thought until it's almost too late. About half of all marriages end in divorce, and most of the others are a bitter disappointment. Very few marriages turn out to be as fulfilling as they could have been.

> **What starts out as a caring and thoughtful relationship often disintegrates into thoughtlessness.**

I'd like your marriage to be one of the exceptions. I've written this book to help you avoid the tragedy of Jim and Karen's marriage and, instead, build a happy marriage that *stays* happy. If you follow my advice, you're likely to enjoy a lifetime of love. My recommendations have helped thousands of people replace marital pain with marital pleasure, and you can be one of them.

But before I show you how to make your marriage a happy exception, I must first explain why Jim and Karen reacted to each other the way they did. At first they loved each other, but eventually they hated each other. How did that happen? It's something you must fully understand if you want to avoid Jim and Karen's tragic experience.

The Love Bank

My years of counseling experience have taught me that when you learn to behave in ways that make your spouse feel great and you learn to avoid behaving in ways that make your spouse unhappy, your spouse will be in love with you. That's how Jim and Karen first fell in love with each other—they made each other happy when they were together, and they did whatever they could to avoid upsetting each other.

To help couples understand this very important fact, I created the concept of the Love Bank. It helps me explain the rise and fall of **romantic love**—the feeling of passion that people should always have in their marriage.

All of us have within us a Love Bank that contains accounts in the names of all of the people we know. It's the way our emotions keep track of the way people treat us. When someone does something that makes us feel good, love units are deposited into their account. And when he or she does something that makes us feel bad, love units are withdrawn. If a person consistently does things

> **Love Bank**
> The way our emotions keep track of the way people treat us.

that make us feel good they build a large Love Bank balance. If on the other hand they do things that make us feel bad and do very little to make us feel good, they end up with a negative Love Bank balance.

Our emotions check our Love Bank regularly to determine who is taking good care of us and who isn't. With that evidence, they encourage us to spend more time with those who make us happy and avoid those who make us unhappy. If someone has a large positive balance, our emotions encourage us to spend time with that person by making him or her feel attractive to us. On the other hand, if someone has a large negative balance, our emotions encourage us to avoid that person by making him or her feel

21

repulsive to us. We have very little intellectual control over these feelings, and they are based almost entirely on Love Bank balances. Those we like have accumulated positive balances and those we dislike have accumulated negative balances.

Once in a while, someone of the opposite sex comes along who makes us feel absolutely sensational. That's because they meet one or more of our most important emotional needs. When that happens, so many love units are deposited that his or her account hits what I call the **romantic love threshold**. Our emotions are so impressed with that high balance that it gives us added incentive to spend more time with that person—it give us the feeling of romantic love. We don't merely find that person attractive—we find that person **irresistible.** And along with that feeling goes a desire to spend our lives with whoever has that high Love Bank balance. Marriage is an easy choice when Love Bank balances are above the romantic love threshold

> **Romantic Love Threshold**
>
> The Love Bank balance needed to trigger romantic love.

What Goes Up, Can Go Down

Before marriage, while a couple is dating, they usually deposit a tremendous number of love units because they're doing things that make each other very happy—they're meeting each other's important emotional needs. They also try to avoid doing whatever might make each other unhappy. They consciously and deliberately want to please each other and avoid anything that would be thoughtless. This mutual effort deposits so many love units that their Love Bank balances rise above the romantic love threshold, and they're ready to marry—they find each other absolutely irresistible and they want to be together for the rest of their lives.

Unfortunately, after marriage most couples, like Jim and Karen, fail to keep their Love Bank balances above the romantic love threshold. They don't do as good a job meeting each other's emotional needs. And sometimes they begin doing things that are irritating and annoying. They don't try as hard to avoid thoughtlessness as they did before marriage. When that happens they lose their feeling of passion for each other.

But it gets worse. As their Love Bank balances drop below zero, what used to be a feeling of attraction turns into a feeling of repulsion. It's not uncommon for a couple that started out feeling that they would love each other for eternity to come to the conclusion that their marriage was the biggest mistake of their lives.

And it's all due to Love Bank balances. If Jim and Karen had simply been able to keep their Love Bank balances above the romantic love threshold, they would have had a marriage full of passion for the rest of their lives. But because they allowed the Love Bank balances to drop below that threshold, they lost their feeling of passion for each other. And by allowing their Love Bank balances to keep falling until they entered negative territory, they eventually came to regret the day they met each other.

> **A couple who started out thinking they would love each other forever may conclude that their marriage was the biggest mistake of their lives—all due to Love Bank balances.**

Marriage Can Make Us Hate the One We Once Loved

Of all the people you know, you are more likely to hate your spouse than anyone else. And your spouse is more likely to hate you than anyone else. What I am telling you is true, and because of it, I want you to take extraordinary measures to avoid this very real danger. Since you may not believe me or think I am exaggerating, I will explain why this is the experience of most married couples.

Many of our relationships are voluntary. That is, we choose which people we'll spend our time with. Our emotions encourage us to choose to be with those who have deposited love units in our Love Bank since they are the ones most likely to keep depositing them. When we surround ourselves with those who treat us well, they keep depositing love units, so we come to like them more and more.

On the other hand, our emotions encourage us to avoid those whose Love Bank accounts are in the red. By avoiding these people, we prevent them from making even more withdrawals. So most people who make us unhappy don't have an opportunity to withdraw as many love units as they might, because once their account is negative, we try to avoid them. That's why we usually don't dislike very many people—we "close their account" before things get that bad.

But there are some people who are not easy to avoid. At work, at home, in our churches, clubs, or community activities, we have to deal with certain people whether we like them or not. And these are the ones we can grow to hate, because they have an opportunity to keep withdrawing love units until their account reaches the hate threshold. That's the negative balance that our emotions use to trigger an intense feeling of repulsion toward someone who has consistently and repeatedly made us unhappy. Just as our emotions give us added incentive (the feeling of love) to be with those with accounts over the romantic love threshold, our emotions give us added incentive (the feeling of hate) to avoid those with accounts under the hate threshold.

The person in the best position to withdraw unprecedented numbers of love units is your spouse.

You might find another job or switch churches to avoid someone who treats you badly enough. Uncles, aunts, cousins, and other members of your extended family can be avoided, at least for most of the year. With greater effort it is possible to avoid brothers and sisters, and even parents.

But a spouse is almost impossible to avoid unless you divorce, especially if you have children. So it should come as no surprise that the person in the best position to withdraw unprecedented numbers of love units is your spouse. And for that reason, you are more likely to hate your spouse than anyone else. Your spouse is the one hardest to avoid—no matter how miserable he or she makes you feel.

Day after day, month after month, year after year, your spouse can withdraw love units by making demands of you, criticizing you, lying to you, annoying you with disgusting habits and thoughtless activities, calling you disrespectful names, and even being physically or verbally abusive to you. And what can you do about it? What can you do to get him or her to stop?

> **All the best intentions, sincere vows, and honest efforts cannot substitute for a substantial Love Bank account.**

You do what most people do: Dish it back as fast as it comes. If you're miserable, then, by golly, you'll *both* be miserable. Your instinct is to destroy the one who is upsetting you and almost all couples respond that way when Love Bank accounts fall into the red.

When a married couple's relationship starts on a downward slide, the loss of love units usually gains momentum. Instead of caring for each other, spouses devise increasingly painful strategies to pay each other back for the last thoughtless act. As negative Love Bank balances increase, the feeling of anger and disrespect increases. Because they live together, a couple cannot avoid each other, and withdrawals continue unabated. The end result is often the violence that comes from a deep and pervasive hatred.

The secret to avoiding this tragedy, of course, is to keep Love Bank balances above the romantic love threshold. And if they happen to drift below that threshold, couples should make a special effort to redeposit them and avoid losing any more. All the best intentions, sincere vows, and honest efforts cannot substitute for a substantial Love Bank account. The Love Bank determines whom we marry, and it usually determines whether or not we'll be divorced. Therefore it is tremendously important to understand how to build Love Bank accounts and how to avoid withdrawals once deposits have been made.

What Are Love Busters?

Whenever you do something that makes your spouse unhappy, you withdraw love units. But let's face it, it's impossible to avoid all the bumps and bruises of life, especially *marital* bumps and bruises. Even in the best marriages, spouses hurt each other now and then.

Occasional mistakes do not drain a Love Bank, as long as they're seen as mistakes. An apology quickly heals the wound and the deposits continue unabated.

But when a mistake turns into a habit, repeated again and again, Love Bank balances are at great risk. In these situations, apologies mean very little because nothing is done to keep the love units from flowing out of the Love Bank. I call these habits that drain the Love Bank **Love Busters,** because they do more to ruin romantic love than anything else.

Through years of marriage counseling, I've been made aware of a host of Love Busters. Most of them fall into six categories: selfish demands, disrespectful judgments, angry outbursts, dishonesty, annoying habits, and independent behavior. Because each of these categories is so important, I will discuss them one at a time in the following chapters and show you how to overcome each of them.

> **Love Busters**
>
> Habits that drain the Love Bank.

Then, in the second part of this book, I will show you how these Love Busters prevent couples from resolving common marital conflicts. You'll also see how easy it is to resolve these conflicts once Love Busters are overcome.

The Parable of the Net

Marriage is like a fishing net. Each day fishermen use their nets to catch fish and sell them at the market.

One fisherman takes his fish from the net every day but lets debris from the ocean accumulate. Eventually so much debris is caught in the net that he can hardly cast the net out of the boat, and when he does, it's almost impossible to retrieve. Finally, in a fit of anger, he cuts the net loose and goes home without it. He's unable to catch and sell fish again until he buys another net.

Another fisherman removes debris every time he retrieves the net with the fish he caught. Each time he casts his net, it's clean and ready to catch more fish. As a result, he catches and sells enough fish to support himself and his family.

In this parable, the fish are emotional needs met in marriage and the debris are Love Busters, habits that cause unhappiness.

Bad marriages are like the first fisherman's net. Angry outbursts, disrespectful judgments, annoying behavior, selfish demands, and dishonesty accumulate over time. The burden of the unhappiness they cause ruins a couple's willingness and ability to meet each other's emotional needs. Eventually the marriage supplies no benefits to either spouse and ends in divorce or emotional separation.

Good marriages are like the second fisherman's net. Love Busters are eliminated as soon as they appear, making it easy for the spouses to meet each other's emotional needs. Love grows because the Love Busters are tossed overboard.

The Chapters of Jim and Karen's Marriage

Let's think once more about Jim and Karen's marriage. Their story consisted of five stages—chapters we'll call them. They progressed through the first three chapters even before I counseled with them. In the **first chapter** they met each other's emotional needs, deposited love units, and were in love with each other. In the **second chapter** they stopped meeting some of these important emotional needs and their deposits were fewer and farther between. Their frustrations with unmet needs opened the **third chapter**. Instead of solving their problems thoughtfully, they chose to hurt each other. This selfish strategy poked gaping holes in their love bank accounts, and love units poured out.

But there are very important fourth and fifth chapters to Jim and Karen's story. In the **fourth chapter** they learned to stop hurting each other. They no longer made demands, showed disrespect, or became angry when they didn't get their way. They also learned how to get what they needed from each other by making thoughtful decisions that took each other's feelings into account. And they learned to be honest with each other instead of creating secret and independent lives.

This book will teach you the lessons that Jim and Karen learned in the fourth chapter of their book of life—the lessons of avoiding Love Busters. Before you can ever hope to rebuild your Love Bank balances, you must first learn to stop making Love Bank withdrawals.

But to make their book of life complete, in the **fifth chapter** Jim and Karen relearned how to meet each other's important emotional needs. That helped them deposit so many love units that they both broke through the romantic love threshold once and for all. The lessons that they learned in their fifth chapter of life are described in this book's companion, *His Needs, Her Needs.*

If you find yourselves in Jim and Karen's third chapter of life, with an unfulfilling marriage that has led you to respond with demands, disrespect, and anger, or if you have just given up on ever having the kind of marriage you need and have created an independent lifestyle that ignores each other's feelings, this book is for you. I will focus attention on the tragic mistakes that Jim and Karen made. When they chose to hurt each other in response to their frustration, they chose to withdraw love units from each other's Love Banks. That choice created hate where there was once love.

Once they were in the downward spiral of thoughtlessness that triggered hate that, in turn, triggered even more thoughtlessness, meeting each other's emotional needs was completely out of the question. They didn't feel like helping each other—they felt like hurting each other. Besides, even if they had made a heroic effort to meet each other's needs, it wouldn't have done much good. It would have been like pouring water into a sieve. All the love units they deposited would have drained right out of their Love Banks—their efforts to care for each other would have been wasted. Love Bank deposits make sense only after the avoidance of Love Busters can be guaranteed.

In marriage you have an unprecedented opportunity to make your spouse happy. You do that whenever you meet his or her most important emotional needs. But you are also in a position to make your spouse miserable, more miserable than anyone else can. In all too many marriages, people choose to make each other miserable. When they come to me with their marital problems, my ultimate goal is to teach them how to make each other happy. But before I can get to that goal, I must first teach them how to stop hurting each other.

By the time you finish this book, you will know how to protect your spouse from yourself and your Love Busters. You'll be able to plug up the leaks in your Love Bank so that deposits will accumulate until you are passionately in love with each other—essential for a happy and fulfilling marriage. Once you learn these lessons, your efforts to meet each other's needs will reap huge dividends. The love units you deposit in each other's Love Bank will accumulate, and just like Jim and Karen, you'll be in love with each other again.

Key Principles

- All of us have within us a Love Bank that keeps track of the way people treat us. When someone does something that makes us feel good, love units are deposited into their account. And when he or she does something that makes us feel bad, love units are withdrawn.

- Our emotions check our Love Bank regularly and encourage us to spend more time with those who make us happy and to avoid those who make us unhappy.

- When someone of the opposite sex makes us feel absolutely sensational by meeting one or more of our most important emotional needs, his or her account hits the romantic love threshold. We don't merely find that person attractive—we find that person irresistible.

- Our emotions encourage us to avoid those whose Love Bank accounts are in the red. But it's not easy to avoid our spouse, so they may keep withdrawing love units until their account reaches the hate threshold.

- It's not uncommon for a couple that started out feeling that they would love each other for eternity to come to the conclusion that their marriage was the biggest mistake of their lives—all due to Love Bank balances.

- Love Busters are habits that drain the Love Bank. They fall into six categories: selfish demands, disrespectful judgments, angry outbursts, dishonesty, annoying habits, and destructive independent behavior.

Consider This . . .

1. Discuss the tragic events of Jim and Karen's marriage. Are there any similarities between their marriage and yours? If you had been advising them during the first year of their marriage, what would you have suggested to them? Would that same advice have helped your marriage?

2. Try to explain the Love Bank to each other in your own words. Most couples have trouble discussing Love Bank withdrawals, because it often sounds like criticism. How could you let each other know about withdrawals that are taking place in a way that would be constructive?

3. There are many who believe that the feeling of love cannot be sustained in marriage. What do you think? If you believe that it can be sustained, is it important enough for both of you to do what it takes to keep your Love Bank balances above the romantic love threshold?

4. How do Love Bank balances affect your willingness to meet each other's emotional needs? How do they affect your temptation to hurt each other? When your Love Bank balances are low, what should you try to do that you don't feel like doing for each other? What should you try to avoid doing that you feel like doing to each other?

5. What are Love Busters? Why do I emphasize habits rather than isolated behavior?

WHAT IS
MARITAL ABUSE?

AND WHY ARE WE TEMPTED TO BE ABUSIVE?

I defined a **Love Buster** in the last chapter—it's a habit that drains the Love Bank. To put it another way, it's **repeated** behavior of one spouse that causes the other spouse to be unhappy. This definition is very important because it focuses attention on habits instead of isolated one-of-a-kind mistakes. While it's true that you make Love Bank withdrawals whenever you do anything to make your spouse unhappy, I've chosen to focus on habits because they multiply the effect of a single mistake—bad habits will drain your Love Bank much more quickly than single mistakes. If you're in the habit of doing something that hurts your spouse, you'll continue to lose love units until you change the habit or until your spouse doesn't love you anymore.

> **Habits multiply the effect of a single mistake.**

The first three Love Busters I will introduce to you—selfish demands, disrespectful judgments, and angry outbursts—are all examples of marital abuse. They are habits that represent typical, yet very hurtful, approaches to problem solving in marriage. If you want something from your spouse, or if you are in conflict, it's tempting to use these Love Busters to try to get your way.

Each one of these Love Busters illustrates the way one spouse deliberately hurts the other in a selfish effort to gain control. Instead of searching for mutually acceptable solutions to a problem, one spouse tries to impose a solution that is to the other spouse's disadvantage. And it's backed up with punishment if there is resistance.

Abusive strategies will make getting what you need less likely.

Any one of these three Love Busters qualifies as an abusive attempt to resolve conflicts, but they tend to appear in a certain escalating order. The first to appear is usually **selfish demands**—one spouse tells the other what to do. If that doesn't get the job done, **disrespectful judgments** often take their place—one spouse tries to impose his or her way of thinking on the other spouse in an effort to eventually force compliance. And if that doesn't work, **angry outbursts** are the final and most abusive step toward gaining control—punishing the other spouse until compliance is attained.

I want you to get what you need from each other because that's essential for a happy and fulfilling marriage. But these three abusive strategies will not help you. In fact, they will make getting what you need *less* likely. And if you use these Love Busters to try to resolve your conflicts, you will lose your love for each other.

One of my greatest hurdles in helping couples overcome abuse is for them to identify and understand it. When I try to persuade spouses to stop being abusive toward each other, I run into the same roadblock almost every time. The perpetrator of abuse usually does not recognize it for what it is. I often hear the shocked reaction, "I'm not being abusive—it's my spouse who's being abusive to me!" Or, "Don't I have a right to express my feelings?"

If spouses do not know when they are being abusive and why they are doing it, it's impossible to stop abuse from taking place. So before we look specifically at the three most common forms of abuse in marriage—demands, disrespect, and anger—I will explain what abuse is and why we tend to do it to our spouses.

What Is Abuse?

I define abuse in marriage as a **deliberate** effort of one spouse to cause the other to be unhappy. Control of a spouse's behavior, attitudes, beliefs, and opinions is usually the motive, although the one doing the abusing rarely acknowledges it. The perpetrator of abuse usually knows that his or her actions cause unhappiness but often views it as the "right" thing to do, or "for the spouse's own good." And the abuser will rarely admit that the abuse is a deliberate effort to make his or her spouse unhappy. Instead, the abuser claims the spouse's unhappiness as an unforeseen or unintentional outcome. "I didn't mean to hurt you," or "you shouldn't feel bad," is often the reaction of an abusive spouse.

> **Abuse**
> Deliberate effort of one spouse to cause the other to be unhappy.

There are, of course, many habits and activities in marriage that **unintentionally** cause the other spouse to be unhappy. These causes of unhappiness are also Love Busters because they can create massive Love Bank withdrawals and I will be encouraging you to overcome them in the later chapters of this book. But I want to begin by helping you overcome the deliberate Love Busters, because they hurt your spouse in two ways: First, your spouse is hurt by the act itself, and second, your spouse is hurt because he or she knows it was deliberate.

Because abuse is such a tricky concept in marriage, I will devote this entire chapter to helping you see it for what it really is and why we are all tempted to be abusive. That way, you will be better able to understand and identify your own abusive instincts and habits.

> **Deliberate Love Busters hurt your spouse in two ways.**

If your spouse has ever accused you of being controlling, manipulative, or abusive, you owe it to your spouse, and yourself, to read this chapter carefully so you will know what he or she is talking about. And I hope that by the time you are finished, you will make a commitment to protect your spouse from your abusive habits.

To better understand the nature of abuse and why those who are abusive rarely see it for what it really is, let me give you a short course on the two parts of your personality. I call these two the Giver and the Taker.

Getting to Know Your Giver and Taker

Have you ever wondered if your spouse has two personalities? One that's caring and considerate, and one that seems impossible to get along with? I'm sure you've not only noticed, but you've probably been very disappointed, or even horrified, by the impossible one.

We all have them and they make marriage much more difficult than it should be. To help you understand why you may be having so much trouble communicating and why you are tempted to be abusive when you try to resolve conflicts, I'm going to reveal these two parts of your personality to you—the Giver and the Taker.

> **The Giver**
>
> The part of someone's personality that is concerned only about the happiness of others.

The Giver is the part of you that is kind, generous, thoughtful, and caring. It follows this rule: **Do whatever you can to make others happy and avoid anything that makes others unhappy, even if it makes you unhappy.** In other words, the Giver encourages you to do things for others even if it means doing it in self-sacrificing ways. It's the part of you that wants to make a difference in the life of someone else. And it grows out of a basic instinct that we all share, a deep reservoir of love and concern for those around us.

But this is only half of the story. The other half is the Taker. It's the part of you that's concerned about your own welfare and your own happiness. It follows this rule: **Do whatever you can to make yourself happy and avoid anything that makes you unhappy, even if it makes others unhappy.** It's the part of you that wants you to get as much out of life as possible. And it grows out of your basic instinct for self-preservation.

By themselves, the Giver and Taker are both shortsighted. Your Giver's concern is only for others, often at the expense of yourself, while your Taker's concern is only for yourself, often at the expense of others.

But the Giver and the Taker don't usually work in isolation of each other. In everyday life, your Giver and Taker usually solve

34

problems together. They recognize your need to give and take simultaneously. For example, when you buy groceries you give money and take groceries. You don't give more money than the grocer asks for and you don't take groceries without paying for them. Instead, you strike a fair bargain where the grocer is satisfied with the money you give and you are satisfied with the groceries you purchase in return.

In marriage, however, a very strange thing happens to the way your Giver and Taker operate. They often work independently

> **The Taker**
>
> The part of someone's personality that is concerned only about his or her own happiness.

of each other. Either the Giver's in charge, encouraging you to give unconditionally to your spouse, or the Taker's in charge, encouraging you to take what you want from your spouse without consideration of your spouse's interests or feelings.

When your Giver is in charge, you're loving and considerate and you tend to make personal sacrifices to see to it that your spouse is happy and fulfilled—your Taker makes no effort to defend your personal interests. You love unconditionally when your Giver guides you, because your Giver doesn't care how you feel. Regardless of how badly you are treated and how little you get in return, your Giver wants you to keep on giving.

But when the Taker's in charge you're tempted to be rude, demanding, and inconsiderate. All you seem to think about is yourself and what your spouse should be doing to make you happy. You expect your spouse to make sacrifices for you because your Taker doesn't care how your spouse feels. Regardless of how badly you treat your spouse and how little you give in return, your Taker wants you to keep on taking.

I want to emphasize that this is normal behavior in marriage. You might think you're married to a crazy person or you may think you're crazy. But let me assure you, marriage is one of the very few conditions in life that bring out the pure Giver and Taker in each of us. And that usually makes us seem much crazier than we really are.

It should come as no surprise to you that it isn't the Giver that ruins marriages—it's the Taker. But the Giver plays a very important role in creating the problem. When the Giver encourages us to give our spouse anything he or she wants, it sets up the Taker for its destructive acts. After you've been giving, giving, giving to your spouse and receiving very little in return, because you haven't bargained for much, your Taker rises up to straighten out the situation. It sees the unfairness of it all and steps in to balance the books. Instead of coming to a more equitable arrangement, where you bargain to get something for what you give, the Taker just moves the Giver out of the picture altogether. It says "I've been giving enough; now it's time to take!"

> **Marriage is one of the very few conditions in life that bring out the pure Giver and Taker in each of us.**

Sound familiar? We've all been through it. But it doesn't work. All our Taker does is arouse our spouse's Taker. And the first thing you know, we're having a fight.

Since the Taker has no concern for your spouse's feelings, it encourages you to let your spouse suffer if you can gain something for yourself. *You've been suffering for your spouse's happiness,* your Taker whispers to you. *It's about time your spouse did a little suffering for your happiness.*

In fact, it will even encourage you to **cause** your spouse to suffer, if that's what it takes to get your way. And that's what abuse is really all about—deliberately hurting your spouse so that you can have what you want. If you have ever made demands of your spouse, shown disrespect, or had an angry outburst, you have yielded to your Taker's abusive way to solve problems.

Your Taker not only tries to encourage you to do whatever it takes to make you happy, it also defends you when its tactics get you into trouble. When your spouse sees your actions as selfish and abusive, your Taker gives you logical arguments to deflect criticism. It tries to make your selfish behavior seem rather thoughtful. Even when you are having a fight with your spouse, it gives you the words to justify your abuse. And when the fight is over, it helps you forget what you did and gives you memories that make your abusive behavior seem downright compassionate. By the time you discuss the incident with your spouse, your Taker has you believing that you were Mother Teresa.

This all sounds insane, but it isn't. It is the way we all behave, so that makes it normal. When I try to get to the bottom of what goes on when spouses fight, the Takers of both spouses distort the event to such an extent, you'd think they were describing completely separate incidents. How could two people remember the same event so differently? Their Takers are the culprits.

Our Giver and Taker Make Us Look like Idiots

Some of the smartest people I know become idiots when faced with marital conflict. I've seen this happen in case after case. An intelligent man listens to his wife talking about her needs and her desires and her interests, and it's as if she's speaking a foreign language. A brilliant woman hears her husband describe his perspective and she just doesn't get it.

What makes marital communication so tough? Is it that men and women just can't communicate with each other? Or is there something about marriage that blurs their thinking?

As I already mentioned, I'm thoroughly convinced that it's marriage itself, or more specifically a romantic relationship, that makes communication so difficult. It's not the differences between men and women. The men I counsel have very little trouble resolving conflicts with women when they're not in a romantic relationship. And their wives are just as good at negotiating with men other than their husbands. It's conflicts they have with each other that seem so impossible to

> **A romantic relationship makes communication so difficult.**

resolve. And that's because their Giver and Taker are working at odds with each other. Instead of striving for fairness, they are either entirely selfless or entirely selfish.

Bear with me a little longer as I go on to explain to you how the Giver and Taker can turn you into an abusive spouse. Not only do these two influence your thinking, they also change your approach to marital negotiation. I call each approach a state of mind, and each one has its own unique negotiating rules and emotional reactions. But regardless of the state of mind, the way your Giver and Taker encourage you to negotiate is unfair and ineffective. I call these three states of mind in marriage intimacy, conflict, and withdrawal.

The State of Intimacy

The most essential prerequisite for the state of intimacy is the feeling of being in love and being very happy with the relationship. You have that feeling when your spouse has deposited enough love units to break through the romantic love threshold.

The Giver is usually in complete control of this state of mind. So a spouse is encouraged to follow the rule of the Giver: **Do whatever you can do to make your spouse happy and avoid anything that makes your spouse unhappy, even if it makes you unhappy**. If both spouses follow this rule at the same time, they're both likely to have their emotional needs met, and all is well. Giving to each other seems almost instinctive, and they both have a great desire to make each other happy in any way possible and avoid hurting each other at all costs.

Since you are happy, the Taker has nothing to do, because its job is to make sure you are happy. So the Taker gives the Giver full reign and takes a nap.

> **State of Intimacy**
>
> The state of mind dominated by your Giver, who encourages you to give unconditionally.

Since the Taker has turned things over to the Giver, spouses build trust between each other. They can share their deepest feelings and become emotionally vulnerable to each other because they know that they both have each other's best interests at heart. They feel so close to each other that to hurt the other person would be the same as hurting themselves.

Conversation in the state of intimacy is respectful and nonjudgmental. Couples usually express their deepest love for each other along with gratitude for the care that they're receiving. By lowering their defenses so that they can form a close emotional bond, they feel even greater pleasure when they meet each other's needs.

This is the way most people expect marriage to be—unconditionally loving and caring. When one spouse expresses a desire, the other rushes to fulfill it. There's no thought of repayment. So as long as both spouses are in the same state of mind, there is actually nothing to negotiate. They give each other anything that's possible, and they do it unconditionally.

You might think that this is the way you and your spouse should negotiate with each other, but the problem with this strategy is that it causes one spouse to gain at the other's expense. And that, in turn, can cause substantial Love Bank withdrawals for the spouse making the sacrifice. And if your sacrifice becomes a habit, eventually there will be so many love units lost that your spouse's account will fall below the romantic love threshold and you will no longer be in love with your spouse. When that happens you enter the second state of mind in your marriage.

The State of Conflict

In the state of intimacy you are happy because your spouse has been meeting your most important emotional needs and has been avoiding behavior that upsets you. But if your spouse were to stop meeting your emotional needs, or if your spouse starts upsetting you, or even if the sacrifices you make for your spouse draw too many love units from your spouse's Love Bank account, your Taker will rise from its nap and say "Hey, what's going on? I don't like this." And as quick as you can say

> **State of Conflict**
> The state of mind dominated by your Taker, who encourages you to take unconditionally.

"Bull in a china closet" out comes the Taker along with the Taker's rules and its own emotional reactions to things. You now have an entirely new state of mind—the state of conflict. It's in this state of mind that you will be tempted to be abusive to your spouse.

Remember the Taker's rule: **Do whatever you can do to make yourself happy and avoid anything that makes you unhappy, even if it makes your spouse unhappy**. In an effort to make you happier than you've been, the Taker prepares you for war.

In this state of mind, you demand that your spouse meets your needs. And you demand that your spouse stop doing whatever it is that is upsetting you. You threaten your spouse with punishment until those demands are met.

Your conversation tends to be very disrespectful because the Taker sees no point in respecting your spouse for his or her failure to make you happy. To justify your demands, the Taker creates disrespectful arguments that "prove" your spouse is wrong, and you are right. The unconditional care of the Giver in the state of intimacy is now replaced by unconditional self-centeredness. Your Taker no longer trusts your spouse to look after your own interests, but instead pulls out all the stops to see to it that your spouse treats you fairly. The problem of course is that your Taker is unwilling to treat your spouse with the same fairness expected of your spouse. From your Taker's perspective, fairness is getting your way at all costs.

In the state of conflict, you still feel emotionally connected to each other, and that makes your Taker's thoughtlessness even more painful to your spouse—love units can be withdrawn at a very rapid rate.

You can return to the state of intimacy from the state of conflict if, and only if, you stop hurting each other and start meeting each other's needs again. But this is extremely difficult to do once you're in the state of conflict because all of the instincts of the Taker encourage you to do the opposite. The Taker urges you to return pain whenever you receive it. And that's abusive. And it also encourages you to withhold meeting your spouse's needs until your needs are met.

So for most couples the state of conflict inspires them to be shortsighted. Instead of stopping the pain they are causing each other, they create even more pain. Instead of wanting to meet each other's needs, they want their own needs met before they'll do anything. Our Takers would rather fight than try to make the other spouse happy.

When you're in the state of conflict your Taker tries to make your spouse meet your needs with demands, disrespect, and anger. And if that doesn't work, your Taker will suggest a new strategy: withdrawal. It tries to convince you that your spouse is not worth the effort.

The State of Withdrawal

In the state of conflict, the Taker's strategy is to fight. But in the state of withdrawal, its strategy is flight. Abuse is rare in this state of mind because the Taker doesn't want you to try to get anything from your spouse. Demands, disrespect, and angry outbursts are pointless because they are used only when the Taker wants something. Emotional defenses are raised, and there is no longer an emotional bond. You don't want your spouse to meet your emotional needs anymore, and you certainly don't want to meet your spouse's emotional needs.

I've spent quite a bit of time and effort trying to understand how emotional needs are actually met in marriage. One of my observations is that they are met only when we are emotionally vulnerable to somebody who meets those needs. But when we're in the state of withdrawal, we raise emotional defenses so high that our spouse cannot get love units through the barrier. We don't allow ourselves to be that vulnerable. So even when our spouse makes an effort to do something we had demanded in the state of conflict, by the time we are in the state of withdrawal it deposits few if any love units.

> **State of Withdrawal**
>
> The state of mind dominated by your Taker, who encourages you to emotionally withdraw from your spouse, neither giving nor taking.

Negotiation is difficult in the state of intimacy because our Giver encourages us to give unconditionally. We don't negotiate in our own best interest. We are willing to give what our spouse wants at our expense.

Negotiation gets much worse in the state of conflict because our Taker encourages us to take unconditionally—we don't negotiate with our spouse's best interests in mind.

But in the state of withdrawal, there's no negotiation at all. There are no discussions, no bargaining, not even arguing. In the state of withdrawal we are unwilling to do anything for our spouse or even let our spouse do anything for us in return.

Some people think that withdrawal is a form of abuse. By refusing to discuss an issue, or even by physically walking away, it feels like a punishment. But in most cases, even though withdrawal may be painful to the other spouse, it is not really punishment. Instead, it is giving up. When one spouse sees no hope in the future of the relationship, escaping into withdrawal seems the only choice possible. It's not abuse—it's escape.

States of Mind Are Contagious

These three states of mind that we've been talking about—intimacy, conflict, and withdrawal—are not usually experienced by both spouses at the same time. But each spouse's state of mind can draw the other spouse into it.

One spouse in the state of intimacy may inadvertently upset the other spouse enough to cause that spouse to enter the state of conflict. That's when criticism, complaints, nagging, and arguments usually start. And as these negative reactions escalate for the spouse that's in the state of conflict, enough love units are lost to drag the other spouse from the state of intimacy into the state of conflict as well. And then both spouses behave negatively and selfishly.

Each spouse's state of mind can draw the other spouse into it.

Typically, if they fail in their efforts to resolve their conflict, and if the unpleasant efforts of their Takers escalate, one spouse will usually escape into withdrawal first and raise his or her emotional barrier. The spouse that remains in the state of conflict may continue to argue for a while. Sometimes the arguing spouse can goad the withdrawn spouse back into the state of conflict, but it's more likely that the arguing spouse will simply give up and join the other spouse in the state of withdrawal. At that point, they are emotionally divorced.

The Road Back to Intimacy

Fortunately, for most couples, that's not where it ends. Someone eventually comes to his or her senses and realizes that divorce is not really what they want. So they use their intelligence to dig themselves out of the hole they find themselves in. And their intelligence convinces them that they must ignore the advice of their Takers to be successful.

An apology, something the Taker would **never** want you to make, is one of the best ways to begin the trek back to intimacy. Whatever it was that each spouse did to drive the other into withdrawal should be acknowl-

> **An apology is one of the best ways to begin the trek back to intimacy.**

edged and a promise to avoid it in the future should be made. It's usually what was said during the arguments they had while in the state of conflict. Furthermore, each spouse must also come to grips with what their original conflict was all about, what drove them from the state of intimacy into the state of conflict.

Recovery from withdrawal is something you must become skilled in accomplishing for each other, because every married couple goes through this painful experience once in a while. The less it happens the better, and the quicker you can recover from it the better.

The passage from intimacy through conflict to withdrawal can seem almost effortless to a couple. One day they're in a state of bliss but before they know it they're ready to divorce. On the other hand it takes quite a bit of work to climb back up that hill. While it's true that one of you can pull the other one back up, it's a whole lot easier when you're both working together.

Abuse Happens in the State of Conflict

Later in this book I will show you how to keep you and your spouse in the state of intimacy as much as possible. But right now I want to focus your attention on the state of conflict, because that's the state of mind where abuse is most likely to take place.

Whenever you feel neglected by your spouse, or feel that your spouse is treating you unfairly, or even feel that your spouse is being abusive, it's very likely that you are in the state of conflict. And if you want your spouse to do something to straighten things out, then you are definitely in the state of conflict. That means the rule you are likely to follow is, ***do whatever you can to make yourself happy and avoid anything that makes you unhappy, even if it makes your spouse unhappy.*** That rule will tend to dictate the way you approach the problem and want the problem to be solved.

Instead of bargaining fairly with your spouse, discussing alternatives and trying to take your spouse's feelings into account as you negotiate, you will try to impose your solution on your spouse. You will try to make your spouse do things your way, whether he or she likes it or not. And that's abusive.

Abuse tends to prevent couples from solving any of their problems, because the abuse itself becomes their greatest problem. Instead of negotiating a fair resolution to conflicts as they arise, couples ignore important issues because they are afraid to raise them. As problems pile up, they become increasingly incompatible and eventually give up hope of ever being happy together.

Take my word for it: if you want a happy marriage, you must be able to discuss your differences safely and enjoyably, with each other's interests in mind. Any tendency toward the Taker's abusive ways of handling problems will prevent you from having what you need in your marriage—a loving and caring relationship.

If you want a happy marriage, you must be able to discuss your differences safely and enjoyably.

The Taker's rule ruins any relationship because it is totally self-serving. But in marriage it is particularly devastating because escape from its negative consequences is so difficult. As I mentioned in the last chapter, if your spouse cannot avoid your constant withdrawal of love units, eventually he or she will hate you. Instead of having your spouse's loving and caring Giver to face each morning, you will draw out the very worst side of your spouse.

"But what about me?" you may ask. "My spouse is drawing out the worst side of me!"

That may be true, but the solution to the problem is not to return fire for fire. If you want to return to intimacy, you must avoid following the Taker's rule at all costs, even when you are being mistreated. And if you do that, you will have overcome abuse.

In the next three chapters I will help you avoid the Taker's favorite approaches to problem solving: selfish demands, disrespectful judgments, and angry outbursts. Each of them follow logically from the Taker's rule, and they are each a form of marital abuse. Instead of using those flawed strategies, I will help you negotiate fairly, especially when you find yourself in the state of conflict.

Key Principles

- Abuse is the deliberate effort of one spouse to cause the other to be unhappy. It hurts your spouse in two ways: by the act itself and by the knowledge that it was deliberate.

- The three abusive strategies to get your way in marriage are selfish demands, disrespectful judgments, and angry outbursts.

- The Giver is the part of our personality that is concerned only about the happiness of others. The Taker is the part of our personality that is concerned only about the happiness of ourselves.

- Marriage is one of the very few conditions in life that bring out the pure Giver and Taker in each of us, and that makes marital negotiation very difficult, because neither part of our personality knows how to negotiate.

- Intimacy is the state of mind dominated by your Giver, who encourages you to give unconditionally. Conflict is the state of mind dominated by your Taker, who encourages you to take unconditionally. Abuse tends to take place when you are in this state of mind. Withdrawal is the state of mind dominated by your Taker, who encourages you to emotionally withdraw from your spouse, neither giving nor taking.

- In marriage it is very easy to fall from intimacy to conflict to withdrawal. But it is difficult to climb back from withdrawal to conflict to intimacy.

Consider This . . .

1. How do I define marital abuse? The problem with my definition is that the person doing the abusing rarely acknowledges that it's **deliberate**. So when one of you does something that hurts the other, you can hide behind the excuse that it was unintentional. Has this issue ever come up in your marriage? I'll make it easier for you to identify your abusive habits in the next three chapters.

45

2. Have you been able to identify the Giver and Taker in each of you? Some couples give each other two names when they discover these two entirely different personalities. Have you ever done that?

3. The rules of the Giver and Taker define the way they approach life. What are those rules, and how do they influence the way you treat each other?

4. What are the three states of mind in marriage? Can you identify them in yourselves? When was the last time you were in the state of intimacy? The state of conflict? The state of withdrawal?

5. Have either of you ever felt abused by the other? Have you noticed how difficult it is to discuss the problem? If so, that's because you are usually in the state of conflict when the problem arises. The Taker's rule dominates your discussion, and you are not willing to do anything to try to stop the abuse or even acknowledge it. And you are certainly not willing to apologize. In fact, the discussion itself is likely to turn abusive. And yet, if you ever want to solve problems in your marriage, you must eliminate all abuse in your marriage. If you are committed to end abuse in your marriage, take the next three chapters very seriously, because they will help you identify and eliminate it.

part two

THE SIX
LOVE
BUSTERS

S E L F I S H
DEMANDS

WHO WANTS TO LIVE WITH A DICTATOR?

In an effort to provide for his new family, Jim spent so much time at work that he had neglected to meet Karen's emotional needs. It was an innocent mistake, but it led to her loss of love for him, which, in turn, caused her to lose interest in sex. That was a serious problem for Jim, and he didn't know how to solve it.

Karen didn't help. Instead of telling him what was bothering her, she claimed not to understand the problem herself. In response to his frustration, Jim made an almost fatal mistake— he used demands to try to solve the problem. As a result of this fateful course of action, their relationship took such a nosedive that it almost crashed. His demand for sex not only failed to address their underlying problems, but it brought their lovemaking to a complete stop.

Jim and Karen's struggle with sex is fairly common in marriage, but the way it turned out may seem a little extreme to you. So let's look at a less severe situation that also illustrates the inappropriateness of demands in marriage. You may have experienced something similar—possibly as recently as last week.

Imagine yourself cleaning up after dinner with your kitchen a mess, kids running wild, and a husband sitting watching TV (if you are a husband, imagine how you would feel being the wife in this situation). You are feeling very neglected and wonder how he could sit there so oblivious to your need for help. At the very least, you think, he could offer to calm the children down, or dry the dishes. But instead he is just sitting there while a myriad of things need to be done.

Out of utter frustration, you walk up to the TV, turn it off, point your finger at your spouse, and say, "I'm giving you a choice: you can either watch the children for me or you can clean up the kitchen, but you are *not* watching television."

Selfish Demands

Commanding your spouse to do things that would benefit you at your spouse's expense, with implied threat of punishment if refused.

Most women listening to my example would consider this approach to the problem both courageous and wise. By taking control, she will get the job done, and the husband will be doing something that he should have volunteered to do in the first place. But if you have ever been on the receiving end of a demand, you can probably see the fly in this ointment.

Demands Seem Reasonable

If you're in the habit of making demands of your spouse, it's not surprising. Demands seem reasonable when we are frustrated. And most couples make demands unless they're taught to avoid them. That's because the Taker within all of us encourages us to use demands as a way to solve a problem, especially in marriage. Remember the Taker's rule: *Do whatever you can to make yourself happy even if it makes your spouse unhappy.* With that rule in mind, demands make sense.

Demands begin when you are in the state of conflict. You are frustrated about something, and your Taker comes to your rescue. It wants you to be happy, even if at your spouse's expense. So it takes the direct approach—it demands "cooperation." If your spouse happens to be in the state of intimacy at the time, with his or her Giver in charge, your Taker gets whatever it wants without a bit of resistance.

That's one of the main reasons that demands are so common in marriage and less common in all other relationships. In marriage your spouse is more likely to submit to demands, at least when he or she is in the state of intimacy. So demands are rewarded often enough in marriage to be commonplace. Your spouse encourages you to make demands whenever he or she obliges, even though demands are a very thoughtless way to solve problems.

Then, because you can get away with demands once in a while, you are at risk of developing the habit of making demands, even when you are in the state of intimacy yourself. Your Giver usually tries to discourage demands when it is in charge. But if you make demands often enough when you are in the state of conflict, they become an almost unstoppable habit.

Think for a moment how you and your spouse ask each other for favors. Do you tell each other what to do, as if one of you is a sergeant and the other a private? Do you order each other around when something needs to be done? If so, you may be in the habit of making demands, even when you are feeling very close to each other and your Giver should be in charge. It's an insidious habit that, if left to run amok, can destroy your ability to solve even the simplest problems in marriage.

The instinct of making demands whenever you are frustrated and the habit of making demands even when you are not frustrated, make demands very difficult to overcome in marriage. You may just assume that demands are the way to get things done in your marriage and don't see the damage that it does. Of course, if your spouse is in the state of conflict when you make a demand, your spouse's Taker will respond with intense resistance. Instead of finding a patsy to bargain with, you find yourself battling your spouse's angry Taker who feels it's about time that you start fulfilling your spouse's demands. A fight ensues, and . . . well, I'm sure you've had that experience.

But fights won't stop you from making demands in the future. Your Taker keeps telling you that you have every right to make demands, even if they don't work.

Your Taker Justifies Demands

Overwhelming evidence shows that demands do not solve marital problems. At best, all they gain is short-term gratification, because they are a "solution" at your spouse's expense. Your spouse's Taker will not put up with it indefinitely, and sooner or later you will be frustrated again and resentment will begin to take root in your marriage.

And yet, we are programmed to make demands—they are instinctive when we are in the state of conflict. Demands are one of the Taker's favorite solutions to problems. Remember, the Taker is *your* advocate—it is the part of you that wants you to be happy, that wants you to avoid pain and suffering. And it doesn't mind having someone else suffer so you can get what you need. But because demands inherently cause your spouse to be unhappy so you can be happy, they are a form of abuse. You might think that you would never be abusive, but your Taker gives you all the justification you need to make demands despite their abusive nature.

Demands do not solve marital problems.

In my earlier example, your frustration begins on your ride home from work. You are exhausted from a full day of preparing insurance claims, yet you face an evening of even more work caring for your husband and children.

"Why should you be responsible for all this work?" your Taker whispers in your ear. "Your husband sure has it easy. He doesn't work nearly as hard as you do, and when he gets home from work he expects you to do everything. He spends a leisurely evening at home while you're working yourself to exhaustion. Is that fair?"

Upon arrival at home your Taker keeps up the chatter. "Your husband isn't even telling you when he's going to come home from work. He expects you to have dinner ready for him. He expects the kids to be all cared for, and he doesn't even have the decency to call you and let you know when he's coming home."

When your husband arrives home, he says "hi" to the kids that come rushing to him at the door. And instead of acknowledging you right away, he turns on the television. Eventually he gets around to greeting you and gives you a peck on the cheek.

Your Taker responds, "Is that the only reward he can think of for all the work you've done? Hey, he's expecting you to be his slave!"

Your Giver may step in once and a while and argue on behalf of your husband. "He's had a hard day too. He needs to relax."

But no sooner does your Giver get the words out than your Taker pushes your Giver away and counters, "Are you nuts? This guy's been relaxing all day. You're the one that needs to relax, not him."

Remember what I said in the last chapter about the relative strength of the Giver and Taker. The happier you are, the stronger your Giver becomes, but the more frustrated you are, the stronger your Taker becomes. So if you were to find yourself in the situation I've been describing, your Giver would not have much of a chance to argue on behalf of your husband because it would be relatively weak. Your Taker's arguments, however, would be deafening.

Your Taker gives you all the justification you need to make demands.

I agree with the Taker that it's not fair for you to do all the work at home after a hard day at the office. Your Taker's goal, that you should be relieved of some of these responsibilities, is reasonable. But I object to the way the Taker wants to go about solving the problem. The Taker wants you to take control and demand a change. That's because it doesn't care how your husband feels any more than your Giver cares about how you feel. The Taker's solution isn't any fairer than the Giver's solution that you do all the work yourself.

But wait a minute, you might be thinking. *The wife is not demanding that the husband do all the work. She is demanding that he share in the work, which is his responsibility. She will still be doing her fair share.*

What makes your Taker's solution a demand is that your husband is given no choice. You might think that your solution is fair, but it's only fair when both of your Takers think it's fair. Your Taker is in no position to evaluate your husband's interests—they can be evaluated only by his Taker, and it has not been consulted. The alternatives that have been presented, watching the children or drying the dishes, are created by *your* Taker to relieve *your* burden.

And when it comes to fairness, you can't ever trust the advice of only one of your Takers.

A fair solution to any marital problem must take both of you into account. You must somehow solve the problem of who does what after work in a way that makes you both happy. That solution is the one that is most likely to become a habit, and once it does, it will reinforce your love for each other. On the other hand, if your solution makes one of you unhappy, it won't work in the long run, and it will erode your love for each other. If you want to be in love, it makes a lot of sense to create a lifestyle that works well for both of you.

> **A fair solution to any marital problem must take both of you into account.**

Use the Policy of Joint Agreement to Find Fair Solutions

To help you and your spouse make fair decisions, I encourage you to follow a policy I created with that goal in mind. I call it the **Policy of Joint Agreement**. *Never do anything without an enthusiastic agreement between you and your spouse*. Let me repeat that policy to you with emphasis. Never do **anything** without an **enthusiastic** agreement between you and your spouse. The purpose of this policy is to remind you how important it is for you to take each other's interests and feelings into account whenever you make a decision. That way, you will be making fair decisions.

But the Policy of Joint Agreement does more than help you make fair decisions. It helps you deposit more love units and avoid withdrawing them. Since just about everything that you and your spouse do is going to affect each other, either depositing love units or withdrawing love units, it makes a lot of sense to pay attention to which of those things your decisions are doing. Are they depositing love units? Or are they withdrawing love units?

We're not plugged into each other's feelings in marriage. We have no way to directly experience the way we affect our spouse. The only thing we know for certain is how our spouse affects us. So couples need a special rule to force them to share information with each other regarding how they are being affected. The Policy of Joint Agreement is that rule.

Before you make a decision, you should ask your spouse, "How would you feel about this?" If your spouse's response is an enthusiastic "Yes!" it means that the decision you make is not only going to be good for you, it's going to be good for your spouse, too.

Many of our decisions set a precedent. Once the decision is made, it's likely to be repeated again and again. That's why it's especially important to follow the Policy of Joint Agreement for something we would like to become part of our lifestyle, such as how we share responsibilities when we come home from work.

In my example of the exhausted wife and the television-watching husband, there are a host of decisions that have to be made about what they do between 4 o'clock in the afternoon and 7 o'clock in the evening. Clearly, the Policy of Joint Agreement has not been applied to this part of the day, or it would not be turning out the way it does. And as a result, neither the husband nor the wife is depositing very many love units in each other's Love Banks. The husband is making withdrawals from the wife's Love Bank because of his habit of watching TV when he comes home each evening. But the wife is also making withdrawals from the husband's Love Bank by being so upset whenever she comes home to face all the extra work. She's certainly no treat to be around at the end of the day.

> **The Policy of Joint Agreement**
> Never do anything without an enthusiastic agreement between you and your spouse.

The point I want to make as clearly as possible is that while this couple needs to change what they do after work, demands will not lead to a mutually satisfying solution. They lead to a solution where one person tries to gain at the other's expense. From the wife's perspective, turning the TV off and getting the husband to help a little is a fair solution to the problem. But the husband's Taker doesn't see things the same way. In fact, the husband regards his wife's demands as controlling and abusive. In the actual case from which I took this example, he left the house and went back to work, with his wife in tears as he left.

After having counseled thousands of couples, I don't know of a single example where demands have created the ultimate solution to a problem. Instead of leading to a solution, demands lead to resentment and in some cases an aversive reaction. When people are forced to do something they do not want to do they often develop a very negative emotional reaction to the very thought of it. That's what an aversive reaction is. It often takes the form of a very sick feeling in the pit of the stomach whenever thinking about having to do something that's been associated with pain or suffering.

That's what happened to Karen when she tried to meet Jim's demand for sex. She developed an aversion to sex, and then they didn't have any sex at all. Karen was not only resentful that Jim would force her to have sex with him, but she also developed an emotional reaction to sex that made it an absolute nightmare for her. Her husband's demand for sex actually made it less likely that Karen would meet his sexual need.

> **It's only when you enjoy doing something that it can become a habit.**

It's only when you enjoy doing something that it can ever become a habit. So even when a selfish demand seems to work in the short run and you get your way, it would have been better for you to have never made the demand in the first place, because whatever it is you're trying to get your spouse to do is now going to be associated with a negative experience. It will not only withdraw love units, but it'll make it less likely for your spouse to do it next time.

I want you to be able to get what you need in your marriage, and I want you and your spouse to be in love with each other. But you're not going to have either one of those if you're in the habit of making demands. You won't have your needs met and you won't be in love. So let me help you eliminate demands entirely. And then let me suggest an alternative to selfish demands: thoughtful requests. That will not only help you get what you need in your marriage, but it'll do it in a way that will build the love that you and your spouse should have for each other.

Turning Selfish Demands into Thoughtful Requests

People feel used when you show no consideration for their feelings. And your spouse is no exception. Even when your

spouse has agreed to help you, he or she can come away feeling resentful if you start ordering him or her around. So when
you want your spouse to do
something for you, make a
request, not a demand. The difference between the two is found
in your concern for your spouse's
feelings and your willingness to
accept "no" for an answer, at least
temporarily.

Thoughtful Requests

Asking your spouse to do something for you, with a willingness
to withdraw it if there is reluctance. The request must be
preceded by "How would you
feel if you were to . . ."

You are not the boss, and your
spouse is not your slave. And yet,
you both need to help each other in a myriad of different ways. I
want you to meet each other's needs and help each other, but I
want you to learn to do it in ways that are not controlling or abusive. Instead, I want you to help each other with enthusiasm. And
you can learn to do that if you turn your selfish demands into
thoughtful requests.

Step 1: Explain what you want and ask how your spouse feels about doing it.

This first step makes all the difference in the world. Suddenly
the focus is not just on what you want, but also on how your partner feels. That's considerate; that's thoughtful. Now your spouse
doesn't feel taken for granted. You have shown that his or her
feelings matter to you.

In many cases, the thoughtful request itself will make your
spouse willing to do what you've asked. Your concern for his or
her feelings deposits love units, and your spouse
will want to make you happy. Besides, just knowing that you care makes the task more enjoyable.

But don't bask in this bliss too long, because it
isn't always that simple. If thoughtful requests pro-
duced instant agreement, most of us would have
given up demands long ago. Sometimes a spouse
still finds the request unpleasant to fulfill. What
then?

ACTION
STEP

Explain what you
want and ask how
your spouse feels
about doing it.

Step 2: If your spouse has a problem with your request, withdraw it in its present form.

Thoughtfulness is more than how you ask for something. If you really care about your spouse's feelings (as your thoughtful request indicates you do), you want him or her to *enjoy* doing what you've asked. You will not take "well, all right, I guess" for an answer. If your spouse balks at helping you, withdraw the request.

This second step will not be taken by anyone who believes his or her spouse owes favors, has a duty to meet needs, or must do what he or she is told. In other words, if you are controlling or abusive, you will not follow this second step. But if you are to stop abuse in your marriage, this step is crucial.

In counseling abusive spouses, I must first convince them that they do not have the *right* to make demands. Indeed, some assume that their wedding vows gave them this right. But we have already seen how demands choke the feelings of love. And let me add that selfish demands are basically immoral. We do not have the right to gain at anyone else's expense, and that's what demands are all about.

Being considerate is not just a word game. It means behaving in a way that takes other people's feelings into account. If you suspect that your spouse will find it unpleasant to meet your request, you're being thoughtless if you persist.

This leaves many people in a quandary. They do not want to be thoughtless, but without demands, how can their basic emotional needs be met?

I've encountered a few people who simply refuse to do anything for their spouse unless they're threatened with punishment. They suffer from a pervasive character disorder that limits their ability to care for others, and their marriages are usually frequent and of short duration. But even in these cases, demands do not solve the problem for the long term.

Fortunately, in the vast majority of couples I've seen, reciprocal care is instinctive, and demands are unnecessary if requests are made thoughtfully. With this in mind, I encourage couples to take one

ACTION STEP

If your spouse has a problem with your request, withdraw it in its present form.

final step when a request has been withdrawn because it was rejected in its present form.

Step 3: Discuss other ways your spouse could enthusiastically help you.

ACTION
STEP

Discuss other ways your spouse could enthusiastically help you.

Your spouse probably wants to help you—even when he or she refuses your request. It isn't the helping that's being refused—it's the form the help takes. If the requested task is unpleasant, there may be another way to get the job done that is enjoyable. For example, if Jim wants Karen to help him clean out the garage, she may object because of his timing. Suppose she's been looking forward to spending that time on another project that's more important to her. After she declines his initial request, he may ask if she would be willing to help at some other time. It may turn out that she doesn't mind helping him the following weekend.

But what if she can't imagine *ever* helping with the garage? What if Karen sees that as Jim's job and his alone?

This is where the Policy of Joint Agreement gets a workout. Jim must not demand his way, even if he is demanding that Karen come up with an alternative to his original request. He should approach this discussion seeking a solution to which Karen will enthusiastically agree. Together they can brainstorm the situation, looking for arrangements that will satisfy them both.

Later in this book, I will focus attention on how to arrive at mutually enthusiastic agreements. But for now, I want you to understand that they are not only a good alternative to getting you what you need in marriage, they are also the only alternative that is not controlling and abusive. If you want consistent help from each other, there is no better way to get it than through an enthusiastic agreement.

Thoughtful Requests Build Habits

If you only expect to get the help you need when you're exhausted you're not likely to create the habits that you need in your spouse. If you really feel that you need help with the dishes once in a while, it makes a lot of sense to go to the trouble of creating the habit of you and your spouse doing the dishes together every night in a way that would be enjoyable for both of you. That way when Tuesday night rolls around and you're exhausted, it's a done deal. You get the help you need because it's something you've already negotiated with each other and you're doing it in a way that doesn't require sacrifice from either one of you.

The husband that's sitting there watching television while his exhausted wife is slaving away at the dishes isn't a lazy husband. He's a husband that's in the habit of watching television. This man could just as easily be in the habit of helping his wife with the dishes and enjoying it just as much as watching television. The problem is, when he's already in the habit of watching television, he's going to be very upset with a wife who simply turns the television off and demands that he start washing the dishes. That isn't the way to get the job done. It creates anger and resentment, and you lose a lot of love units while those dishes are being dried.

But if you explain the need in a thoughtful way and get into the right habits, the evening that this husband and wife spend together with their children could be enjoyable because they've created it to be enjoyable. They've thought it through and they decide to do things for each other that they find enjoyable. And that enjoyable routine is repeated night after night.

Keeping Your Requests Thoughtful

Let each other know when you drift from thoughtful requests back to selfish demands. And try not to react defensively when your spouse gives you feedback. You may be surprised the first time your spouse reminds you that you are making a selfish demand. From your perspective, you were making a request, not a demand. But if you have been in the habit of making demands, you're likely to continue making them without even thinking. And only your spouse will be able to recognize the difference between a selfish demand that's disguised as a thoughtful request and a genuine thoughtful request.

You may complain that you didn't mean to make a selfish demand, that you meant to make a thoughtful request. But that's not the point. The point is that your spouse has interpreted what you've asked for as a demand. Until your spouse starts interpreting what you ask as requests, you're going to have to work on not only your intent, but also your wording.

Adopt a policy of zero tolerance for selfish demands.

And don't make the mistake that many couples make where you begin arguing about whether something was or wasn't a selfish demand. As far as I'm concerned, whoever is making the request must convince the other spouse that it's not a demand. If the spouse receiving the request is completely honest, you're going to learn quite a bit about how to adjust to his or her feelings. And in so doing you're going to be in a great position to create a lifestyle that's full of passion for both of you.

Quite frankly, your effort to convert demands into requests is a great way to communicate what it is you need. As you both learn to accommodate each other's needs in a way that would be enjoyable to both of you, you will eventually be in the habit of getting what you need most from each other voluntarily, instead of trying to do it in ways that are controlling and abusive. Ultimately you want to receive help without even having to ask. In other words, you want your spouse to form the *habit* of helping you (as you develop a habit of helping your spouse). Demands cannot accomplish this. Demands may get the job done in the present but they sabotage the future.

Demands are the strategy of your Taker, who doesn't care at all about the feelings of your spouse. But you care about your spouse, so don't follow the instincts of your Taker. Get into the habit of doing the intelligent and caring thing for each other. Make thoughtful requests, not selfish demands. If you can eliminate selfish demands from your marriage, you'll have eliminated one of the most important reasons that couples fall out of love with each other.

Key Principles

- If you command your spouse to do things that would bene-fit you at your spouse's expense, with implied threat of pun-ishment if refused, you are guilty of making selfish demands. The Taker encourages you to make selfish demands.

- Selfish demands are abusive and controlling, but they seem reasonable to make when you are frustrated because your Taker gives you all the justification you need to make demands.

- Selfish demands are more common in marriage than in other relationships. To overcome the habit, your spouse should avoid meeting your demands even when he or she is encouraged to do so by the Giver.

- A thoughtful request is asking your spouse to do something for you, with a willingness to withdraw the request if there is reluctance. The request must be preceded by "How would you feel if you were to . . ."

- Thoughtful requests will help you create habits that provide the care you need from each other. Selfish demands, on the other hand, will not lead to habits that give you what you need in the long run.

- You should have zero tolerance for your selfish demands.

Consider This . . .

1. What is the difference between a selfish demand and a thoughtful request? Have you been able to identify selfish demands in your marriage? When one of you makes a selfish demand does the other spouse bring it to your attention? What have the consequences of such feedback been? Do you tend to punish each other for com-plaining about demands, or do you appreciate the feedback?

2. What is the Policy of Joint Agreement? Why is it important for you to make decisions that take each other's feelings into account? Why is an enthusiastic agreement important? It's because I want you both to benefit from each agreement you make with each other that I require enthusiastic agreement. Do you agree with me?

3. Are you both willing to eliminate selfish demands and replace them with thoughtful requests? If you are in the habit of making demands, it will take practice to avoid them. I suggest that you each make a worksheet titled, "Selfish Demands," so that whenever one of you feels the other has made a demand, you write it on your worksheet. Be sure to avoid arguing about whether or not you have made a demand. Remember, the one who feels it was a demand defines it. It's up to the one who made the demand to learn to rephrase it so that it is regarded as a thoughtful request.

4. Make a second worksheet titled, "Thoughtful Requests." Write down each instance of what you considered to be a thoughtful request. And make as many requests of each other as you want. The practice will do you good. But don't be disappointed if you are denied your request in the form in which it was presented. It will give you opportunity to consider other options so your spouse can give you what you need in a way that follows the Policy of Joint Agreement.

5. How comfortable are you in making requests of each other? When spouses are in the habit of making selfish demands, they are often reluctant to make as many requests of each other as they should. They tend to use demands as a last resort to getting what they think they deserve and forget about asking for what they simply need from each other. By learning how to make thoughtful requests, you will probably be asking for more and receiving more from each other than you did when you were making demands.

chapter four

DISRESPECTFUL
JUDGMENTS

WHO WANTS TO LIVE WITH A CRITIC?

Linda was raised by parents who worked long hours but never seemed to get ahead. Poor educational background was the main reason for their low income—neither parent graduated from high school. But their large family—five children—was also a contributing factor. Linda, her three brothers, one sister, and their parents shared a small house and just about everything else throughout her childhood.

After graduating from high school, Linda found a job as a receptionist, which paid enough to support her. So at eighteen, she moved away from home, rented an apartment, bought her own car, and felt on top of the world.

Tom, a new executive, found Linda very attractive. At first, he just greeted her whenever he passed her desk, but the greetings turned into conversations and before long he was regularly having lunch with her. Eventually they fell in love.

Tom was well educated, having earned advanced degrees in both law and business administration. When he met Linda's family, he was immediately accepted and respected by them all. Her father was especially pleased that she chose to date such an intelligent man.

At first, Tom had respect for Linda and her family as well. But as their romance developed, he began making critical remarks about the decisions made by members of her family. Then, occasionally, he began to criticize Linda's decisions. Since he was so well educated, she assumed in most instances that he was correct and she was wrong. It bothered her whenever he made these critical remarks, but it happened so seldom that it did not have much effect on her love for him.

Before long they were married, and after the honeymoon Tom and Linda returned to work as husband and wife. But their relationship at work changed the very first day: Linda found herself working with her worst critic, who also happened to be her husband.

Now that they were married, Tom became more critical than he was before. He would bring the smallest errors to her attention and coach her on improving her posture, telephone etiquette, and other office skills.

Of course, she became increasingly unhappy at work and eventually decided to quit. She used the excuse of wanting to prepare for having children, but her real reason was to escape Tom's incessant criticism. Her income, after taxes, was not enough to make much of a difference in their standard of living anyway, since Tom earned enough to support them both. Besides, she was raised to value the role of a homemaker and full-time mother.

But as soon as she quit her job, she went from the frying pan into the fire. At home Tom became even more critical than he'd been at work. He expected her to develop a high level of homemaking skills and critically evaluated her work each day. Her performance rarely met his standards, so she just gave up. Before long, she was spending the day watching television and sleeping.

Since his lectures on homemaking didn't seem to help, Tom turned his attention to subjects of motivation and ambition. When he came home from work, Linda had to suffer through Tom's self-improvement courses. Their discussions became so one-sided that she eventually stopped trying to explain her point of view.

Tom rationalized his efforts to straighten Linda out as his way of caring for her. He would explain to her that he was doing her a favor by helping her overcome weaknesses. In the end, he told Linda, she would thank him for his "coaching."

But the truth was that he was being controlling and abusive. He wanted things done his way, and he didn't really care how Linda felt about it. He was trying to turn her into his personal slave. But instead of simply making demands on her, he used a more sophisticated approach to abuse—he showed disrespect in an effort to shame her into doing what he wanted. He knew that his criticism was making her unhappy, but he did nothing to protect her. His "help" was causing her to become very depressed, and his lectures made massive Love Bank withdrawals. Before long Linda had lost her feeling of love for Tom.

> **Disrespectful Judgments**
>
> Attempts to "straighten out" your spouse's attitudes, beliefs, and behavior by trying to impose your way of thinking through lecture, ridicule, threats, or other forceful means.

Linda became so depressed that Tom decided that she needed professional help. He made an appointment to speak with me alone, to determine my competence. After I passed his test, he brought her with him to the second session and wanted to be included in the interview. But I asked to speak with Linda alone while he remained in the waiting room. Within two sessions, however, I had Tom join her—for marriage counseling.

You're Always Right?

Have you ever tried to straighten out your spouse? Occasionally we're all tempted to do that sort of thing. At the time, we think we're doing our spouse a big favor, to lift him or her from the darkness of confusion into the light of our "superior perspectives." We think that if our spouse would only follow our advice, he or she could avoid many of life's pitfalls.

Yet our effort to keep our spouse from making mistakes usually leads to a much bigger mistake, one that destroys the feeling of love. The mistake is called *disrespectful judgments.*

A disrespectful judgment occurs whenever someone tries to *impose* his or her way of thinking or way of doing things on someone else. If you ever try to force your spouse to accept your point of view or do something the way you want it done, you're just asking for trouble.

Most of us feel that our judgment is correct. When we hear others express opposing views or doing something differently than the way we are accustomed to doing it, we sometimes feel that their opinions and behavior will get them into trouble someday. If it's your spouse disagreeing with you, naturally you want to save him or her from the pain that this mistake will create. So you try to change your spouse's opinion.

But disrespectful judgments do not really come from our Giver's compassion for others—they come from our Taker's desire to help us get what we want. The Giver doesn't try to impose anything on people—it tries to accommodate people's opinions and behavior. It's the Taker that's unaccommodating and rigid, trying to get what's best at the expense of others. And when demands don't work, the Taker encourages us to use a more sophisticated form of control next—disrespectful judgments.

If Tom had understood his true motives for trying to straighten out Linda, he would have known that he was trying to get his way at her expense. He wanted her to do things his way at work, and then when she quit, he wanted her to do things his way at home. The ruse of care was used to hide his controlling and abusive ways. Linda knew that whatever he was doing hurt her terribly, but she was duped into thinking it was somehow good for her.

Even though Linda believed that Tom was doing the right thing by trying to straighten her out, his disrespectful judgments still destroyed her love for him. There are many who can see through the deception of the Taker, and when their spouse makes disrespectful judgments they know it's based on selfishness. In their case, the Love Buster is exposed for what it is. But even when a spouse is deceived into thinking that disrespect is motivated by care, the result is the same—it destroys the feeling of love. That's because disrespect always hurts. In the case of selfish demands, it's relatively easy to see how a demand represents an effort on your part to gain at your spouse's expense. But in the case of disrespectful judgments, your own self-centeredness is usually hidden. The Taker tries to fool both you and your spouse into thinking that you're doing your spouse a favor. But disrespect never grows out of compassion—it grows out of selfishness.

While you may think that you have all the answers to the world's questions and that your perspective is better than your spouse's, unless you fully understand your spouse's perspective, you're in no position to judge it. The more you understand your spouse's attitudes and beliefs, the more you'll understand and appreciate why your spouse feels the way he or she does. And the less likely it is that you'll try to straighten him or her out.

> ### Respectful Persuasion
>
> Blending your value systems, giving each one's wisdom an opportunity to override the other's foolishness.

If you show respect for your spouse's opinions and ways of doing things, you may still see the need for change, but you will discuss any conflicting issue with a willingness to change your own mind, too. In the process, the two of you learn something from each other. That's how *respectful persuasion* works.

In marriage the blending of a husband and wife's value systems and behavior brings benefit to both. Each partner brings both wisdom and foolishness to the marriage. By respectfully discussing beliefs and values, the couple has an opportunity to create a superior system. But the task must be approached with mutual respect if it is to work. Without that respect, the husband and wife cannot improve their values and behavior—and they will lose their love for each other.

Ridicule Doesn't Work Either

Tom's efforts to straighten Linda out were not her only problem. Whenever she expressed an opinion, Tom tended to make fun of her. He thought her ideas were so stupid that they were funny, and told her so whenever she tried to express herself.

While disrespectful judgments are usually an effort to try to show that you're right and your spouse is wrong, sometimes in marriage the sole purpose of disrespect is entertainment. For some, whenever they ridicule their spouse, they're not trying to change his or her opinions or behavior, but rather using the situation as something to laugh at—something that they find funny.

When it comes right down it, almost all humor is ridicule of one form or another. Most jokes are designed to point out the foolishness of people's thinking or behavior. But in marriage making your spouse the butt of ridicule is extremely dangerous. Not only is it very hurtful to the one being ridiculed, but if you're not careful, the tables can be turned and the ridiculed spouse can return ridicule in a way that doubles the pain. Some spouses raise ridicule to an art form where they use every opportunity to make fun of each other. But it's not fun for the person being ridiculed. In fact, it makes massive Love Bank withdrawals.

> **Almost all humor is ridicule of one form or another.**

In marriage you have an opportunity to know each other's deepest secrets and greatest weaknesses. You know some of your most embarrassing moments, which leave both of you very vulnerable to each other's ridicule. It's extremely important for you to know each other so well that you thoroughly understand your weaknesses. But that creates a vulnerability and responsibility that's almost unprecedented in life. The price of learning each other's deepest secrets should be a guarantee never to use that information to hurt or try to make fun of each other.

I hope you're beginning to see what disrespectful judgments really are: an instinctive way to make your spouse feel miserable. Disrespect is a real Love Buster.

The Road to Recovery

When Linda became depressed, Tom assumed that she had not learned the lessons he tried to teach her, so he pressed them with even greater diligence. But the harder he pressed, the more depressed she became. He was so convinced he was right that he was oblivious to the suffering he was inflicting on her.

The first time I spoke with Linda, she explained how unpleasant her life had become since she married Tom. She used to enjoy housework, and looked forward to raising children. But now that Tom expected her to become a professional home economist, a whole lifetime of failure loomed before her. Raising children no longer appealed to her, because it would only increase the ways that Tom could criticize her. She felt useless and trapped. And if that wasn't bad enough, her sexual attraction to Tom had disappeared entirely. Everything he expected of her, including lovemaking, had become impossible to perform.

In my session with Tom, I explained to him that, in his effort to help his wife, he'd apparently overlooked her emotional reactions. Perhaps his advice would have helped Linda if her feelings had been taken into account. But because he overlooked her feelings, his advice was useless. Her depression was, in part, caused by his flawed approach to helping her.

Since there was a part of Tom that cared a great deal for Linda and wanted her to be healthy and happy (his Giver), he was willing to test my theory. If she recovered from her depression, he was willing to make the changes permanent. By this time, even his Taker was looking for a new approach, because her depression was making him unhappy. Anything he could do to make her more cheerful would be in his best interest.

I focused attention on the way Tom and Linda made decisions. Until they came to my office, Tom tried to make many of Linda's decisions for her. And he rarely consulted her about her feelings on those issues. Linda had very little confidence in her own judgment, and the longer she'd been married, the more convinced she became that Tom was smarter—so she let him make all the decisions.

Use the Policy of Joint Agreement to Overcome Disrespectful Judgments

If Tom was to overcome his disrespectful judgments, Linda had to become an equal partner in their decision making. He needed to respect her perspective on each issue they faced and give her equal power in coming to final decisions. So I ventured forth with a plan to teach Tom how to make decisions that would respect Linda's opinions.

Before training them in respectful decision-making, I gave Tom and Linda the rule I introduced to you in the last chapter, the Policy of Joint Agreement: *Never do anything without an enthusiastic agreement between you and your spouse.*

This rule gave Tom a new perspective on how to make decisions with Linda. From then on, he could never force his way of thinking on her, because that approach would not result in her enthusiastic agreement. He could not shame her; he could not talk over her; he could not ridicule her. None of those would lead to an enthusiastic agreement. If he wanted to change her mind or behavior, he had to *respectfully persuade* her. And he had to be so persuasive that she would enthusiastically agree with him.

Up to the day Tom was introduced to the Policy of Joint Agreement, he rarely discussed his plans with Linda and didn't feel he needed her approval. He believed he was being thoughtful when he merely told her what he was doing, and when he bothered to get Linda's reluctant agreement to his plans, he felt he was going the extra mile!

But from that day forward, everything Tom did had to meet with Linda's *enthusiastic* agreement. I knew he'd find the rule incredibly difficult to follow at first, and I expected him to make many mistakes. But it would set him on a course that would eventually lead Linda out of her depression and ultimately save their marriage.

After Tom and Linda agreed to follow the Policy of Joint Agreement, we focused attention on the details of their joint decision-making. To get an enthusiastic agreement with Linda, Tom had to learn to treat her opinions and behavior with respect. At the same time, Linda needed help in developing a higher regard for her own perspective and feelings.

Turning Disrespectful Judgments into Respectful Persuasion

Put yourself on the receiving end of disrespectful judgments. Few conversations are more irritating than those in which someone tries to force his opinion on you, and so you're seldom swayed by those who badger you. You end up wondering, *Why should I consider the point of view of someone who's so insensitive?* You don't *want* to be persuaded by someone who doesn't even consider your perspective, let alone understand it.

On the other hand, when someone makes an effort to consider your opinion before presenting his or her own, you're far more open to an alternative view.

One of a salesperson's first lessons is to understand the need of the prospective buyer before presenting a product. The prospective buyer will consider the product if it meets a need, *but if he or she doesn't need it,* the salesperson wastes everybody's time.

How often have you been called on the telephone (in the evening) by a telemarketing salesperson who wants to sell you a new telephone service? "I'm satisfied with my existing service," you answer, trying to explain that you have no need. But instead of politely ending the conversation, the telemarketer begins to read the sales pitch as if you had not spoken. I react to such an approach by mentally labeling that company as one I will never do business with, even if they offer me *free* telephone service!

First determine why your point of view would be an improvement.

If you want to persuade your spouse to your way of thinking, you must first determine why your point of view would be an improvement. If your perspective would make life easier or more successful, then your appeal should be seriously considered. But if it makes *your* life easier *at your spouse's expense* (which is often the case), your selfish motives will make your position very weak.

In most cases, we want our spouse to change perspective for selfish reasons. We want something we haven't been getting. But if we follow the Policy of Joint Agreement, wanting only what our spouse can do with enthusiasm, there must be something in it for him or her, too.

If you eventually come to the conclusion that what you want is in your best interest, but not in your spouse's best interest, you will have to regroup and figure out a way for your spouse to benefit. Or else, drop the subject and move on.

Unless your spouse can also benefit from what you want, it's not something that's good for your relationship. But if you're certain that your perspective would be of value to your spouse, you need to introduce evidence to prove it. People are usually willing to try something for a while, and that may give you the chance to test the value of your perspective.

There are five steps that I suggest you can follow to replace disrespectful judgments with respectful persuasion.

Step 1: Express your conflicting opinions to each other with respect and understanding.

The first step in any marital conflict is to define the conflict with respect and understanding. When you have a disagreement, can you clearly explain *your spouse's* opinion as well as you can explain your own? Many needless arguments arise because spouses misunderstand each other.

Being able to state *your own* position clearly is crucial in helping your spouse understand your motives and true objectives. For example, if I want my wife to wear her seat belt, I might tell her that I care about her safety and it makes me nervous when she drives without her belt buckled up. This type of explanation helps her understand the emotional reasons behind my opinion.

In response to my concern for her welfare, she may explain to me that she doesn't wear a seat belt because it makes her feel confined and wrinkles her clothes. Explaining her position in emotional terms takes the issue away from the philosophical debate. It turns out that she is not opposed to people wearing seat belts. In fact she believes it is a good idea to wear them. She just doesn't feel it's necessary for *her.*

In this example, we are not in disagreement over the principle itself. We merely disagree over the application of the principle to my wife's behavior.

In fact most arguments are like this—not rooted in different beliefs but in differing *emotional reactions* to the application of beliefs. If Joyce *feels* bad when she wears seat belts, she will tend not to wear them.

If I tell her to wear seat belts, and wearing them makes her feel uncomfortable, I am losing love

ACTION STEP

Express your conflicting opinions to each other with respect and understanding.

73

units in two different ways: First, people usually don't like to be told what to do; second, wearing seat belts makes her feel uncomfortable, and I'll be blamed for that unpleasant feeling whenever she buckles up.

If I want to avoid losing love units, *she* must believe that my opinion is in her best interest. And she must learn to wear seat belts in a way that is not uncomfortable for her. I try to achieve that objective in the second step.

Step 2: Explain why you feel your opinion is in your spouse's best interest.

Why do husbands and wives have so much trouble discussing their differences? It's usually because the discussion is so unpleasant. Rather than discovering each other's emotional needs and working together toward mutual need satisfaction, they tend to show disrespect for each other. How long can a conversation like that last before someone wants to run and hide?

In the first step, you are to explain your opinions to each other with respect. But the second step will take an extra-special effort if you are to remain respectful. That's because this step is your first try at trying to change your spouse's mind. How can you do that with respect? After all, if your spouse were right to begin with, you wouldn't be trying to change his or her mind.

I suggest you begin by showing respect for the opinion of your spouse, even though your goal is to try to change it. You might say, "Even though I don't agree with you, I know you have good reasons for your opinion. But I would like to suggest some other reasons that may change your mind."

Some people have great difficulty making the above statement because they don't believe their spouse has any good reasons for his or her opinions. This attitude reveals an underlying misunderstanding. As I mentioned earlier, the more you understand people, the more reasonable their opinions are.

ACTION STEP

Explain why you feel your opinion is in your spouse's best interest.

Respect is crucial in persuasion, but it isn't something that your Taker would have ever come up with. Remember your Taker isn't interested in how other people feel or how other people will benefit.

74

Your Taker's only interested in how you're going to feel. So your Taker's strategy for persuasion is to try to force your spouse into your way of thinking without looking after your spouse's interests. Your Taker wants to make your spouse accept your point of view because it's good for you. If he or she doesn't go along with it, your Taker will then try to punish your spouse. So respect is completely unintuitive to your Taker. And if your persuasive efforts have been guided by your Taker lately, it'll be unintuitive to you as well. But let me assure you if you want to persuade your spouse to your point of view in a respectful way you must demonstrate convincingly that it's in your spouse's best interest.

Using our seat belt example, I would be foolish to shout at Joyce, "Can't you see how stupid you are when you don't wear your seat belt?" That would not only be an ineffective and antagonizing statement, it would also reflect my own ignorance of her reasons for not wearing it. Instead, I might explain how unpleasant her life could become if she were thrown through the windshield. I might also point out her risk of being fined if the police stop her. On a more positive note, I could suggest that, once she adjusts to a seat belt, she will have greater control over her car and may feel more secure in her seat. I could even suggest wearing clothes that don't wrinkle when she drives or leaving her jacket in the back seat.

Respectful persuasion never involves an attack on your spouse's defenses. Joyce may disagree with me, saying that some people have been killed because they use seat belts—sometimes they are unable to unlock the strap to escape a burning automobile. I should accept the reasonableness of her defense. Remember, her initial problem was that seat belts made her feel confined. It's reasonable for her to fear being locked in a burning automobile, unable to escape.

Thus far in our discussion, I have tried to explain how my position is in Joyce's best interest, and she has explained that she doesn't agree with me. If I were to attack her explanation, it would probably get me nowhere. Instead, it's more prudent to take another approach: Simply ask her to test my opinion for a brief period of time to see if she likes it. This is the third step of respectful persuasion.

ACTION STEP

Suggest a test of your opinion.

Step 3: Suggest a test of your opinion.

A final argument in defense of your position is "Try it. You'll like it!"

People often make a big mistake in marital "discussions" when they try to force each other to make a committed change rather than a temporary one. Joyce is not convinced that my opinion is correct for her, so expecting her to make a commitment to my position is ridiculous! But her curiosity about my opinion and her respect for me may encourage her to risk a test of my opinion.

I might suggest to Joyce that she try to wear her seat belt each day for a week and see how she feels about it at the end of the week. In advance of the test, I would explain that habits take time to develop, so if she is comfortable with the first week's test, she may need to extend the test for a few more weeks so that she will develop a habit of seat belt wearing.

In some situations, a test is not possible. For example, investing all your retirement savings into a new business pretty well commits you to the program, once you make the decision. But most examples of disrespectful judgments that I have encountered as a marriage counselor could have been reformulated to accommodate a test.

Step 4: If the test fails to persuade, be prepared to drop the subject.

Clearly understand the bargain: If your spouse is not comfortable with your position after the test, you may ask for yet another test. But if your spouse feels the first test was sufficient, you must agree to drop the subject. At this point in respectful persuasion many couples forget the rules. The focus of attention should be on being *respectful,* not on *persuasion.* If your test is ineffective in persuading your spouse, you may have another opportunity someday, but at this point you should back off.

If on the other hand your test is successful, resist the temptation to force a commitment to your position. If your spouse finds that your opinion works, it will automatically be incorporated into his or her judgment.

If Joyce were to try wearing her seat belt each day for a week and by the end of the week she were to find the experience reasonably comfortable, she would probably be willing to extend the test for a few more weeks, as we had originally agreed. The problem would probably take care of itself without further intervention on my part.

ACTION STEP

If the test fails to persuade, be prepared to drop the subject.

But if Joyce did not find that my test worked for her, I would be in no position to insist on another test or, worse yet, try to force my position on her. I may discuss the outcome of the test with her, trying to understand what went wrong, and I can ask if she would be willing to try another one. But if she refuses, I should thank her for her willingness to try my first test and leave the subject alone.

Remember, the goals of respectful persuasion are (1) to avoid making Love Bank withdrawals and (2) to resolve conflicts—in that order. That way you will have many opportunities to resolve conflict because the process will be painless. But as soon as you do anything that your spouse finds unpleasant, it's no longer respectful persuasion, and it's unlikely to be repeated very often. The entire process must be pleasant and nonthreatening or your spouse will try to avoid it entirely. If you feel you must persuade your spouse at all costs, the cost will be love units, and you will be less likely to persuade. Even if I force my wife to say she agrees with me and force her to do what I want, I cannot force her to love me. Only the process of respectful persuasion can protect my account in her Love Bank.

Now at this point you may be feeling that if you drop the subject you'll be very unhappy with the outcome. But I want you to be aware of a very important fact—you do not have to change each other's minds about something to create behavior that makes each other happy. Remember, it's what you do for each other that will make you happy or what you do to each other that will make you unhappy. So in your efforts to create a more passionate marriage, one where you'll find each other absolutely irresistible, your focus of attention should be on each other's habits and not necessarily on each other's beliefs, opinions, and attitudes.

ACTION STEP

Give your spouse an opportunity to persuade you.

My mother is a social and fiscal liberal and my father is a social and fiscal conservative. They had many discussions about their differences, but it never led to a resolution. Yet throughout their lives they respected each other's opinions and were in love with each other. You don't have to agree on everything to have a great marriage.

Step 5: Give your spouse an opportunity to persuade you.

Respectful persuasion is a two-way street. Joyce has the right to try to influence my judgment just as much as I have the right to try to influence hers. Technically she has every right to try to convince me that wearing seat belts is a *bad* idea. Since most of us are convinced we should make a habit of wearing them, it's not a very reasonable illustration. Still, none of us has a corner on truth and we all can improve our judgments. Being open to the possibility that our loved one may be right about anything is a critical step toward respectful persuasion.

If I want to persuade my wife, I must be willing to let her persuade me. I must be open to the possibility that she could be right and I could be wrong about any issue we discuss. And I should be willing to test her opinion, just as she is willing to test mine.

Disrespectful Judge or Respectful Persuader?

How can you know if you're a perpetrator of disrespectful judgments? Ask your spouse. You may not realize how you come across. But you are disrespectful if your spouse thinks you're disrespectful. That's the deciding factor.

I've made up the following questionnaire to help identify this particular Love Buster. Ask your spouse to answer these questions honestly. If your spouse identifies you as one who makes disrespectful judgments, you'll probably be tempted to make yet another disrespectful judgment and claim that he or she is wrong! Believe me, in this situation your spouse is the best judge by a long shot.

If you feel terribly uncomfortable having your spouse complete the questionnaire, or if your spouse would prefer not to, then do your best to answer the questions *as you think your spouse would.*

The scoring of this questionnaire is simple. Unless all your spouse's answers are 1, you're probably engaging in disrespectful judgments. Almost all of us are guilty of this from time to time, so don't be alarmed if you get some 2s or 3s. But if your spouse gave you any 4s, 5s, 6s, or 7s, you're probably at risk of losing some of the romantic love in your marriage.

Disrespectful Judgments Questionnaire

1. Does your spouse ever try to straighten you out?

2. Does your spouse ever lecture you instead of respectfully discussing issues?

3. Does your spouse seem to feel that his or her opinion is superior to yours?

4. When you and your spouse discuss an issue, does he or she interrupt you or talk so much it prevents you from having a chance to explain your position?

5. Are you afraid to discuss your point of view with your spouse?

6. Does your spouse ever ridicule your point of view?

Don't make the mistake of winning the battle only to lose the war. An important part of romantic relationships is the support and encouragement lovers show each other. Disrespectful judgments do the opposite. If they have crept into your marriage, make an effort today to eliminate their destructive influence.

I encourage you to adopt a policy of zero tolerance when it comes to disrespectful judgments. Take my word for it, if you're in the habit of being disrespectful to each other, whatever hope you might have of changing each other's minds about crucial issues is a sheer fantasy. People don't change their minds after being shown disrespect. Instead, they go into a defensive mode and they're less likely to be persuaded. On the other hand, I think

Adopt a policy of zero tolerance for disrespectful judgments.

it is very important for both of you to gain from each other's wisdom. There's a real sense in which both of you should probably be straightened out by each other in a way that's respectful.

I want you to be able to influence each other. But I want you to do it effectively and in a way that doesn't destroy your love for each other. Each of you has quite a bit to offer the other.

When I discussed demands with you in the last chapter, I pointed out the fact that the expression of your needs to each other was so important that it was absolutely essential for you to learn to do it effectively. Demands are a very ineffective way to get your needs met. And so I encouraged you to use the more effective thoughtful requests.

We have the same situation here. I think it's extremely important for you and your spouse to influence each other's thinking. And the primitive instinct of your Taker, disrespectful judgments, just won't get the job done. Instead I'd like you to break the habit that your Taker's taught you and replace it with the new habit of respectful persuasion, so that whenever you have a disagreement about a belief or a value or an attitude or a behavior, you'll be able to resolve that conflict in a way that will take each other's feelings into account.

Key Principles

- Disrespectful judgments are attempts to "straighten out" your spouse's attitudes, beliefs, and behavior by trying to impose your way of thinking through lecture, ridicule, threats, or other forceful means.

- When selfish demands fail to get you what you need from your spouse, your Taker's next approach is to use disrespectful judgments.

- Disrespectful judgments are abusive and controlling, but your Taker disguises them as a way to care for your spouse by changing his or her unproductive attitudes, beliefs, and behavior.

- Respectful persuasion requires a blending of your value systems, giving each one's wisdom an opportunity to override the other's foolishness.

- Failure to reach agreement on attitudes and beliefs will not destroy your love for each other, as long as you follow the Policy of Joint Agreement whenever you make decisions. But being disrespectful about your differing views will destroy your love for each other.

- You should have zero tolerance for your disrespectful judgments.

Consider This . . .

1. What is the difference between disrespectful judgments and respectful persuasion? Have you been able to identify disrespectful judgments in your marriage? When one of you makes a disrespectful judgment does the other spouse bring it to your attention? What have the consequences of such feedback been? Do you tend to punish each other for complaining about disrespect, or do you appreciate the feedback?

2. Review the Policy of Joint Agreement with each other. What is it? Why is it important for you to make decisions that take each other's feelings into account? Why is an enthusiastic agreement important?

3. Are you both willing to eliminate disrespectful judgments and replace them with respectful persuasion? If you are in the habit of being disrespectful, it will take practice to avoid it. I suggest that you each make a worksheet titled, "Disrespectful Judgments," so that whenever one of you feels the other has been disrespectful, you write it on your worksheet. Be sure to avoid arguing about whether or not you have been disrespectful. Remember, the one who feels you have been disrespectful has an important point to make, and you should try to understand it. It's up to you to change your approach so that it is interpreted by your spouse as respectful persuasion.

4. Make a second worksheet titled "Respectful Persuasion." Write down each instance of what you considered to be an instance of respectful persuasion. And try to persuade each other as much as you want. The practice will do you good. But don't be disappointed if you are

not persuasive. It will give you opportunity to understand what your spouse considers convincing and what doesn't work.

5. How comfortable are you in trying to persuade each other? When spouses are in the habit of being disrespectful, they are often reluctant to try to change each other's minds as often as they should. They tend to use disrespect as a last resort to getting what they think they deserve and forget about trying to persuade each other to get what they need. By learning how to respectfully persuade, you will probably be challenging each other's opinions and behavior more often and receiving more wisdom from each other than you did when you were being disrespectful.

chapter five

ANGRY
OUTBURSTS

WHO WANTS TO LIVE WITH A TIME BOMB?

Jill's father was kind and generous 99 percent of the time. But during that other 1 percent, he terrorized the entire household with his anger. So even though Jill's boyfriend, Sam, lost his temper once in a while, she considered him well-mannered compared to her father's outrageous behavior. Sam didn't hit anybody, he didn't break furniture, and he was never arrested for disorderly conduct—he was a real gentleman!

Before they married, Sam directed his anger away from Jill. He'd curse other drivers on the road, he'd fume over his boss's foolish decisions, and he'd become irate when salespeople failed to wait on him quickly. Jill did many of the same things, so she just chalked this up to human nature.

One morning soon after they were married, both Sam and Jill overslept and were running late. As they scurried about, getting dressed, Sam suddenly had a problem.

"Jill, I'm out of clean shirts," he shouted.

She didn't quite know how to respond. Since they both worked, Jill and Sam usually shared the washing and ironing of clothes, but they had come to no formal understanding about who did what. Sam was a very generous person, and so most of the time he would do it all, but Jill would help him once in a while. It bothered him that Jill did not do all of the laundry, because in his home that's what his mother had done.

Jill tried to lighten up the situation. "I don't think any of mine will fit you," she joked.

"Was that supposed to be funny?" Sam shot back.

"Wear the one you wore yesterday," Jill suggested, trying to be helpful.

But Sam had already decided that she was at fault. "You had to notice that I was out of shirts last night," he bellowed.

"Me, notice your shirts? Please, get serious." With that she turned to finish getting ready herself.

"I'm not done talking to you. You knew I was out of shirts, didn't you?"

"No," she said, "I didn't know you were out of shirts. But even if I did, it's your problem, not mine."

With that, Sam flew into a rage, complete with recriminations, condemnations, and obscenities.

Jill started to cry. This was the first time Sam had directed his anger toward her. Although he was not being physically violent, it hurt her deeply. Sam left the room, and nothing more was said about the incident.

This angry outburst was the first of many Jill would endure during the first year of their marriage. The pattern would always be the same: Sam would have a problem, assume that Jill should have done something to solve it, and when she did not, he would lose his temper. Then she would cry, and he would back off. As time passed, however, the frequency and intensity of these outbursts increased.

They were planning to have children, but Jill wisely chose to see a marriage counselor first. She was afraid Sam's anger would eventually turn into the mayhem she had witnessed as a child.

Jill was wise to see a marriage counselor for another reason. Sam's angry outbursts had punched a hole in her Love Bank—it had sprung a leak. After one year of marriage, she was losing her feeling of love for Sam.

Every time Sam lost his temper, he was punishing Jill. This was doubly painful for Jill—she not only suffered from his punishing anger but also from the shocking realization that he was *trying* to hurt her. The man who had committed himself to her protection had become her greatest threat.

Why do couples destroy the love they have for each other with angry outbursts? In most cases, the problem begins with the false assumption that their spouse must do this or that for them. Control is ultimately behind every angry outburst. And when a spouse does not do what is expected (selfish demand), recriminations usually follow. Sam thought that Jill was an uncaring person, or she would have washed and ironed his shirts. That's a disrespectful judgment. Then, once she was deemed to be uncaring, his angry outburst was justified as punishment for her attitude.

> **Angry Outbursts**
>
> Deliberate attempts to hurt your spouse because of anger, usually in the form of verbal or physical attacks.

An angry outburst is usually an effort to teach a lesson—the one partner feels hurt and angrily tries to show the other how that feels. But in most cases, the angry spouse does not expect this punishment to ruin their love—after all, they promised to love each other forever.

They may have made the promise, but it was one they could not keep. People's feelings for each other are determined, not by promises, but by the Love Bank. When couples deliberately try to hurt each other, they deplete their Love Bank accounts. Romantic love becomes the victim of their anger.

Escalating Abuse

So far in this book I've talked with you about two types of Love Busters, selfish demands and disrespectful judgments. Now I want to help you overcome a third Love Buster: angry outbursts.

I've taken these first three Love Busters in sequence because they represent an escalation of control and abuse in marriage. Remember, control is making your spouse do what you want,

> **Demands, disrespect, and anger represent an escalation of control and abuse in marriage.**

and abuse is hurting your spouse intentionally. Neither of these should be tolerated in marriage.

Selfish demands are usually where abuse begins, because they force your spouse to do something for you that he or she is reluctant to do. In other words, you're trying to gain at your spouse's expense. You're willing to let your spouse suffer to get what you want.

The next level of abuse in most marriages is disrespectful judgments. In fact, they usually come on the heels of a failed selfish demand. If you can't force your spouse to do what you want with a demand, then your Taker will encourage you to escalate the abuse with disrespectful judgments.

If you stop to analyze the fights that you and your spouse have I think you'll see what I mean. You'll find that they often begin with demands and from there disrespectful judgments quickly follow. And if neither you nor your spouse has the sense to end a fight, this next Love Buster, angry outbursts, is sure to rear its ugly head. It's usually the final stage in the escalation of abuse, where couples consciously and deliberately do all they can to hurt each other.

Anger: A Threat to Your Spouse's Safety

I've listened patiently to husbands who have sworn never to hit their wife again, but by the next time I see them, they've inflicted even more bruises and broken bones. One man claimed to be "cured" in a religious service of his violent tendencies, then tried to kill his wife a short time later. Another man attempted to kill his wife three times before she finally divorced him. I have witnessed many cases of murdered or permanently injured men and women who gave their spouse one chance too many.

Your anger is the greatest threat to your spouse's safety. But even if the weapons you use in an angry outburst are not life threatening or disabling, you can still inflict a great deal of fear. Without a doubt it's a Love Buster.

Anger is the feeling that other people cause your unhappiness and they'll keep upsetting you until they're punished. They can't be reasoned with; the only thing they understand is pain and personal loss. Once you inflict that punishment, they'll think twice about making you unhappy again!

Anger's solution to a problem is to punish the troublemaker. This emotion overrides intelligence, which knows that punishment usually doesn't solve problems; it only makes the people you punish angry, which causes them to inflict punishment on you.

Anger also wins out over your commitment to provide safety and security for your spouse. When you become angry and try to hurt your spouse, your marriage is no longer safe. You are failing to protect your spouse from yourself.

Each of us has a private arsenal of weapons we can use when we're angry. If we think someone deserves to be punished, we're able to unlock the gate and select an appropriate weapon. Sometimes the weapons are verbal (ridicule and sarcasm), sometimes they're devious plots to cause suffering, and sometimes they're physical. But they have one thing in common: the ability to hurt people. And we can hurt our spouse more than anyone.

Each of us has a private arsenal of weapons we can use when we're angry.

Most of the angry husbands and wives I've counseled have fairly harmless arsenals—like Sam's outbursts. Others are extremely dangerous. Many of my clients have been arrested for physical abuse, and some have spent time in prison for beating their spouse. Most are remorseful at first but after they go through a time of hand-wringing, the conversation usually turns to lessons their spouse needs to learn. The bottom line for most of these clients is that they believe their spouse deserves the punishment.

Without a doubt, anger is the most destructive strategy of your Taker to get what you want. Most of the people that I've counseled who are perpetrators of angry outbursts don't see their anger as a real problem. As far as they're concerned, the real problem is their spouse's behavior that triggers their angry outbursts. "If she'd just stop being so annoying, I wouldn't get angry." "If he'd be a little more thoughtful and considerate I wouldn't lose my temper." In other words, most of the people who have angry outbursts feel that the other person made them do it.

That's the way the Taker thinks. Your Taker wants you to be happy and wants your spouse to make you happy. And it will use any tactics necessary to accomplish that objective. Of course, angry outbursts don't really accomplish that objective very well, but the Taker thinks it's worth a try. The fact that your angry outburst is destroying your spouse's love for you is of no consequence to your Taker. It's not interested in your relationship; it's interested in getting your way. And it mistakenly thinks that your anger will somehow get your spouse to do what you want.

Another reason that you lose your temper is to even the score. Let's suppose your spouse has done something that upsets you. Your Taker tries to convince you that your spouse needs to suffer the same pain that you suffered. So you let your spouse have it. Your anger isn't a solution to a problem; it's justice. If you didn't lose your temper, your spouse would get away with his or her thoughtless behavior.

Angry people tend to have a very elevated sense of injustice. They feel that people in general and their spouse in particular just aren't treating them fairly. But some of this feeling of injustice comes from the fact that they don't really negotiate to get what they need the most in life.

Let's get back to my case study of angry outbursts. Sam was under the illusion that if he gave sacrificially to Jill, she would give sacrificially to him. If she really cared about him, she would notice that his shirt inventory was down and get right to work washing and ironing shirts. Sam felt that he would do the same for Jill if the roles were reversed.

Sam was a generous man, and that was part of the problem. His Giver made so many sacrifices for Jill that his Taker wanted Jill to make a few sacrifices for him just to be fair. When Jill expected something of him, he went ahead and did it regardless of the pain or suffering that it might cause him. So he felt it was only fair for her to do the same.

When our own sacrifices are not reciprocated, it can make us feel used and very angry. We think we have a right to feel angry, because an obligation was not fulfilled. But when the Giver gives unconditionally, it really doesn't create an obligation at all. That's the problem with unconditional love—it does not require any reciprocity. In fact, when we do something for our spouse out of generosity, our spouse is to assume that it's unconditional, that he or she doesn't have to do anything in return for our sacrifice.

But the Taker does not see our generosity in the same way as our Giver sees it. It wants something for our effort and encourages us to have an angry outburst when nothing is forthcoming. It wants justice.

But anger doesn't provide justice; it provides pain and suffering to the very person that you promised to love and cherish. Instead of evening the score, it withdraws love units. It lowers your account in your spouse's Love Bank. Your angry outburst simply causes your spouse to love you less. And some forms of anger are so dangerous that your spouse shouldn't even live with you until you can guarantee his or her protection.

> **Anger doesn't provide justice, it provides pain and suffering.**

When angry outbursts reach extreme levels it's often too risky for the spouses to live together during therapy. Even successful therapy does not suddenly end abusive acts but brings about only a gradual decrease. This can be tolerated if we were dealing with, say, name-calling—an occasional slipup during the therapeutic process will not threaten the safety of a spouse. But it's quite another matter when the occasional failure takes the form of attempted murder.

I offer a plan to overcome angry outbursts in this chapter. And in most cases, the plan can be followed without the need for separation. But if your arsenal of weapons puts your spouse in physical danger, I strongly suggest following the plan while separated, because you will most certainly have failures from time to time as you overcome this abusive habit. Only when your spouse's physical safety can be guaranteed should you live with each other again.

I hope you've come to agree with me that an angry outburst in any form leaves your spouse unprotected from the worst of you. No one should have to put up with your angry outbursts, especially your spouse. So if you've decided to end your verbal or physical attacks on your spouse once and for all, you're ready for the next step, which is to better understand why you have angry outbursts in the first place.

Overcoming Angry Outbursts

Sam was not so sure he had a problem with angry outbursts but that's a common perspective of those who can't seem to control their temper.

Anger is deceitful: It lets you forget what really happened and offers you a distortion of the truth. When Jill described one of Sam's angry outbursts to me, he shook his head in disbelief. "It just didn't happen that way," he said in all sincerity. "I don't understand why you would tell Dr. Harley such a thing."

Of course, I wasn't at the scene, but experience has taught me to give the benefit of the doubt to the victim. When couples have tape-recorded their fights, the one having the outburst is usually amazed at what he or she said.

As a clinical psychologist, I view an angry outburst as a form of temporary insanity. What is said and done is often about as irrational as a psychotic episode, and when it is recorded, the one having the angry outburst usually agrees with my assessment once he hears and sees himself in action.

The fact that the details of the angry outburst are often forgotten or remembered falsely is also typical of a psychotic episode. Insane behavior usually takes a detour around our intelligence and has us behave in very primitive and irrational ways. Then it either fails to give us any memory of what we did or gives us an inaccurate memory that makes it seem more rational than it was.

Anger is deceitful and it is also cunning: It tries to convince you that an angry outburst is an appropriate reaction. Sam felt that Jill "made him" angry. If she had been more considerate, he would not have lost his temper. So it was her fault.

Many of my violent clients, both men and women, have told me that their spouses had it coming to them, that they deserved the angry reaction their thoughtless behavior aroused.

How do you go about stripping anger's deceit and cunning from outbursts so that anger can be seen for what it is? It's an ugly monster. How do you remove the screen that it hides behind?

Step 1: Identify instances of angry outbursts and their effects.

Sam had to begin with the facts. Did he have a problem with anger or didn't he? My first step in helping him overcome angry outbursts was to uncover the monster—describing Sam's angry reactions and their effects on Jill. The person in the best position to describe the problem was Jill.

So I had Jill answer the following questions:

1. On a scale from 0 to 6, with 0 indicating no unhappiness and 6 extreme unhappiness, what number most accurately reflects how much unhappiness you experience when your spouse attacks you with an angry outburst?
2. How often does your spouse tend to attack you with an angry outburst?
3. When your spouse attacks you with an angry outburst, what does he or she typically do? List the ways you are attacked.
4. Which of the ways you are attacked cause you the greatest unhappiness?
5. When did your spouse first attack you with an angry outburst?
6. Have your spouse's angry outbursts increased or decreased in intensity and/or frequency since they first began?
7. How do recent angry outbursts compare with those of the past?

I've counseled many who, after reading their spouse's answers to these questions, simply laugh. They are amazed that their spouse would write down what they believe are lies about their behavior. The deceit and cunning of their anger blind them to the truth. In some cases, they even lose their tempers as they are reading the answers.

If your spouse completes this questionnaire and you are tempted to view it as sheer fantasy, remember what I said about anger's deceit and cunning. Your spouse is in a much better position to record what you do when you are angry, so accept his or her word for it at this stage of the program. You must see anger for what it is: a threat to the safety and security of your spouse—and your marriage.

Jill's answers to these questions defined the problem and made it clear that Sam was making her unhappy with his angry outbursts. That was reason enough to do something about it. As Sam and I looked over Jill's answers, tears came to his eyes.

Sam saw that Jill had rated her unhappiness a 6, "extremely unhappy." He didn't want her to be unhappy and certainly didn't want to be the cause of her unhappiness.

What he had seen as an honest expression of his frustration, she interpreted as an ambush, a painful attack. His method of communicating his feelings had turned him into her worst enemy.

Sam's vicious attacks on Jill's character and judgment (disrespectful judgments) were weaved into his angry outbursts. He would tell her how selfish she was, how he was doing everything for her and she was doing nothing for him. He also would berate her abilities, charging that her only value was in her figure, not in her head.

His rantings simply weren't true. She did many things to prove her care for him and she was a highly skilled legal secretary, in great demand because of her knowledge and clerical ability. Sam's angry outbursts were filled with irrational statements made to hurt her, not to solve his problem.

Jill described the shirt incident as the first time she felt attacked by his angry outbursts. She had been a witness to his anger prior to that incident but until then it had not been directed toward her. She went on to describe his recent attacks and how they had become more frequent and more abusive. Jill also said that she was unwilling to raise children in an environment overshadowed by the threat of violence.

After Sam finished reading Jill's answers to the questions, he agreed to stop losing his temper. He made no excuses and, for once, agreed with her interpretation of the problem. We were ready to go to the next step.

ACTION STEP

Understand why angry outbursts take place.

Step 2: Understand why angry outbursts take place.

Now it was Sam's turn to answer a few questions. Why did he do it? Why did he lose his temper? I gave him the following questions to answer before our next appointment.

1. What are the most important reasons that you use angry outbursts to punish your spouse?
2. When you use angry outbursts to punish your spouse, what do you typically do?
3. When you use angry outbursts to punish your spouse, what hurts your spouse the most?
4. After you use angry outbursts to punish your spouse, do you usually feel better about the situation than before you used them? Why or why not?
5. Do you feel that punishment evens the score and that without it your spouse wins and you lose? Explain.
6. Do you ever try to control or avoid using angry outbursts to punish your spouse? If so, why do you do it? How do you do it?
7. If you were to decide never to use angry outbursts to punish your spouse again, would you be able to stop? Why or why not?
8. Are you willing to stop using angry outbursts to punish your spouse? Why or why not?

There is something about all of these questions that should jump out at you. Do you see it? Each question assumes that angry outbursts are *intended* to be a punishment. As it turns out, one of the ways people deceive themselves about anger is to interpret it as something other than punishment. One of my clients called it an expression of his creativity—another viewed anger as a cry for help. I probably haven't heard them all but I've heard hundreds of ways that perpetrators of violence have downplayed what anger really is. It's punishment, pure and simple.

The purpose of angry outbursts is to inflict pain and suffering on the target. Any other interpretation is part of anger's deception. When the deception is removed and you see it for what it is—punishment—it's much easier to ask the question *why?*

Sam understood that he was punishing Jill whenever she was the target of his anger. As he answered the questions in the privacy of his home, he began to uncover the reasons. After they were married, he had a growing feeling that she was more important to him than he was to her. He was very generous with her, but he did not see the same generosity returned by her. He made sacrifices for her regularly, but she did not make the same sacrifices for him.

And her career seemed to be the most important thing in her life. His feelings were hurt whenever she made her work a higher priority than his interests. So whenever he lost his temper, he attacked her career, which he felt was coming between them. But he also attacked Jill.

As we went through his answers, he realized that he was using anger to even the score, to make her feel some of the pain he felt. He admitted that after an outburst he felt a little better. At least he had expressed his frustration instead of keeping it bottled inside of him.

After Sam made the commitment to control his temper, he didn't think it would be difficult to achieve. He would just have to make the decision to stop and that would be that. Most people with angry outbursts feel that way. Some are right, but time would tell if Sam was being realistic.

He had seen the error of his ways, and he had decided to change. But was that enough?

ACTION STEP

Try to avoid the conditions that tend to trigger angry outbursts.

Step 3: Try to avoid the conditions that tend to trigger angry outbursts.

Before Sam left my office, I gave him a few more questions to answer for our next session. They concerned the angry outbursts we had been discussing in the assignment he had just completed:

1. In the instances of angry outbursts that you identified earlier, describe the conditions that seemed to trigger them. Include your physical condition (amount of sleep, physical health, etc.), setting, people present, behavior of those people, your mental state, and any other relevant information.
2. What changes in any of those conditions or efforts to avoid those conditions might help you stop angry outbursts in the future?
3. What changes identified in question 2 can be made with your spouse's enthusiastic agreement?
4. Describe your plan, which can be made with your spouse's enthusiastic agreement, to change or avoid the conditions. Include a deadline that also meets with his or her enthusiastic agreement.

Almost all of the conditions that tend to trigger an angry outburst usually begin with two very serious mistakes. The first mistake is to assume that caring people make sacrifices for each other. Remember the Policy of Joint Agreement? *Don't do anything without an enthusiastic agreement between you and your spouse.* That means if you're doing something for your spouse that you regard as a sacrifice, you're not following the Policy. Caring couples consider how they both feel simultaneously, and neither expects or wants the other to suffer for them. It's only the uncaring side of us that expects our spouse to make sacrifices on our behalf.

But the problem goes beyond making sacrifices. It's also a misunderstanding regarding agreements. The person prone to angry outbursts often feels that there's an unspoken understanding: That if I do this for you, you'll do this for me. But when that agreement isn't made clear and isn't understood by the other spouse, disappointment is sure to follow. So one of the points that I made to Sam was that he must learn to avoid making sacrifices for Jill, and then to make sure that agreements are clearly understood by both of them.

Another point that I made to Sam was that his angry outburst often came at the tail end of a series of mistakes. The first mistake is to think that you have the right to tell your spouse what to do with a demand. Once that mistake is made and your spouse is unwilling to comply with your demands, you have an angry outburst as your version of "or else." If your spouse doesn't do what you demand, out comes the arsenal of weapons.

Or, if your spouse tells you to do something for him or her "or else," that very Love Buster can trigger an angry outburst in **you**. When the "or else" means that you're going to be punished by your spouse for failing to deliver on his or her demand, that may be all the incentive you need to unlock the door of your arsenal of weapons.

So an angry outburst can often be a reaction to your spouse's failure to meet your demand or your reaction to your spouse's demand of you. In either case the demand itself is the error. Since neither of you should be making demands on each other, by getting rid of demands altogether you'll be getting rid of a very important condition that triggers your angry outbursts.

The same thing can be said for disrespectful judgments. If your spouse makes a disrespectful judgment about you, it's very likely to be the condition that triggers your angry outburst. On the other hand, if you make a disrespectful judgment about your spouse, and your spouse tries to defend him or herself, you may find that you will have an angry outburst as a way of trying to penetrate your spouse's defenses. As is the case in demands, it's the disrespectful judgment that's the mistake that leads to an angry outburst. By eliminating disrespectful judgments in your marriage, again you get rid of one of the important conditions that lead to angry outbursts.

Another condition that can trigger angry outbursts is your physical state of mind. You may find, for example, that when you wake up in the morning you may tend to lose your temper with very little provocation. A glass of orange juice may be all it takes for you to pull yourself together and gain control of yourself. If that's the case, your first item of business every morning should be to go to the refrigerator and have a glass of orange juice.

Physical surroundings may also affect your tendency to lose your temper. For example, battling traffic on your way home from work may put you in such a foul mood that nobody would want to have dinner with you, especially your spouse. So either changing your work schedule or changing the route you take to get home might make a world of difference in the attitude that you have most evenings.

You'll find that if you create a lifestyle around the Policy of Joint Agreement, where the events of your day are compatible with both your sensitivities and the sensitivities of your spouse, you'll greatly reduce the conditions that tend to trigger your angry outbursts.

When a husband and wife come to an agreement, I want it to be an *enthusiastic* one. Halfhearted, self-sacrificing arrangements generally fall apart the first time they're tested. So any changes that would help Sam control his temper had to be agreed to enthusiastically by Jill.

Sam felt that mornings were worst for him and that he tended to wake up irritable. Little things that Jill would do or say bothered him terribly at that time of the day. Later in the day, he seemed to have a completely different outlook on life, and he could handle irritations much better.

Jill's job was Sam's greatest source of frustration. Whenever she talked about it, particularly when she talked about her boss, it drove him nuts. He saw her job in general and her boss in particular as great threats to their future. Sam was fearful that Jill would eventually have an affair with her boss.

It is quite common for jealous husbands or wives to be angry with their spouse. The threat of something or someone coming between them makes them furious. Their anger, of course, doesn't begin to solve the problem. In fact it tends to drive their spouse into the arms of anyone who will save him or her from their terror experienced in marriage. Whether or not Sam had anything to fear from Jill's boss, his anger greatly increased the risk of an affair.

Angry outbursts are an inappropriate way to approach a marital conflict. It makes the solution much more difficult. The conflict that Sam had with Jill over her work and her relationship with her boss could be resolved, but not with the threat of an angry outburst.

So I encouraged Sam to resolve his conflict with Jill *after* he had learned to control his temper, rather than making it a *condition* to control his temper. It's like negotiating with terrorists. Whatever

ACTION STEP

Find an individual or support group to help you learn to control your temper.

they demand, you cannot let them have it. They must remove the threat to innocent citizens before you discuss a resolution. Otherwise they will use that threat every time they want something.

Sam's early-morning irritability was another matter entirely. Jill was perfectly willing to avoid discussing conflicts with him in the morning, and Sam also agreed. So they decided that their morning conversation would be limited to "please pass the milk," avoiding any unpleasant topics.

Step 4: When you cannot avoid conditions that trigger angry outbursts, find an individual or support group to help you learn to control your temper under those conditions.

The first line of defense against angry outbursts is to eliminate those conditions that tend to trigger your angry outbursts. But what if you can't eliminate those conditions? Or what if your spouse seems uncooperative? What if he or she refuses to stop doing the things that irritate you? How can you control your temper under those conditions? I've found that when a person simply can't avoid the conditions that trigger their angry outbursts, in order to keep their cabinet of weapons locked up, they usually need to find an individual or support group that will provide them encouragement and accountability in avoiding angry outbursts.

The goal of most anger management groups is to help people avoid an angry outburst when they're irritated the most and when others seem to be the most insensitive. I teach couples that I counsel that they can overcome angry outbursts even when the other spouse would make a mistake that would tend to trigger one.

Angry outbursts in marriage should be avoided at all costs, because they represent an extreme form of abuse. And a mistake of the other spouse should never be viewed as an excuse. While eliminating the conditions that tend to trigger an angry outburst makes them much easier to control, you should learn to avoid losing your temper regardless of what he or she does. This means that when you feel irritated, instead of venting your anger, you walk away. You leave the situation that's causing you to be angry, even if it means leaving your spouse for a while.

If you find that you can't guarantee your spouse's safety because you can't control your temper, then you shouldn't be with your spouse until you can guarantee that safety. In many of the situations I've encountered, I've encouraged a couple to physically separate until the spouse that has a bad temper can learn to control that temper to such a degree that avoiding an angry outburst can be guaranteed 100%. This is particularly true in cases where an angry outburst threatens a spouse's physical safety.

Sam had made a commitment to control his temper regardless of the conditions. In other words, even though Jill seemed to put her career interests before Sam's interests, he agreed not to express his frustration with an angry outburst.

From the perspective of an angry spouse, the solution is simple: *Stop doing what irritates me and I'll control my temper.* But any anger management therapist knows that a plan like that gets a person nowhere. The truth is, there are many situations in life, especially in marriage, where we cannot make others do what we want them to. People will do irritating things, there's no getting around it.

The goal of anger management is to avoid an angry outburst when you're irritated the most, when people seem the most insensitive. To achieve that objective, it's a good idea to find a person or group to hold you accountable. For Sam, I was that person. But an anger management group would also have been effective.

Although Sam thought he would have no trouble controlling his temper, just to be on the safe side he agreed to call me three times a week. I still met him for weekly appointments, but his five-minute calls were for support and accountability.

Step 5: Measure your progress.

Before Sam left my office, I invited Jill to join us and handed her a form with these instructions:

Please list all instances of your spouse's angry outbursts and acts that you consider punishment for something you did. These include verbal and physical acts of

ACTION
STEP

Measure your progress.

99

anger and threatened acts of anger toward you, cursing you, and making disrespectful or belittling comments about you. Include the day, date, time, and circumstances, along with a description of each angry outburst.

I asked Jill to keep a record of how well Sam kept his commitment to control his temper. Measuring progress is the most critical step in this plan to overcome angry outbursts, and the victim is usually the best one to do the measuring. Jill, more than anyone else, would know when Sam slipped up. Her documentation would be a big help in understanding precisely what it was that bothered her so much.

Before they left my office, I told Sam that he would have to accept as truth whatever Jill wrote down. He was not to argue with her about her interpretation of his behavior, but just try to avoid doing it in the future. I warned him that there would be some surprises the first week.

Sure enough, when he called me the first time for his five-minute session, she had already written down two instances of angry outbursts—and one of them was in the parking lot on the way out of my office.

"Why is she doing this to me?" Sam complained. "I didn't lose my temper. All I did was tell her that we didn't need to go through all of this. Can't I express my feelings anymore?"

I hadn't seen Jill's report, so I didn't know what he had said. But I explained that this was one of the surprises I had warned Sam about. It was important for him to understand exactly how Jill interpreted his "expression of feelings." To her it was punishment. I suggested that to be on the safe side, he should not express his frustration to her but to me instead.

Two days later, I talked to him again on the telephone, and he proudly announced that Jill had made no new entries since my last conversation with him. For the very first time he realized that his expression of frustration with Jill threatened her and made her unhappy. He would need to learn how to talk to her in a way that would make her feel safe.

When I saw Jill and Sam for their next appointment, I talked with Jill first and read the entries in her progress report. She explained how difficult it had been to be truthful, because she was afraid that the report itself would cause Sam to lose his temper. It's true. Some of my clients have reacted to the report with angry outbursts. One man actually tore it up when he read it because he did not agree with his wife's analysis.

Whenever that happens, it brings into focus the seriousness of the client's problem. In some cases a more intense plan of action must be created to address the fact that the anger is out of control. Sometimes I encourage couples to separate until a client can prove enough control to guarantee the spouse's safety.

I encourage you to have your progress measured, just as Jill measured Sam's progress. As was also the case with selfish demands and disrespectful judgments, your spouse is the best judge of whether or not you've had an angry outburst.

It's very common for someone having an angry outburst to view it as something else. For example, you may interpret raising your voice when you're having a disagreement with your spouse as simply an expression of concern. But your spouse may interpret it as an angry outburst. If that's the case you should try to avoid raising your voice when you're having a discussion. Your spouse may be very sensitive to your anger and may be greatly affected by even the slightest hint of your becoming angry.

Remember what the point of all of this is. You want to avoid affecting your spouse negatively. So if you have a habit that your spouse interprets as anger, get rid of it. Don't quibble about whether it is an angry outburst or not; the point is that it's causing your spouse to suffer and it's a habit that you can eliminate. Adjusting to each other in marriage is simply developing habits that make each other happy and eliminating those that make each other unhappy.

At this point you might ask the question, How long should my spouse go on documenting any instances of my angry outbursts? My answer is, For the rest of your life. Of course if you're successful there won't be any instances to document. But if you ever do something in the future that your spouse interprets as an angry outburst, he or she should have the right to bring it to your attention, and you should have the responsibility of apologizing to him or her for something that you'd promised not to do and then reviewing that strategy that you developed to see what went wrong. Did you follow the plan? Is there a new condition that triggers angry outbursts that you need to consider? Whenever you have an angry outburst, you might need to revise your plan so that you can avoid that sort of thing in the future.

Eventually, Sam was able to stop being verbally abusive, and he was able to reduce his feeling of anger toward Jill. He explained to me how he did it.

"I know what makes me feel angry. It is thinking that Jill doesn't really care about me and all she cares about is herself. But if I can relax and tell myself she really does care and that we will be able to work out our problems eventually, I don't feel as angry."

Jill really did care about Sam and wanted to have a family with him someday. She was definitely on his side and wanted him to succeed in controlling his anger. Within a few weeks, they were engaged in serious negotiations about the way her work affected him, and she made some very important changes to accommodate his feelings. His anger had driven her away from him, and now that he proved he could protect her from it, she was drawn closer to him, something he had wanted all along.

They also came to some very important agreements regarding child-rearing techniques. I warned them that Sam's anger could easily be directed toward their children, and that would also withdraw love units from Jill's Love Bank. So they both agreed that any discipline would be mutually agreed to, *enthusiastically* agreed to, or it wouldn't happen.

People with a predisposition to anger are also predisposed to bad marriages and, ultimately, divorce. But if you can recognize anger for what it really is, a monster, and learn how to protect your spouse from it, you not only save your marriage, but you also save yourself from a life of endless searching for someone you can get along with.

Despite what some people think, controlling your anger does not lead to serious emotional problems. I've counseled hundreds of people who have been successful in protecting their spouse from their angry outbursts, and none of them went crazy. Instead, they felt a lot better about themselves, and their spouses felt downright emancipated.

As I've said over and over, anger has no place in marriage. While it is a normal human reaction, it is also a destructive reaction, and you must protect your spouse from it if your spouse is to be happy and secure living with you.

Selfish demands, disrespectful judgments, and angry outbursts very often blend into each other. Sometimes it's a little difficult to know what is a selfish demand, and what is a disrespectful judgment, and what is an angry outburst, because in many arguments you have them all at once. When a spouse is making a demand he might also be disrespectful and angry all at the same time. That's one of the reasons that I put these three Love Busters on a continuum of abuse. All three of them represent ways that your Taker tries to get what you need by taking advantage of your spouse.

These three strategies are all very instinctive and can be seen in most of us when we're just a year old. Demands, disrespect, and anger are strategies to get our way that we're all born with. But just as they're inappropriate for children, and we try to teach children to avoid them, they're certainly inappropriate in marriage. If your parents didn't do a very good job teaching you to

> **Adopt a zero-tolerance policy for angry outbursts.**

avoid demands, disrespect, and anger, for the sake of your marriage and your spouse you need to learn to avoid them now. And you can learn to avoid them.

I've seen many marriages turn completely around because spouses have decided to take a zero-tolerance attitude toward their own anger, disrespect, and demands. And when that happens, it opens you up to negotiations that really work, where you and your spouse really do get what you need from each other. You see, I don't advocate giving up anger, disrespect, and demands with nothing to replace them. I want you to give these Love Busters up and then replace them with methods that really do accomplish the objectives that you have. I want you to have what you need in your marriage. It's just that anger, disrespect, and demands simply won't get that for you.

Later in this book I'll show you how you can get what you really need in your marriage by negotiating with your spouse effectively. And effective negotiation is only possible with the Policy of Joint

Agreement. It's only when you and your spouse make decisions that are in your mutual interests that you'll both be depositing love units into each others Love Banks simultaneously. You not only resolve your conflicts, but you resolve them in a way that builds your passion for each other.

Your love and passion for each other is more important than whether or not you resolve your conflicts.

It's very important to remember that your love and passion for each other is more important than whether or not you resolve your conflicts. Because if you're in love with each other, you'll have what you really want the most in your marriage. On the other hand, if all your conflicts are resolved and you're not in love with each other, you'll feel cheated. So if you remember that very important principle, that how you treat each other will determine how you feel about each other, you'll take my advice and completely eliminate from your marriage demands, disrespect, and anger.

Key Principles

- An **angry outburst** is a deliberate attempt to hurt your spouse because of anger, usually in the form of verbal or physical attacks.

- When selfish demands and disrespectful judgments fail to get you what you need from your spouse, your Taker's next approach is to use angry outbursts. It is the third and final escalation of abuse as a strategy for getting your way.

- Angry outbursts are abusive and controlling, but your Taker justifies them by trying to convince you that your spouse made you lose your temper.

- You should have zero tolerance for your angry outbursts. If my plan to help you overcome them doesn't work, seek professional help to guarantee your spouse' safety.

Consider This . . .

1. What is an angry outburst? Have you been able to identify angry outbursts in your marriage? Does the one having the angry outburst see it for what it really is, an abusive and controlling habit? When one of you has an angry outburst, does the other spouse bring it to your attention? What have the consequences of such feedback been? Do you tend to punish each other for complaining about angry outbursts, or do you appreciate the feedback?

2. Describe your arsenal of weapons. What do you tend to do when you have an angry outburst? Which weapons are the most offensive to your spouse?

3. Do you understand the conditions that tend to trigger your angry outbursts? How do selfish demands and disrespectful judgments tend to trigger them? You will notice that when your spouse makes a selfish demand or disrespectful judgment about you, it can make you feel angry. And when you make a selfish demand or disrespectful judgment without getting what you want from your spouse, it can also make you feel angry. But feeling angry and having an angry outburst are not the same. No one can avoid feeling angry once in a while, but we can all avoid angry outbursts. What is the difference between the two?

4. If you are in the habit of having angry outbursts, it will take practice to avoid them. I suggest that you each make a worksheet titled "Angry Outbursts," so that whenever one of you feels the other has had one, you write it on your worksheet. Be sure to avoid arguing about whether or not it has taken place. Remember, the one who feels you have had an angry outburst has an important point to make, and you should try to understand it. It's up to you to change your approach so that what you do and say is not interpreted by your spouse as an angry outburst.

5. If either of you cannot seem to gain control over your angry outbursts, I suggest you find professional help. Most hospitals and mental health clinics offer anger management therapy that has proven to be effective. But not all therapy is equal, so be certain that the therapist you select is recommended by doctors or social service agencies who have witnessed first-hand their effectiveness in treating this serious problem.

chapter six

DISHONESTY

WHO WANTS TO LIVE WITH A LIAR?

Jennifer found it easy to be honest with Ed about her feelings—while they were dating. He was a great guy, always trying to make her happy, so her accolades far outweighed her complaints. On the few occasions when he did something that upset her, she mentioned it briefly, and he quickly made accommodations.

The first time Jennifer was dishonest with Ed about her feelings was during their honeymoon. They were having dinner together in a restaurant that was on the beach. The evening was beautiful and from where they were seated, they could watch the waves crashing onto the sand.

Then Ed's cellular phone rang, and the mood suddenly changed. Ed had given his number to some of his best customers, and one of them wanted help with a problem.

Ed excused himself to talk to his customer, leaving Jennifer to enjoy the scenery and her dinner—alone. Half an hour later Ed returned, with apologies for the interruption.

Though Jennifer was deeply offended by the way Ed had treated her, she did not tell him how bad she felt. Instead, she told him how much she was enjoying the scenery.

That call at dinner was not the only one that interrupted their honeymoon. Ed received several calls, once while he and Jennifer were making love. Jennifer was hurt that Ed was trying to conduct business during their honeymoon, but she never let him know. She wanted him to be successful in his business and felt she had to learn to adjust.

Because of his demanding job, Ed left Jennifer alone three nights each week. This bothered her but she didn't want him to worry, so she let him think she was happy with the arrangement.

By the time they had children, both Ed and Jennifer had become increasingly preoccupied with the ever-escalating responsibilities of life. Their marriage suffered because they neglected each other's emotional needs, but neither Ed nor Jennifer thought it right to complain. In fact, they had read marriage books that warned them to avoid complaining. Their dishonesty was now mutual and growing.

Ed felt unfulfilled with their sexual relationship, but he understood the pressure Jennifer was under. After a long day of childcare, he knew she'd be tired when he came home from work late at night. He felt that it would be unfair to expect her to meet his sexual needs whenever he felt amorous. So he didn't tell her about his increasing sexual frustration.

Jennifer was also frustrated with Ed's neglect of her. Once in a great while, when he came home after another late night at the office, she'd admit, "I'm feeling lonely."

Ed would react a little defensively, "It took me longer than I thought to close the sale. We have bills to pay, you know."

"Yeah, I guess you're right." Jennifer would drop the subject and Ed would think she was satisfied with his answer. But she wasn't. She had told him how she felt, and he didn't seem to care.

And Ed even told Jennifer how he felt about their sexual relationship—once. When Jennifer explained that the children made her too tired at night, he said he understood. And he did, but the problem still bothered him.

Meanwhile, both Ed and Jennifer were innocently creating incompatibility. Slowly but surely they were growing apart because neither one said anything when his or her emotional needs were not met. Eventually, they were no longer in love with each other.

Radical Honesty Is Essential in Marriage

Ed and Jennifer's problems were a result of their failure to follow one of my cardinal rules of marriage—spouses must be radically honest with each other. By radical honesty I mean that they must be completely honest with each other about their feelings, their past experiences, their present activities, and their future plans. There are three very important reasons that radical honesty is essential in marriage.

> **Radical Honesty**
>
> Complete honesty about one's feelings, past experiences, present activities, and future plans.

Radical honesty provides a clear road map for marital adjustment. A husband and wife who are honest with each other can identify their problems very quickly and, if they know how to negotiate with each other, dispose of them very quickly. Sometimes dishonesty covers up both the problems themselves and the solutions to those problems. Honesty is simply revealing the facts. The more facts you have, the better your understanding will be of each other. And the more understanding you have, the more likely it is that you'll come up with solutions to your problems. Ed and Jennifer drifted into a loveless marriage because they failed to reveal their feelings well enough to understand the problems that they faced.

Radical honesty is also important because it meets an important emotional need. For many, radical honesty deposits so many love units that they fall in love with the person who's open and honest with them. In other words, for those people to be in love, there must be a clear and unobstructed view into the mind of their spouse.

But there's a third important reason for radical honesty in marriage, and that's the reason I will showcase in this chapter. Dishonesty is a Love Buster. When one spouse is lying to the other spouse or trying to cover the truth in some way, the spouse that's lied to is almost invariably offended. And that offense causes massive Love Bank withdrawals.

At the point we left Ed and Jennifer, dishonesty had prevented them from making adjustments to each other's emotional needs.

And the honesty that could have helped them bond with each other was missing. But there was more dishonesty that was yet to be revealed. In fact, the scope of their dishonesty was so great that it almost ended their marriage. This happened in several ways.

Types of Dishonesty

There are four types of dishonesty in marriage: (1) protection, (2) looking good, (3) avoiding trouble, and (4) compulsion. While the motives and excuses are very different for each type, the result is the same—your marriage suffers.

Protector Liars

In my opening illustration, Jennifer and Ed were practicing a very common type of dishonesty when they failed to reveal their negative reactions: protection. They were trying to care for each other, to protect each other from the pain of criticism. In many marriages, people keep unpleasant information from their spouses, perhaps a health scare or a financial setback. I call these people "protector liars," and most of us fit this category at least once in a while. Almost everybody can think of times when they have withheld their true feelings or unpleasant information to avoid upsetting their spouse.

> **Protective lying denies a spouse crucial information.**

It seems quite innocent, doesn't it? But the problem with protective lying is that it does not protect—it *denies* a spouse crucial information. As Ed and Jennifer "protected" each other from the truth about their feelings, they were both making huge withdrawals of love units *without knowing it*. Ed's work schedule was siphoning love units out of Jennifer's Love Bank, but she didn't let him know how it was affecting her. Each time Jennifer turned down Ed's sexual advances, she was making withdrawals in Ed's Love Bank, but he pretended there was nothing wrong.

How would you feel if your bank stopped giving you monthly statements on your checking account but continued to deduct fees for overdrafts without informing you? You'd be outraged.

109

"When our customers run out of money in their accounts," the bank manager might say, "we try to protect them from that unpleasant information." That's crazy! That's exactly the time you *need* information, so you can make some deposits and avoid bouncing checks.

The same is true in marriage. If Jennifer and Ed had known how often they were withdrawing love units, they could have made adjustments to prevent further losses. But without that information, they were blindly drifting into incompatibility.

Trying-to-Look-Good Liars

If lying to protect was the only type of dishonesty to infect Jennifer and Ed's marriage, that would have been bad enough. But dishonesty in marriage can take several forms, and Ed also suffered from a second type of dishonesty—lying to look good.

Some people are dishonest because they want to be seen as better than they really are. To leave a favorable impression, these "trying-to-look-good" liars fabricate achievements and abilities so that others will have higher regard for them. Most of us want to put our best foot forward, but this type of liar misrepresents the facts. For some, it's just an embellishment of something that actually took place, but for others, the entire event is a lie.

> **"Trying-to-look-good" liars fabricate achievements and abilities to impress others.**

Ed was a trying-to-look-good liar. It started when he first dated Jennifer. He knew that she had done well in school, so he made up stories about his school achievements. As far as she knew, he was among the top in his class. But the truth was that he was an underachiever. Granted, he had the ability to get good grades, but he never really gave it much effort. Those A's and B's that he told her he earned were actually C's and D's. He hardly made it through high school, but who ever checks school records?

Then, during their marriage, Ed continued to exaggerate his achievements, especially those at work. When Jennifer asked him how his day went, he often made up stories about sales he made and commendations he received from his supervisor. She would tell him how proud she was of him and to keep up the good work.

His stories were so convincing that he believed some of them himself. On one occasion when he was asking for a raise, he reminded his supervisor of an outstanding sale he had recently made, only to remember halfway through the conversation that it was merely one of the stories he had told his wife. It was embarrassing to him when he had to admit it never happened, but he got out of the situation by blaming his poor memory and dropping his request for a raise.

But Ed knew it was not really a memory problem—it was an honesty problem. He had developed the habit of lying to make himself look better than he really was. He thought he could keep up the deception throughout his marriage, but bad habits have a way of tripping us up eventually.

Avoid-Trouble Liars

Dishonesty has a way of spreading like a virus. One lie can lead to another, and one type of lying can lead to another type of lying. Ed's lying to look good created problems for him that led to yet a third type of dishonesty—lying to avoid trouble. It arises from the threat of being caught doing something wrong.

What is right and wrong, of course, is often in the eyes of the beholder, so "avoid-trouble liars" often feel that their own shady actions are appropriate but they know that others will judge them harshly if they were to know about them. In marriage, these people do things they know their spouse disapproves of, but to avoid their spouse's judgment, they lie.

Jennifer suspected that Ed was embellishing his sales record, and so one day she mustered up the courage to call his supervisor to get the facts. What she heard was devastating. He had not only been lying to her about his outstanding sales record, but he had been fired six weeks earlier for poor performance. Ed's supervisor had warned him several times that if his sales did not improve they could not continue to employ him, and they finally had let him go.

For six weeks, Ed left the house each day pretending to go to work. But instead of going to his old job he was looking for a new one. He had hoped to find something quickly and tell Jennifer that he quit the old job for a better offer, so that she would be none the wiser.

Was Ed's lie to protect Jennifer, to make himself look good, or to avoid trouble? Sometimes a lie has many motives, and in this case, there could be an argument made for a little of all three. But Ed was definitely avoiding trouble. If he were to tell Jennifer he had been fired, his lies about his sales would unravel and he would be seen as the underachiever he really was.

Another couple I counseled also suffered from the ravages of avoid-trouble lying. Always short of cash, Sally hated begging Steve for money. So she opened her own bank account by forging her husband's signature on a ten-thousand-dollar loan application. She planned to make the payments with the money she earned working part-time. Steve suspected that something was going on, because she seemed to have a new outfit just about every week. But she claimed that she was simply finding incredible bargains.

> **Avoid-trouble liars lie so that they can get away with their thoughtlessness.**

Sally's plan might have gone undetected if she hadn't spent all the money and then missed a payment on the loan. When Steve got a call from the bank, the cat was out of the bag.

"None of this would have happened if Steve hadn't been so cheap" was Sally's excuse. According to her, she had a right to spend more money than Steve gave her, and so she took matters into her own hands. She justified her dishonesty as necessary for her survival.

People who have affairs often feel the same way about their behavior. With their spouse unwilling to meet their needs, they are "forced," they claim, to find another who is willing. Most people caught in affairs are more upset about the fact that they were caught than they are about the pain they've caused their spouse and children. While admitting that they hurt their spouse, very few actually feel guilty about it. They tend to believe that if their spouse had met their needs in the first place, they would not have had to go to the trouble of finding someone else.

Avoid-trouble liars usually don't lie because they're *ashamed* of their actions; they lie so that they can get away with their thoughtlessness. Since their spouse would not understand or accept the truth and would certainly cause a great deal of trouble, these liars simply avoid trouble by covering up their illicit deeds. Ironically, when caught in a lie, an avoid-trouble liar will often *keep* lying to get out of the trouble *that* causes. When these lies don't work, he or she tries to avoid trouble by dodging responsibility. "I wouldn't have to lie if you'd just mind your own business," such liars protest. And their excuses go on and on.

Lying is bad enough, but trying to shift blame to the offended spouse is adding insult to injury. A humble and contrite apology is the only appropriate response to an uncovered lie. But most liars make matters worse by trying to defend their indefensible act.

Born Liars

When Jennifer first learned about all of Ed's dishonesty, she thought that she had married a compulsive liar—the fourth type of dishonesty. But, thankfully, that was not Ed's problem. Compulsive lying is very different from those we have discussed so far, and it is fairly easy to identify.

I call those who lie about anything and everything, whether they have a good reason to lie or not, "born liars" because they don't seem to be able to control it nor do they know why they do it. These people often lie about trivial experiences and don't seem to know what is true and what is a lie. Even solid evidence to the contrary does not always dissuade them.

Born liars often live double lives. Occasionally you'll read a news story about a con artist who has finally been caught after passing themselves off as a doctor or lawyer or marrying two or more people. These people are usually born liars. When caught red-handed in a crime, they sincerely deny any involvement and can even pass lie detector tests. Such liars are fascinating to psychologists such as myself, but for obvious reasons they're impossible as marriage partners. Since

Born liars lie about anything and everything.

honesty is essential in marriage, and these individuals simply cannot tell the truth, their marriages are usually very short-lived.

This fourth category, compulsive lying, is obviously the most extreme form of dishonesty, and thankfully, very few of the spouses I counsel are born liars. It is almost impossible to treat this kind of dishonesty because the person doing the lying rarely sees it as dishonesty. I believe it is a mental disorder that has a neurophysiological cause, and, short of brain surgery, I doubt that it can be cured.

Since this form of lying should be quite obvious to anyone with an inquisitive mind from the first date on, compulsive liars usually do not get very far in romantic relationships. Those who end up with two marriages usually target those who have little or no interest in their personal lives. It's rare for anyone to be that disinterested.

If you and your spouse struggle with dishonesty, chances are that it falls into the categories of lying to protect, to look good, or to avoid trouble. Fortunately, these three types of dishonesty *can* be overcome—without resorting to brain surgery.

Can Honesty Be a Love Buster?

As you contemplate what your marriage might be like if you practice radical honesty, you may be wondering if honesty isn't, in some cases, a Love Buster. Aren't there times when a couple can be *too* honest with each other, and when it would be better to avoid conflict by keeping a spouse in the dark?

That's what Ed and Jennifer believed. They assumed their relationship would suffer harm if they expressed their true feelings. And on the surface, this argument seems to make sense. Love Busters are those actions that make your spouse unhappy; so if your expression of honesty troubles your spouse, it must be a Love Buster, right?

But if you take a closer look, you find that the Love Buster isn't honesty itself, but the behavior that honesty reveals. Confessing to an affair will certainly upset your spouse, but it isn't the confession that's upsetting. It's the affair!

In most cases, dishonesty merely post-
pones your spouse's discovery of the truth,
and once it's revealed, the fact that you lied
will do even more damage to your relationship. Then your spouse will be upset by both
your thoughtless behavior and your dishonesty. And of the two, your dishonesty will

> **Dishonesty merely
> postpones your
> spouse's discovery
> of the truth.**

usually hurt your spouse more than whatever it was you were
trying to conceal. Dishonesty in marriage, once discovered, causes
incredible pain. That's why it's dishonesty—not honesty—that is
a Love Buster.

Don't Wrap Your Honesty in Love Busters

While it's true that honest disclosures are often painful, couples often make them much more painful than they need to be.
That's because their disclosure is often a Love Buster in disguise.

In reaction to Ed's failure to be home with Jennifer evenings,
suppose she had greeted him at the door by throwing a dish at
him? "You never have time for me anymore, you selfish jerk! I
don't know why I ever married you!" She gets points for honesty,
but her angry outburst ruins it all. Ed will never hear the genuine
feelings she is expressing, because he's running for cover.

Or, suppose that Ed decided to take the same approach to his
sexual frustration as Jim did in my opening illustration—by
demanding sex. That's one way to get your feelings out on the
table, but it's honesty wrapped in demands. And all it would communicate is brutal selfishness, not an unmet emotional need.

Many people wrap their honest feelings in the poison of Love
Busters. When Takers respond and havoc results, they go back to
bottling up their feelings. "I tried being honest and look where it
got me." It's not easy expressing honest feelings without angry
outbursts, disrespectful judgments, or selfish demands, but you
can learn to do it.

"I'm the least important person in your life; you'd rather be
with anyone else but me" is a disrespectful judgment because you
are telling your spouse how he or she feels. The truth is you don't
know how your spouse feels, unless he or she tells you.

115

"I become upset when I'm left alone at night" is an honest feeling, because you are telling your spouse how *you* feel.

"If you don't start spending more time with me soon, I'll find someone else to spend time with" is a selfish demand.

"I'd like to spend more time with you" is an honest feeling.

In conquering the Love Buster of dishonesty, you must do more than reveal the truth. You must make sure you express it in a way that informs without needlessly causing harm.

How Honest Should You Be?

You may agree with me that spouses should be honest with each other, but you may wonder how far honesty should go. For couples I counsel, I have written a rule to describe the depth of honesty I want them to experience. I call it the Policy of Radical Honesty: Reveal to your spouse as much information about yourself as you know—your thoughts, feelings, habits, likes, dislikes, personal history, daily activities, and plans for the future.

> **Policy of Radical Honesty**
>
> Reveal to your spouse as much information about yourself as you know: your thoughts, feelings, habits, likes, dislikes, personal history, daily activities, and plans for the future.

To help explain this rule, I have broken it down into four parts:

1. *Emotional Honesty:* Reveal your emotional reactions—both positive and negative—to the events of your life, particularly to your spouse's behavior.
2. *Historical Honesty:* Reveal information about your personal history, particularly events that demonstrate personal weakness or failure.
3. *Current Honesty:* Reveal information about the events of your day. Provide your spouse with a calendar of your activities, with special emphasis on those that may affect your spouse.
4. *Future Honesty:* Reveal your thoughts and plans regarding future activities and objectives.

To some extent this rule seems like motherhood and apple pie. Who would argue that it's *not* a good idea to be honest? But in my years of experience as a marriage counselor, I have regularly encountered clients who believe dishonesty can be a good idea under certain conditions. Even some pastors and counselors advise dishonesty on occasion.

To those who argue that dishonesty can be justified under certain circumstances, I must say that my Policy of Radical Honesty leaves no room for exceptions.

> **The Policy of Radical Honesty leaves no room for exceptions.**

But because there are so many out there who *advocate* dishonesty in marriage, I need to build a case for my position. Let's take a careful look at each of the four parts of this rule, beginning with emotional honesty.

Emotional Honesty

Most couples do their best to make each other happy. But their efforts, however sincere, are often misdirected. They aim at the wrong target.

> **Emotional Honesty**
> Reveal your emotional reactions—both positive and negative—to the events of your life, particularly your spouse's behavior.

Imagine a man who buys his wife flowers every night on the way home from work. What a wonderful thing to do—except that his wife is allergic to them. Because she appreciates the gesture, though, she never mentions her allergies but just sniffles in silence. Soon, however, she begins to dread the thought of her husband coming home with those terrible flowers. Meanwhile, he's getting bored with the marriage because she is always feeling lousy and never has energy to do anything. But of course he won't tell her that.

This couple's marriage is in trouble, not because of any lack of effort, but because of their ignorance—ignorance caused by dishonesty. He thinks he's doing a good thing by bringing home flowers, but he doesn't realize that's the cause of her malaise. Let's say that, in his effort to show even more love for her, he brings home more and more flowers. Ultimately she's collapsed on the couch, gasping for breath, surrounded by flowers, while he wonders what went wrong.

Of course, this is a preposterous story, but it portrays the way many couples misfire in their attempts to please each other. Their lack of honesty keeps them from correcting their real problems.

You need accurate data from each other.

Some people find it difficult to express their emotional reactions, particularly the negative ones. But negative feelings serve a valuable purpose in a marriage. They are a signal that something is wrong. If you successfully steer clear of angry outbursts, disrespectful judgments, and selfish demands, your expression of negative feelings can alert both you and your spouse to an adjustment that must be made.

Honesty enables a couple to make appropriate adjustments to each other. And adjustment is what a good marriage is all about. The circumstances that led you into your blissful union will certainly change, if they haven't already, and you need to learn to roll with the tide. Both of you are growing and changing with each new day, and you must constantly adjust to each other's changes. But how can you know how to adjust if you're not receiving accurate information about these changes? You'd be flying blind, like a pilot whose instrument panel has shorted out.

You need accurate data from each other. Without this, unhappy situations can go on and on—like the flowers piling up in the allergic woman's home. But if you communicate your feelings to each other, you can correct what you're doing wrong before it becomes a habit.

If Jennifer had told Ed how his behavior was affecting her on their honeymoon, for instance, he could have made an adjustment to accommodate her. If he had told her he was becoming dissatisfied with their sexual relationship, she could have adjusted for him. Instead, their dissatisfaction continued and grew, putting their marriage in jeopardy.

In addition to expressing negative emotions honestly, do not overlook the expression of positive feelings. These are generally easier to communicate, yet many couples have not learned to communicate them well. And by this failure, they miss an important opportunity to *deposit* love units. Whenever your spouse

makes *you* feel good, if you express those feelings clearly and enthusiastically, you'll make
your spouse feel good, knowing that his or her
care is appreciated.

> **Without honest
> communication,
> failure is guaranteed.**

The mere communication of feelings does
not assure that all the necessary adjustments
will be made. There is still work to do. But without honest communication, failure is *guaranteed.*

Historical Honesty

Should your skeletons stay in the closet?

Some say yes: Lock the door, hide the key, leave well enough
alone. Communicate your past misdeeds only on a need-to-know
basis.

But I say your spouse always needs to know. Whatever embarrassing experiences or serious mistakes are in your past, you need
to come clean with your spouse
in the present.

Ed made a serious mistake when
he lied to Jennifer about his aca-
demic achievements. He told her
that he had earned high marks in
school, when in fact the opposite
was true. Granted, she may have

> **Historical Honesty**
> Reveal information about your
> personal history, particularly
> events that demonstrate per-
> sonal weakness or failure.

chosen not to marry him if he had told her the truth about his past
while they were dating. But she had a right to that information.

Ed deliberately misled Jennifer into thinking that he had been
an achiever when in fact he had serious problems motivating
himself to fulfill responsibilities. His tendency toward underachievement in his teen years followed him as an adult to his
sales job, where he could not motivate himself to make the sales
calls that were required of him. But by keeping his history a
secret, he was unable to adequately confront his problem and
find solutions that would accommodate his predispositions.

Your personal history holds significant information about you—
information about your strengths and weaknesses. For your
spouse to make necessary adjustments to you, he or she needs to

understand both your good and bad points. Where can you be relied on? Where do you need help?

A man who has had an affair in the past is particularly vulnerable to another one. If a woman has been chemically dependent in the past, she'll be susceptible to drug or alcohol abuse in the future. If you express your past mistakes openly, your spouse can understand your weaknesses, and together you can avoid conditions that tend to create problems for you.

No area of your life should be kept secret.

No area of your life should be kept secret. All questions asked by your spouse should be answered fully and completely. Periods of poor adjustment in your past should be given special attention, because problems of the past are commonly problems of the future.

Not only should *you* explain your past to your spouse, but you should also encourage your spouse to gather information from *those who knew you* before you met. I encourage couples who are considering marriage to talk with several significant people from each other's past. It's often an eye-opener!

I include in this Rule of Historical Honesty the disclosure of all premarital and extramarital sexual relations. A husband and a wife *must* confide in each other, regardless of the reaction.

"But if I tell my wife about all the bad things I've done, she'll never trust me again."

"If my husband finds out about my past, he'll be crushed. It will ruin his whole image of me."

I have heard these protests from various clients, all ashamed of things they have done. Why dig it all up? they ask. Let that old affair stay buried in ancient history! Why not just leave that little demon alone? I answer that it's not a little demon but an extremely important part of their personal story, and it says something about their character.

But what if you haven't strayed since it happened? What if you've seen a pastor regularly to hold you accountable? Why put your spouse through the agony of a revelation that could ruin your relationship forever?

If that's your argument, I'd say you don't give your spouse much credit! Honesty does not drive a spouse away—*dishonesty* does.

People in general, and women in particular, want to know exactly what their spouses are thinking and feeling. When you hold something back, your spouse tries to guess what it is. If he or she is right, then you must continually lie to cover your tracks. If wrong, your spouse develops an incorrect understanding of you and your predispositions.

Maybe you don't really want to be known for who you are. That's the saddest position of all to be in. You'd rather keep your secret than experience one of life's greatest joys—to be loved and accepted in spite of known weaknesses.

While revealing your past is a good thing to do, it's not always painless. Some spouses have difficulty adjusting to revelations that have been kept secret for years—the saints they thought they married turn out to be not so saintly. To control the emotional damage, you may want to make your revelations in the presence of a professional counselor. Some spouses with emotional weaknesses may need some personal counseling to help them adjust to the reality of their spouse's past.

In many cases the spouse reacts more negatively to the long-term deception than to the concealed event. The thoughtless act might be easily accepted and forgiven, but the cover-up is often harder to accept.

You may be daunted by the idea of revealing your past and that's understandable. But let me assure you that I've never seen a marriage destroyed by truth. When truth is revealed, there are often negative reactions and some shaky times, but ultimately the truth makes marriages stronger. On the other hand, dishonesty destroys intimacy, romantic love, and marriages.

Current Honesty

In good marriages couples become so interdependent that sharing a daily schedule is essential to their coordination of activities. But in weak marriages they are reluctant to reveal their schedules because they often engage in behavior that they want to keep from their spouse. They hide the details of their day, telling themselves, "What he doesn't know won't hurt him," or "She's happier not knowing everything."

Even when activities are innocent, it's extremely important for your spouse to understand what you do with your time. Make sure you're easy to find in an emergency or when your spouse just wants to say hello during the day. Give each other your daily schedule so you can communicate about how you spend your day. Almost everything you do will affect your spouse, so it's important to explain what you do.

> **Current Honesty**
>
> Reveal information about the events of your day. Provide your spouse with a calendar of your activities, with special emphasis on those that may affect your spouse.

If Jennifer and Ed had established a habit of exchanging daily information early in their marriage, his six-week deception would have been almost impossible to arrange. They would have called each other throughout the day to keep each other informed regarding any changes in their schedules, and she would have called his office the very first day to discover he was no longer employed. But then, if they had practiced the Policy of Radical Honesty, his motivational problem probably would have been resolved years earlier. Instead of taking on a career in sales, which requires incredible self-motivation, he would have chosen a career where underachievement is tolerated.

Honesty is a terrific way to protect your spouse from potentially damaging activities. When you know that you'll be telling your spouse what you've been up to, you're far less likely to get into trouble.

Future Honesty

After I've made such a big issue of revealing past indiscretions, you can imagine how I feel about revealing future plans. They're *much* easier to discuss with your spouse, yet many couples make plans independently of each other. Why?

Some people believe that communicating future plans just gives a spouse the opportunity to quash them. They have their sights set on a certain goal, and they don't want anything to stand in their way. Others just think their spouse wouldn't be interested.

Regardless of how innocent your plans are, when you fail to tell your spouse about them, you're engaging in a Love Buster. You may be trying to avoid trouble in the present, but eventually the future will arrive and your plans will be revealed. At that point your spouse will be hurt that you didn't communicate what you were planning. And that will withdraw love units.

> **Future Honesty**
>
> Reveal your thoughts and plans regarding future activities and objectives.

The Policy of Joint Agreement—*Never do anything without an enthusiastic agreement between you and your spouse*—is certainly relevant in discussions of your future plans.

"If I wait for my wife to agree," a husband might say, "we'll never accomplish anything. She's so conservative, she never wants to take any risks, and so we miss every opportunity that comes along." But isn't that approach, in essence, a disrespectful judgment, forcing the husband's opinion on the wife? If he genuinely respects her, he will want her input on the decision—and even more than mere input, her enthusiastic agreement!

"Oh, but the plans I make are best for both of us," a wife might say. "He may not understand my decision now but once he sees how things turn out, he'll thank me for going ahead with it." But to make plans independently and conceal them from your spouse is still a Love Buster. Granted, you won't lose love units until later, but you *will* lose them. Even if your plans work out, your spouse will still feel bad about not being included in the planning.

Creating an Environment for Honesty

How well do you encourage honesty? You may say that you want your spouse to be honest, but do your own values promote it? Do your reactions convey an appreciation for the truth, even if it's painful? To see how you rate, answer these questions:

1. If the truth is terribly upsetting to you, do you want your spouse to be honest only at a time when you are emotionally prepared?

2. Do you keep some aspects of your life secret, and do you encourage your spouse to respect your privacy in those areas?
3. Have you defined your boundaries, and do you encourage your spouse not to cross them?
4. Do you like to create a certain mystery between you and your spouse?
5. Are there conditions under which you would not want honesty at all costs between you and your spouse?
6. Do you ever have angry outbursts when your spouse is honest with you?
7. Do you ever make disrespectful judgments when your spouse is honest with you?
8. Do you ever make selfish demands when your spouse is honest with you?

If you answer "yes" to any of the first five questions, you tend to compromise on the value of honesty. Apparently you feel your marriage is better off with dishonesty in certain situations. That little crack is all dishonesty needs to slip into your marriage and run amok. You see, there are always "reasons" to be dishonest. As soon as you allow one, it begins to blur into all the rest, and before you know it, you have a dishonest relationship.

If you answered "yes" to questions 6, 7, or 8, you are punishing honesty and inadvertently encouraging dishonesty. The way to help your spouse learn to be truthful is to minimize the negative consequences of his or her truthful revelations. If your spouse is forced to agree with you just to survive, you invite dishonesty. Your spouse will learn to agree with anything to avoid a fight—and then do what he or she pleases. But what if there are no fights? No judgments? No demands? If you can eliminate these Love Busters, you'll make it much easier for your spouse to be honest with you.

Overcoming Dishonesty

Step 1: Identify what type of liar you are (protector, try to look good, or avoid trouble) and what parts of honesty you have difficulty achieving (emotional, historical, current, and future).

If dishonesty has crept into your marriage, you may not be entirely aware of it. In the case of an angry outburst, the offended spouse can identify the offense as soon as it happens. But in the case of dishonesty, sometimes the offended spouse does not know that it's occurred until months later when he or she has the evidence for dishonesty firmly in hand. So the first step in overcoming this Love Buster is to reveal it as the monster that it is. If you really want to become honest, you must first reveal the *fact* that you've been dishonest. And you must reveal the *way* in which you tend to be dishonest.

Are you a protector liar, a trying-to-look-good liar, an avoid-trouble liar, or all three? And do you tend to lie about your emotional reactions, your past history, your present activities, your future plans, or all four? By revealing the fact that you have been dishonest, you take the first and extremely important step that requires radical honesty. It's only as you reveal dishonesty that you're able to usher it out the door.

Step 2: Understand why you have been dishonest.

After you have admitted your dishonesty, the next step is to understand what motivates you to be dishonest, and why dishonesty has established itself in your marriage. I suggest that you answer the following questions to help you discover some of the causes of your dishonesty. If both you and your spouse have a problem with honesty, you should both answer these questions. The purpose of this questionnaire is to try to get at the root of why it is you're dishonest and what you think you might do to overcome your dishonesty.

Before you answer these questions, though, reflect on the four parts of honesty. You may wish to answer the questions differently for each of the four. If that's the case, make four copies of the questions on separate sheets of paper.

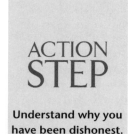

ACTION STEP

Understand why you have been dishonest.

1. What are the most important reasons that you are dishonest with your spouse?
2. How does your dishonesty hurt your spouse (ask your spouse to answer this question)?
3. If you have tried to overcome dishonesty in the past, how did you try to do it?
4. If you were to decide that you would be radically honest with your spouse and would never again be dishonest, could you do it? Why or why not?
5. Are you willing to be radically honest with your spouse? Why or why not?
6. Add any further information that might help you avoid dishonesty with your spouse in the future.

One of the subjects that comes up when people complete this questionnaire is the alleged need for privacy. As a marital therapist, I have never been an advocate for privacy in marriage. As a matter of fact, privacy does the opposite of what I want to see couples do. I want couples to integrate their wisdom and make decisions together. I want them to know each other thoroughly and respond appropriately to each other's needs. So the kind of partnership that I try to create for couples does not allow for privacy, and it certainly doesn't allow for a secret second life where spouses are engaged in potentially offensive behavior behind each other's backs. An affair, probably the most hurtful thing that one spouse could do to another, is almost impossible without a secret second life. And a secret second life is impossible if a couple agrees to radical honesty.

Of course, if you're going to be radically honest, you're also going to have to stop doing the things that would have caused offense if your spouse were to have known about it. If your spouse doesn't like something you're doing, and you've agreed to be honest, you will need to put an end to your offensive behavior. That prospect, of course, will be a serious roadblock in front of your willingness to become radically honest. Your Taker will not like it one single bit. But then, if you leave decisions up to your Taker, your marriage will never amount to much.

Step 3: Create a strategy to overcome dishonesty.

After you know what you want to achieve, the next step is to create a plan to achieve it. To help you arrive at that strategy answer the following questions:

ACTION
STEP

Create a strategy to overcome dishonesty.

1. Describe your dishonesty. Include a description of your feelings, your thoughts, your attitudes, and the way you are dishonest (emotional, historical, present, future).
2. Describe the conditions that seem to trigger your dishonesty. Include physical setting, people present, behavior of those people, and any other relevant conditions.
3. What changes in those conditions would help you avoid dishonesty?
4. Which changes can be made with your spouse's enthusiastic support and agreement?
5. Describe your plans to change these conditions. Include a deadline to make the change complete. Be certain that your spouse has your enthusiastic agreement.
6. Which of the changes described in the third question cannot be made with your spouse's enthusiastic agreement, or cannot be made at all?
7. Describe your plan to overcome dishonesty when those conditions exist. Include a deadline for successful completion of the plan. Be certain that the plan has your spouse's enthusiastic agreement.
8. How will you measure the success of your plan to overcome dishonesty? Does this measure of success have your spouse's enthusiastic agreement?
9. If your plan does not succeed within your designated time limit, will you make a commitment to your spouse to seek professional help in designing and executing an effective plan to overcome dishonesty? How will you go about finding that help?

As I've already mentioned, one of the ways to overcome a bad habit is to simply get rid of the conditions that seem to trigger that habit. You may notice, for example, that there are certain people in your life that tend to encourage you to be dishonest with your spouse. Perhaps you find yourself engaging in certain behavior with those people that usually offends your spouse. And then when your spouse asks about what you've been doing, you lie about it. By simply eliminating these people as friends you may find you've eliminated your dishonesty as well.

You'll probably find that your inquiry into the conditions that trigger your dishonesty tends to focus quite a bit of attention on what I've called a *secret second life*. Of course, I encourage you to completely eliminate a secret second life and by doing so you may find that that's the solution to your problem with dishonesty. If you're simply not doing things that would offend your spouse, you're not going to be as tempted to be dishonest.

But you may find that the conditions that seem to trigger your dishonesty can't be changed. For example, financial pressures may tempt you to be dishonest. When you can't pay your bills you are tempted to keep that fact from your spouse. And you simply can't change the condition of your financial pressure.

In that situation you will need to create a strategy where, under those very conditions that tend to make you dishonest, you practice being honest. You explain to your spouse how difficult it is to reveal the fact that you can't pay your bills and involve him or her in all financial decisions. All the money you earn would be deposited into a checking account that your spouse can clearly see. All the bills that you pay are made with your joint enthusiastic agreement. Any unpaid bills are known and agreed to by your spouse.

If you and your spouse become partners in decision-making, where all the decisions that you make follow the Policy of Joint Agreement, and you don't allow yourself a secret second life, it's much easier to be honest.

Step 4: Document your progress.

When you're ready to put your strategy to overcome dishonesty into action, I encourage you to document your progress. Title a sheet of paper "Dishonesty Worksheet" and use it to list all instances of dishonesty. Generally, the offended spouse completes the worksheet to document progress, but in this case, you and your spouse should complete it together, since there may be instances of your dishonesty that your spouse would not know of if you did not tell him or her.

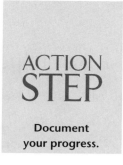

ACTION STEP

Document your progress.

Indicate the day, date, time, description and type of dishonesty, and circumstances whenever you document an instance of dishonesty. If your strategy to overcome dishonesty is successful, you'll find yourself listing fewer and fewer instances of dishonesty. Eventually you'll get into the habit of being completely honest with your spouse, and your spouse will be in the habit of encouraging that honesty by avoiding demands, disrespect, or anger when you are honest.

Once you've been able to overcome this Love Buster, dishonesty, you'll find your relationship improving in many different ways. You'll have not only eliminated this great offense to your spouse, but by being honest you'll have learned to meet a very important emotional need. Your honesty will deposit love units, and your spouse will probably be more in love with you as a result.

You will also have a much easier time resolving conflicts. You'll have a much clearer idea of the problem itself, and you'll have a much better understanding of how you're both reacting. By having the facts on the table, it will be much easier to find solutions that make you happy simultaneously. Without the barrier of unspoken feelings, you'll be able to cut to the chase, understand each other quickly, protect each other's feelings, and create solutions to your conflicts that will help you create a deeper love for each other. And that's my ultimate goal for your marriage. I want you to be in love. And the way for you to be in love is to make each other happy by meeting each other's important emotional needs and avoid making each other unhappy by eliminating Love Busters, such as dishonesty.

Key Principles

- Radical honesty is complete honesty about one's feelings, past experiences, present activities, and future plans. It is essential in marriage because it provides a clear road map for marital adjustment, meets an important emotional need, and prevents massive Love Bank withdrawals.

- There are four types of dishonesty in marriage: (1) protection, (2) looking good, (3) avoiding trouble, and (4) compulsion.

- Honesty is *not* a Love Buster. When thoughtless behavior is revealed, it's the thoughtless behavior, not honesty, that causes unhappiness.

- Avoid wrapping Policy of Radical Honesty: honesty in the Love Busters selfish demands, disrespectful judgments, or angry outbursts.

- Encourage your spouse to be honest by valuing honesty consistently and by avoiding punishment of honesty.

- Remember to reveal to your spouse as much information about yourself as you know: your thoughts, feelings, habits, likes, dislikes, personal history, daily activities, and plans for the future.

Consider This . . .

1. What are the four types of liars? We are all dishonest once in a while. Where are you the most vulnerable? If you were to classify yourself as one of the four types of liars, which would come closest to describing you?

2. What is the Policy of Radical Honesty, and what are the four parts of the policy? Do you agree that you should both follow this policy? If so, why? If not, why not? Hint: You are more likely to want your spouse to be honest with you than to want to be honest with your spouse.

3. If the truth is terribly upsetting to you, do you want your spouse to be honest only at a time when you are emotionally prepared?

4. Do you keep some aspects of your life secret, and do you encourage your spouse to respect your privacy in those areas?

5. Are there conditions under which you would not want honesty at all costs between you and your spouse?

6. Do you encourage honesty, or do you punish it? Repeat the questions I raised earlier (see page 124) to measure negative reactions to honesty.

7. Do you ever have angry outbursts, make disrespectful judgments, or make selfish demands when your spouse is honest with you?

8. If dishonesty has claimed some of the love you could be having toward each other, how do you plan to get rid of it once and for all? Do you think you can follow my four steps to overcoming dishonesty on your own? Or will you need someone to help motivate you and hold you accountable? Try it on your own first as a test of your ability to motivate each other, but if your strategy doesn't get off the ground, or stalls, get help. Be sure that the one you choose has experience helping couples overcome dishonesty and has a proven record of success.

chapter seven

ANNOYING
HABITS

WHO WANTS TO LIVE WITH A DRIPPING FAUCET?

Long before she married Mike, Sharon knew that some of his habits irritated her. For instance, she didn't like the way he sat in a chair. She admired men who sat straight and tall, giving the impression that they were alert and attentive. When a man slouched in his chair, it reminded her of certain fat and lazy relatives.

But slouching was Mike's specialty—especially when he came home after work and parked in front of the TV.

"Mike, it really bothers me when you sit like that," she told him when they were newlyweds. "Please sit up in the chair."

Mike straightened up and continued watching television with a better posture, but a few minutes later he slumped back into the same position.

When Sharon returned to the room, she was always disappointed. "Why do you sit like that, when you know it bothers me?"

Mike would quickly straighten up and say, "Oh, I'm sorry."

"You can't possibly be sorry. You just don't care how I feel."

"Look, Sharon," he'd answer, getting a little irritated. "I've had a hard day at work. Just don't look at me, and you'll feel much better."

Sharon would leave the room in tears, but Mike would be too absorbed in TV to notice. The first few times this happened, Sharon seethed with anger, but after a while she began to doubt herself.

It's such a small thing, she thought. *He needs to relax after work, and I'm just being selfish to expect him to sit in his chair a certain way.*

So she decided to keep her feelings to herself. Whenever she saw Mike slumped in his chair, it still annoyed her, but she didn't say anything. While the marriage seemed peaceful, Mike was losing love units with each slouch.

He never knew what was happening to his Love Bank account, and Sharon may not have been fully aware of it either. She didn't want to nag him about it because she felt he had a right to sit any way he chose, but still it bothered her. As time went on, Mike developed other annoying habits, such as chewing ice and spitting it back into his glass, but as with his sitting posture, Sharon felt she had no right to change him.

When they came to see me for counseling, Mike's poor posture had become only one example of many habits that made him an almost constant irritant to Sharon. She could hardly tolerate being with him for more than a few minutes at a time, because that's how long it took before another annoying habit appeared. Though she didn't believe in divorce, Sharon wanted a separation—she just had to get away from Mike and his bad habits.

Yet Mike's "bad" habits were all essentially innocent. They all fell into the same category as his sitting posture—eating habits, his tone of voice when he disciplined the children, phrases he overused, and the mess he left around the house—they were all ways he did things. None of these habits were "evil" or intentionally destructive, and Sharon knew this. Another woman might be delighted to have him for a husband, but his behavior drove Sharon up a wall. Though she felt guilty about her reaction, it had become so strong and negative that she was sure she'd go crazy unless they split up.

Why Are We So Annoying?

When was the last time your spouse did something that annoyed you? Last week? Yesterday? An hour ago? If you're male, the answer is probably "last week, " if at all. But if you're female, it's more likely to be "this very minute."

For some reason, women seem to find men more annoying than men find women. But, male or female, our annoying habits draw love units out of our spouse's Love Bank every time.

As a marriage counselor, I tell couples that eliminating annoying habits will improve their marriages. This is not rocket science. It only makes sense that you'll get along better if you stop doing things that drive each other to distraction. But you'd be amazed how many couples just don't get it.

> **Annoying Habits**
>
> Behavior repeated without much thought that it bothers the other spouse.

"If Sharon just accepted me for who I am," Mike suggested, "she wouldn't mind it when I pick my teeth after a meal."

"Picking his teeth with his finger," Sharon adds. "And by the time he really gets into it, he's got his whole fist in his mouth."

Couples often sit in my office and try to convince me that they should be able to do whatever they please—that the objecting spouse should adjust to the annoying habits.

Of course, when *we're* annoyed, we usually think others are being inconsiderate, particularly when we've explained how it bothers us and they continue to do it. But when our behavior annoys *others*, we feel we have a right to persist, demanding that others adjust to us.

I often wish I could switch minds: Mike becomes Sharon for a day and feels what Sharon feels when he picks his teeth. If he could only know *how* annoying his habits are, surely he would try to become more considerate. He might argue that it wouldn't bother him if Sharon picked her teeth, but that's not the point. If he could feel what Sharon feels, he would know that.

So one reason we are annoying is that we don't feel what our spouse feels. As a counselor, I try to help couples become more empathetic—see situations through each other's eyes. Sometimes that helps motivate spouses to overcome annoying habits.

But there is another reason that we are annoying—we often don't care how our spouse feels.

Viewed from the perspective of our Giver, we should be trying to eliminate anything that our spouse finds annoying. After all, the rule of the Giver is: *Do whatever you can to make your spouse happy and avoid anything that makes your spouse unhappy, even if it makes you unhappy.* If your spouse doesn't like something you're doing, you should stop doing it even if it would require great sacrifice.

Our problem, of course, is that our Taker doesn't quite see it the same way. Remember the Taker's rule: *Do whatever you can to make yourself happy and avoid anything that makes you unhappy, even if it means making others unhappy.* That rule encourages you to continue any annoying habit that you happen to have. If your spouse says that he or she doesn't like what you're doing, you ask yourself, "Do I like it?" If the answer is "yes," you keep right on doing it.

Remember, the Taker is not concerned about how your spouse feels. It's only concerned about how you feel. *Besides,* your Taker would argue, *I'm not trying to make my spouse feel bad. I'm just being myself. It's up to my spouse to accept me as I am. If he or she expects me to change, it must mean that my spouse doesn't really love me.*

Of course this is a very familiar argument to me, because I've heard it time and time again by the couples that I counsel. When I explain to them that their annoying habits are ruining the love that they could have for each other, I often hear the argument that they want to be loved for who they are, not what they do, especially when what they do is innocent—when it's habits that just come naturally to them.

Quite frankly, all of us are changing habits on a regular basis. Sometimes we do it by design, and sometimes circumstances simply change our habits for us. But we don't really change whenever we change a habit. I'm the same person regardless of how I sit in a chair or how I eat. So if I can convince you that your habits are nothing sacred, that they don't represent characteristics of your identity that will be forever lost if you ever change them, I can then help you avoid the needless loss of love units by simply changing some of your habits, those that your spouse finds annoying.

Habits That Bother Your Spouse Unintentionally Withdraw Love Units

The bottom line is that a couple who wants to stay in love must pay close attention to the way they affect each other. A marriage just doesn't work if either spouse ignores it. Whether it's intentional or not, a couple's behavior will affect the love they have for each other. So if one spouse finds some of the other's habits annoying, they simply have to go. Otherwise their marriage won't be what either one of them wants it to be.

Because annoying habits usually have this element of innocence, couples generally don't view them with the same seriousness as, say, angry outbursts, which are an intentional effort to hurt the other spouse. But if you're to consider the total number of love units lost, it can be argued rather convincingly that annoying habits might be the worst Love Buster of all. Because, unlike angry outbursts, which might occur only once every six months, annoying habits are unrelenting, day after day, week after week, month after month. Your annoying habits and the annoying habits of your spouse are slowly but surely draining your Love Bank. If you and your spouse don't consider them seriously, your Love Bank is going to be like a sieve. Regardless of how fast you keep pouring love units into that Love Bank, they may drain out even faster if your annoying habits are not eliminated.

> **Whether it's intentional or not, a couple's behavior will affect the love they have for each other.**

Most of our behavior is habitual. We may think we act spontaneously and originally, but on closer analysis, we tend to be very predictable. However, we have the power to change—we can turn destructive habits into constructive ones if we have a good reason to do so.

Since annoying habits are more characteristic of men than women, some of my clients have seen it as a male characteristic that women must learn to endure. Men tend to have inherently disgusting habits, they argue, that cannot be understood by most women. Many men don't even consider giving up their annoying habits—that would place them in submission to women, threatening their essential manliness, they maintain.

But this issue has nothing to do with personal characteristics, manliness, or power struggles. We are dealing with the simple issue of *consideration*. If a man wants to live with a woman, it makes sense for him to take her feelings into account. I don't ask men to sacrifice their masculinity. I simply want them to avoid doing something they do not need to do. The following steps will help any couple get rid of the annoying habits that keep them from experiencing the best marriage has to offer.

Overcoming Annoying Habits

Step 1: Identify each other's annoying habits.

The first step in solving any problem is usually to identify the problem, and this is certainly true when it comes to overcoming annoying habits. Both of you must make a list of as many as occur to you. In creating that list, you will be able to think of some of them almost immediately. But other habits will only occur to you when your spouse actually does them. So get out a pad of paper and keep it close by, so you can add to your list when inspiration strikes. Take a few days to complete your inventory.

Beside each annoying habit you list, enter a number between 1 and 10, indicating how intensely you are annoyed (1 = mildly annoyed, 10 = extremely annoyed). The numbers help identify the behavior that is withdrawing the most love units.

When I ask a couple to list each other's annoying habits, the wife's list is almost always longer than the husband's list. In fact for many couples I counsel, the husbands have no entries at all, but it's not uncommon for a woman to list more than fifty habits and activities she finds annoying.

I assure husbands that a long list of irritating behaviors should not lead them to conclude that they are incurably incompatible and that there is no hope. In fact, making the list is the first step toward improving compatibility—resolving problems that have been swept under a rug. They must uncover the dirt before they can vacuum it up.

And yet, this exercise has a high risk for hurt feelings. It's easy for your Taker to convince you that your spouse's long list is an act of disrespect. But it's nothing of the kind. It's simply an honest reaction to habits that you can, and should, change.

ACTION STEP

Identify each other's annoying habits.

137

But if you are not careful, you may actually be disrespectful when you make your lists. Go easy in the way you describe the annoying habits. Remember, most annoying habits are innocent—you happen to find them annoying. The reason you want your spouse to change his or her habits is not necessarily because there is something wrong with the habits themselves. It's because they prevent you from being in love.

I asked Sharon to let me see her list before she showed it to Mike. That's because I wanted to be sure that it did not contain any disrespectful comments. I wanted her descriptions of annoying habits to be simple and nonjudgmental. But she did not heed my advice. Her list still contained many comments such as "you should stop eating like a pig," and "stop being so lazy and learn to pick up after yourself." However, after weeding out her disrespectful judgments, the list described Mike's most annoying behaviors respectfully.

Most annoying habits are innocent.

I'm not there to help you weed disrespectful judgments out of your lists, so check your lists very carefully before you show them to each other. Don't make the same mistakes that Sharon made when she made her first list. Instead, describe your spouse's annoying behavior as simply as possible, without making any value judgments about it. It annoys you, and that's all you need to explain. This was Sharon's list.

Intensity Rating Annoying Habits

10 Slouching in the living room chair

7 Tone of voice when disciplining the children

8 Overusing certain phrases, such as, "you don't say"

9 Leaving toothpaste, toothbrush, shaver, and towel on the bathroom sink

8 Leaving clothes on the bedroom floor after getting ready for bed

9 Stuffing chips into mouth before swallowing the ones already there

7 Chewing ice and spitting it back into the glass

8 Licking the knife at the dinner table

Step 2: Eliminate the easy ones first.

A list of annoying habits usually includes a few habits that can be easily overcome with a simple decision to stop doing them. These are new habits that have not had time to become hard-wired into your brain, or habits that do not provide much gratification.

But the one who is annoyed thinks all bad habits should be easily overcome. Sharon thought that if she told Mike that the way he sat in the chair annoyed her, he could either stop doing it because he cared about her feelings, or he could keep doing it because he didn't care. It didn't occur to her that there was a third alternative— he cared about her feelings but sat in an annoying way anyway because he was in the habit of doing so.

Sharon, like most people, did not understand the control habits have over us. She was under the illusion that we make a deliberate decision to do each thing we do. Truth is, most of what we do is automatic and effortless. One habit follows another, and we really don't give much thought to what we do throughout the day.

Mike did not understand the control habits have over us, either. He thought he could stop doing everything that Sharon listed with a simple decision to stop. But after we discussed each one with an eye to how long he had been doing it and how much pleasure each gave him, we decided that knife-licking might be Mike's easiest habit to overcome.

It turned out that we were right. He had not been licking his knife long, and it also gave him very little pleasure. So from that day on, Sharon never saw him do it again. But he knew that if she ever did, it would be re-entered onto her list.

If you can check off one or more annoying habits that you know will be easy to overcome, it will shorten the time it takes to eventually check them all off the list. Most habits take some time to change, so don't make the mistake of assuming that a simple decision to change is all it takes. Most annoying habits are not that easy to change, and you cannot tackle too many annoying habits at once. That's why, in the next step, I asked Sharon to select the ones that bothered her most.

ACTION STEP

Eliminate the easy ones first.

139

ACTION STEP

Select three annoying habits to overcome.

Step 3: Select three annoying habits to overcome.

You can eventually eliminate all of each other's annoying habits, but to be successful you'll have to focus on only a few at a time. I suggest three at a time. Select the three behaviors that are the most annoying and eliminate those first.

Sharon had a fairly short list of annoying habits. So, after eliminating knife-licking, it would have been tempting to work on all seven of the remaining habits to keep those Love Busters from doing any more damage.

But I did not recommend that to Sharon and Mike. Instead, I suggested that they focus on the three annoyances that got her highest intensity ratings. If more than three have the same high rating, I would have had Sharon select the three that she wanted to see overcome first.

On the list above, there was only one "10"—the way he sat on the chair in the living room. The next most annoying habits, "9s," were chip-stuffing and bathroom-messing. If there had been more 9s, Sharon would have picked the two that she wanted Mike to overcome first.

Step 4: Determine why the annoying habit is there in the first place.

After three annoying habits have been selected, we're ready for the next step. We need to know why each habit formed and what's keeping it there. I use the following questionnaire to help a couple investigate the background of each habit.

1. When did you begin this habit?
2. What are the most important reasons you began this habit?
3. What are the most important reasons you have this habit now?
4. When you engage in this habit, how do you feel?
5. When you engage in this habit, how does your spouse feel?
6. Have you ever tried to avoid this habit? If so, how did you do it?
7. Why didn't it work?

8. What would make the elimination of this habit more likely?

ACTION STEP

Determine why the annoying habit is there in the first place.

The purpose of each question is fairly self-explanatory. Not only do I want a couple to understand the background of the behavior, but I want them to think it through as well. Most spouses engage in annoying behavior for trivial reasons. They may give a more philosophical explanation, but deep down they know that it is there simply because they've gotten used to doing it that way. And when it comes right down to it, they can get used to doing it another way.

At this point you may find my approach to helping you overcome annoying habits to be a bit tedious. Making lists and filling out worksheets may seem to be very foreign to you and unnecessarily burdensome. You may take the position that if you simply decide to overcome this annoying habit you should be able to do it. Why all the paperwork?

Well, the reason that I encourage you to go to all this trouble is because if you don't actually write down the annoying habits that you want to eliminate, you'll forget what it is you're trying to do. And if you don't document your reasons for engaging in an annoying habit, you will have difficulty knowing how to overcome it. In other words, these worksheets that I'm encouraging you to use will make your success far more likely. So bear with me as you're filling out these forms. They may seem unnecessary to you right now, but after you start seeing success, I think you'll agree with me that they're essential.

There are only two more forms to go, so hang on just a little longer!

Step 5: Create a plan to overcome the annoying habit.

Whenever you create a plan to overcome a habit, remember that it is something you do almost unconsciously. The way you eat your cereal during breakfast, take a shower in the morning, and get into your car are instances of automatic, almost effortless habits. Over 95 percent of all you do is in the form of habits, because you really don't think about them, you simply do them. That's why some people think that habits should not be changed. They don't know quite how they got their habits and assume they are for a good reason. But as it turns out, many of your habits have no good reason to be there. It's the way you happened to do something at one point in time, and you have just continued doing it that way ever since.

New habits are formed by simply repeating the new behavior often enough. Eventually you do it without giving it much thought. But if your spouse finds one of your habits to be annoying, it can be overcome by repeating another behavior in its place. It's a simple strategy that will work every time you do it.

There are two approaches that I recommend to overcoming an annoying habit. One is to change the conditions that trigger the habit and learn a new habit under new triggering conditions; and the other is to learn a new habit under the same conditions that trigger the old habit. Of these two approaches, the first, eliminating the conditions that trigger an annoying habit, is much easier to implement than changing the behavior under the influence of the triggering conditions.

I'll give you an illustration of how that works. Sharon was annoyed by the way Mike sat in the living room chair while watching television. For Mike, the conditions of coming home from work and the placement of the chair and television, were triggering conditions. His brain was wired to drive home after work, get out of his car, walk into the house, go straight to his favorite chair, grab the remote control, and start watching TV.

My plan to help Mike overcome his annoying habit began by breaking up his homecoming routine. I suggested that when Mike came home from work each day, instead of going straight to the remote control, he spend about ten minutes sitting down with Sharon and a cup of coffee. They could talk about how the day went and how they're planning to spend their evening. It helped break up his routine, which also changed the triggering conditions. And that made it easier to develop a new habit of how he would sit while he watched TV.

Just that one change made all the difference in the world. It turned out that much of Sharon's irri-

ACTION STEP

Create a plan to overcome the annoying habit.

142

tability about how he sat in the chair had quite a bit to do with his finding the TV more interesting than her. Instead of slouching in his chair, Mike was sitting across from Sharon talking to her about their day. He not only eliminated a habit that caused anger and resentment, but he replaced it with a habit that met one of Sharon's important emotional needs. Mike had a lot of love units to deposit, and talking to Sharon every day after work was a great start.

When it came time to watch TV, Mike sat in a different chair with the TV in a different location. That made it easier for him to form a new habit. The first day, he asked Sharon how she would like him to sit in the chair. She wanted him to sit up straight, but that made him feel uncomfortable. He tried various positions, but nothing except slouching seemed comfortable to him.

Part of his discomfort was due to the fact that *any* new behavior is uncomfortable at first. Whenever a new behavior is introduced to your brain, it must form new neural pathways before it feels natural to you. The more you repeat the new behavior, the more complete the new neural pathways become. Eventually, the pathways

Any new behavior is uncomfortable at first.

are completed, and you have a new habit—automatic and almost effortless.

I knew that Mike sat up straight in his chair at work and it didn't bother him, so he wasn't having a physical problem sitting that way. I suggested that he practice sitting the way Sharon wanted him to sit for just one week to see how he would feel after doing it a few times.

For a few days Mike was uncomfortable coming home and finding that he could not sit in his chair and watch television right away. And he found that sitting down with his wife, talking about his day, was somewhat uncomfortable as well. But after talking to Sharon after work and sitting the way Sharon wanted him to sit for just a few days, Mike agreed that it became much more natural and comfortable for him.

The longer Mike practiced his new after-work routine, the more effortless it became. In fact, he eventually got to a point where he experienced quite a loss when Sharon was not there to greet him when he arrived home. That's the way our habits work. When we're in the habit of doing something, we miss it if we're prevented from doing it.

The example I just used was based on the assumption that you can change the triggering conditions of the original annoying habit. We got rid of the chair and moved the television to prevent the original habit, and that provided the opportunity for a new habit to be formed. But what if you can't get rid of the triggering conditions?

Suppose the chair and the television are just going to stay where they are. And suppose that Sharon was not able to talk to Mike after work to break up his old habit of watching TV right away. How would you go about changing the behavior then? As it turns out, it's much more difficult to do, but it too can be done.

It takes a great deal more willpower to change a habit when the conditions that trigger it can't be changed. We're talking here about the rather trivial habit of watching television after work, but if we were talking about something more serious, like alcohol addiction, the conditions that trigger the addictive behavior, such as having alcohol in the house or meeting with friends that drink, or even driving past a bar on your way home from work, can turn out to be conditions that are just too much to overcome. That's why I encourage most couples to try to eliminate triggering conditions if at all possible.

Step 6: Measure your progress.

Whether a plan is easy or difficult to implement, it helps to document your progress. I encourage the couples I counsel to keep track of how things are going by writing any instance of annoying habits on a sheet of paper. The date, time, and circumstances should also be documented. The spouse who finds the habits annoying should keep the record.

ACTION STEP

Measure your progress.

If a plan is followed perfectly, there is nothing to document. Only instances of failure need to be noted. When couples come for counseling, they bring the progress report with them, and we discuss every failure. If the plan is not proving successful in eliminating the annoying habits, we change the plan.

Honesty is essential in completing this report. All too often, in an effort to be helpful, the annoyed spouse goes easy on the mate and underreports annoying incidents. This gives a false impression of success, which can undermine the entire process.

Over a period of several weeks, the frequency of reported failure usually drops to almost zero. Since I often work on three annoying habits at a time, attention may shift to one of the three that is more resistant to change. But eventually all three are usually overcome.

I don't consider a habit overcome until at least three months have passed with no failure. A phenomenon called "spontaneous recovery" can sometimes cause the habit to mysteriously reappear months or even years after it seemed to end. But in such recurrences, the habit is no longer well formed and can usually be overcome without much effort.

Step 7: Overcome the next three annoying habits on the list.

After you succeed at eliminating the three most annoying habits, you're ready to overcome the next three that are on the list. And you'll find that the next three will be much easier to overcome, because you already know how to get rid of bad habits and form good habits.

But at this point you may ask the question, *Won't this turn out to be an endless task? Just as soon as I've eliminated all the annoying habits on the list, won't more come along? Am I going to be working on this the rest of my life?*

Technically, if you're following the Policy of Joint Agreement, where whatever you do is with the mutual agreement of you and your spouse, any new annoying habits simply won't ever be formed. They'll never get off the ground. You may do something once or twice before you realize that it doesn't meet with your spouse's enthusiastic agreement, but that's not nearly enough repetitions for

ACTION STEP

Overcome the next three annoying habits on the list.

it to become a habit. And it would be very easy for you to stop doing it as soon as you realize that it's annoying.

So as you go through your spouse's list of annoying behavior, and you're also following the Policy of Joint Agreement, eventually you'll be able to overcome every annoying behavior on the list. But remember, it'll be most difficult for you to overcome habits that you've been repeating for years and years. Once these long-standing annoying habits are overcome, the only annoying behavior left will be habits that you've repeated very few times. And those you'll be able to eliminate almost immediately.

Almost everything you do affects each other, so take your annoying habits very seriously. When you learn to overcome annoying habits, you will have eliminated one of the most common ways that spouses lose their love for each other. All you have to do is go to the effort to change a few habits, and it will be just as easy to make your spouse happy as it was to make your spouse miserable. Your annoying habits are not inevitable—they can be changed to make you a much more desirable person.

Key Principles

- Annoying habits are behaviors that bother your spouse that you repeat without giving it much thought.
- We engage in annoying habits because we don't feel what our spouse feels or we don't care how our spouse feels when we do them.
- Whether it's intentional or not, a couple's behavior will affect the love they have for each other.
- Habits are formed by simply repeating the new behavior often enough.
- Any new behavior is uncomfortable at first. Whenever a new behavior is introduced to your brain, it must form new neural pathways before it feels natural to you. The more you repeat the new behavior, the more complete the new neural path-

ways become. Eventually, the pathways are completed, and you have a new habit—automatic and almost effortless.

Consider This . . .

1. What is an annoying habit? I'm sure you have overcome a few already in your marriage. Can you think of things you've done in the past that were annoying to each other that are no longer an issue? How did you go about ridding yourself of those Love Busters?

2. How have your Giver and Taker tried to influence you regarding annoying habits? Remember, the Giver will try to encourage you to accept each other's annoying habits, while your Taker will try to convince you that they should be accepted as a part of your identity. Why do both arguments lead to the loss of love in marriage?

3. Most annoying habits are innocent—you don't do them to upset each other, it just turns out that way. Why can that make annoying habits more difficult to overcome than the other Love Busters we've discussed so far?

4. Does my plan to help you overcome annoying habits seem unnecessarily tedious? If it seems too overwhelming and prevents you from getting started, modify it enough so that you will be willing to follow it for a while. But remember my warning that habits are much more difficult to change than most people think. On the other hand, all habits can be changed. If you follow my plan to eliminate just one annoying habit, you will have learned what most behavioral psychologists like myself have already learned—how to change human behavior. When an annoying habit is overcome, your personal identity remains the same, but you become a much more attractive person.

5. How does the Policy of Joint Agreement prevent the creation of new annoying habits?

chapter eight

INDEPENDENT
BEHAVIOR

WHO WANTS TO LIVE WITH AN INCONSIDERATE JERK?

Brian came to my office with his wife, Kay, wanting to know why she would not make love to him. In my interview with Kay, she admitted that the spark was gone and that she had lost her feeling of attraction for her husband. It wasn't that Brian lacked skill in lovemaking—he certainly knew how to be a good lover. Kay's problem was that she no longer felt emotionally connected to her husband.

Brian had his own friends, hobbies, and, in general, ways of living that were independent of his wife. She was not integrated into his life and was not consulted in the decisions he made. After years of trying to become a part of Brian's life, Kay finally gave up and learned to be just as independent as he was. She lived her life without considering its consequences on him, just as he had not considered the consequences of his choices on her.

While it's true that some of Brian and Kay's decisions were made with each other's interests in mind, there were far too many aspects of their lifestyle that were separated from each other.

What's Wrong with a Little Independence?

At first glance, independent behavior in marriage might seem not only desirable but also essential for a healthy and happy marriage. After all, who wants to be clingy and dependent? And who wants spouses who are clingy and dependent—unable to do anything by themselves or make any decisions of their own?

But independent behavior is not the only alternative to unhealthy dependency. Another, far superior alternative is what I call interdependency, which is behaving in ways that take each other's feelings into account.

> **Independent Behavior**
> The conduct of one spouse that is conceived and executed as if the other spouse did not even exist.

It all goes back to what I have been repeating throughout this book—almost everything you do in marriage will affect each other either positively or negatively, whether or not you intend to do so. So if you want a marriage that makes both of you happy, you must pay close attention to the way your behavior affects each other. And then you must learn to behave in ways that make each other happy and avoid making each other unhappy.

For purposes of this discussion, let me give you my definition of independent behavior in marriage—it's the conduct of one spouse that is conceived and executed as if the other spouse did not even exist. It's independent in that it neglects consideration of the interests and feelings of the other spouse.

Interdependent behavior, on the other hand, is the conduct of both spouses that nurtures and protects each other. It recognizes that in marriage, behavior must be mutually acceptable to guarantee the protection of each spouse's interests and feelings.

It's the difference between a sole proprietorship and a partnership. If you own a business outright, you have the right to make your own business decisions. But if you have a partner

> **Interdependent Behavior**
> The conduct of both spouses that nurtures and protects each other.

who owns an equal share of the business, you should consult with each and come to an agreement before making decisions. Otherwise the business relationship will suffer, and the business itself will suffer. Marriage is definitely a partnership, and if decisions are not mutually agreeable, it will hurt the relationship and the productivity of the marriage.

The Rooms of Brian's House

I used an imaginary house to show Brian how his lifestyle affected Kay. Each room in this house represented one of the roles he played in life. Among the many rooms there was a career room, a leisure activity room, a family room, a religious practices room, and, yes, a marriage room.

Brian's career room was filled with furniture and projects designed to make him a successful production manager. His leisure activity room contained golf equipment and immediate access to friends who enjoy playing golf with him. The family room contained video games and a television set that he used when he spent time with his children. His religious practices room had been made into an Episcopal chapel. And right in the middle of his marriage room was a big bed.

As he made his way through an average day, Brian visited various rooms representing the roles he played. When in any one room, the doors to the others were shut, so that he could focus his undivided attention on the role he played at the time. He found that he did his best when he avoided the distractions of other roles he played in life.

Since Brian regarded Kay and her interests as a distraction, he relegated her to only one room in his house, the marriage room—and that made her feel neglected and resentful. While it was true that Brian gave Kay his undivided attention when he met her in the marriage room and made a special effort to meet her needs, she felt totally neglected the rest of the time. She wanted to be invited into each room, so that she would be fully integrated into his life. But he wanted her to create a house of her own.

So that's what Kay did. In her house, she also had a career room, but it was outfitted with furniture and projects designed to make her a successful accountant. Her leisure activity room was full of gardening books and supplies. Her family activity room contained bicycles and sporting equipment used when she took her children to their after-school sporting events. Her religious practices room was a Baptist chapel. And in her marriage room, there was . . . nothing. She had emotionally bailed out of the marriage, and that's why she was no longer willing to make love with Brian.

Of course, the problems between Brian and Kay were about much more than just sex. Kay's loss of sexual interest may have been the first symptom of a bad marriage that got Brian's attention. But there had been plenty of other warning signs before she refused to make love. She had begged him to spend weekends with her, instead of golfing with his friends. She cried when he refused to participate in their children's school projects and activities. And she felt like a widow taking her children to church each week without their father. His entire lifestyle made her unhappy and caused massive Love Bank withdrawals. And if he had continued his independent behavior much longer, he would have risked divorce.

Why Is Independent Behavior Tolerated?

Unfortunately, Brian and Kay aren't very different from many married couples today when it comes to independent behavior. And this Love Buster threatens to tear many of them apart. But of all the Love Busters we've discussed so far, this one usually sneaks under the radar. Many couples don't see how destructive their independent behavior is to the health of their marriage.

Those on the receiving end of independent behavior are usually aware of how destructive it can be to a marriage, but those who engage in it usually don't regard it as the least bit destructive. Instead, they think that independent behavior actually strengthens a marriage. Without it, they would feel trapped and suffocated. Who they choose as friends, what they do on the job, where they spend their spare time, and even how they pay their bills—these are choices, some feel, that no one, not even a spouse, should have a right to interfere with. They view any attempt to take away their "freedom of choice" as controlling and manipulative, a marriage-wrecker for sure.

Independent behavior also feeds on the mistaken belief of some that it actually makes spouses more attractive to each other. If clingy dependency is viewed as the only alternative to independent behavior, independent behavior **is** usually more attractive. But many ignore the fact that neither of those options creates a happy marriage. Only interdependent behavior achieves long-term marital satisfaction.

Some spouses also feel that they should be blindly trusted in the decisions they make. If their spouse challenges their decisions, they consider it disrespectful. In fact, many of my clients have tried to misapply the Love Buster category, disrespectful judgments, to their spouse's complaints regarding their independent behavior. "If you trusted me and were not so disrespectful, you would not challenge my decisions" is a common defense.

Only interdependent behavior achieves long-term marital satisfaction.

But the most important reason independent behavior is tolerated in marriage is that it's instinctive. Your Taker wants you to be happy at all costs, ignoring the interests of others. So you are born with a predisposition to make decisions that are good for you and bad for your spouse, at least when your Taker is in charge.

And when your Taker encourages you to behave independently of your spouse, it will easily justify your thoughtlessness. After all, your Taker is your defense attorney, and it is always prepared to explain why everything you do on your own behalf is reasonable. It will try to convince you that you have the right to make independent decisions, that those decisions will make you more attractive to your spouse, and that when your spouse challenges your decisions, he or she is being disrespectful. But the bottom line is that whenever you ignore your spouse's interests and feelings, you are eroding the love he or she has for you, and you are destroying your emotional bond.

Brian felt that what he did in the rooms of his imaginary house should not have any impact on Kay, because the doors were closed and she was not present. But present or not, everything he did, even in the privacy of his rooms, affected her. When he went golfing with his friends, he withdrew love units from her Love Bank. His working schedule also upset her, as did the way he chose to interact with their children. Even his religious practices bothered her. Keeping her out in the hallway of his house did not prevent her from feeling the impact of each independent behavior.

Slowly but surely Kay was finding Brian's lifestyle increasingly intolerable. Eventually she woke up to the realization that they had nothing but their children to keep them together.

Brian and Kay made very few demands of each other, were rarely disrespectful, never had an angry outburst, tried to be honest, and didn't even seem to have annoying habits. And they both knew how to meet each other's emotional needs. Their problem was that they had grown apart because of Brian's independent behavior, and that was reason enough for Kay to start thinking about divorce.

To avoid this disastrous outcome, Kay had to become emotionally reconnected to Brian by joining him in each room of his house. She had to be welcome in more than just the marriage room where he expected to have sex with her—he had to integrate her into every aspect of his life.

I told Brian that regardless of his role or responsibility, Kay should be considered in each decision he made. As equal partners, they should create an integrated lifestyle, enjoyable for both of them. That, in turn, would lead to the emotional bonding Kay needed to restore the sexual relationship he had once enjoyed. But their goal was far more important than simply improving sex—they were creating a true partnership in life.

Two Policies That Can Help Create Interdependence

To help Brian create an integrated lifestyle with Kay, two steps were required. First, he had to invite her into each room of his imaginary house, and then he had to come to an agreement with her as to how each room should be decorated.

Earlier in this book, in the chapter on dishonesty, I introduced to you the Policy of Radical Honesty: *Reveal to your spouse as much information about yourself as you know: your thoughts, feelings, habits, likes, dislikes, personal history, daily activities, and plans for the future.* This rule helps couples gain a clear and accurate description of each other's thoughts and activities. So I encouraged Brian to follow this policy in his relationship with Kay. By providing her with information about his daily activities and plans for the future, she was swept into the inner recesses of the life that had been hidden from her.

153

But being honest with her about the details of his life was not enough. If Kay were to be an integrated life partner, Brian's life had to be acceptable to her. So after inviting her into his room by being radically honest, he had to ask if she was comfortable with the way he had it decorated—in other words, did she like the way he was living his life? If she were not enthusiastic about it, it would have to be changed to accommodate her feelings. The room would eventually have to contain furniture and activities that she would enthusiastically accept.

Policy of Radical Honesty

Reveal to your spouse as much information about yourself as you know: your thoughts, feelings, habits, likes, dislikes, personal history, daily activities, and plans for the future.

Brian did invite Kay into his rooms by following the Policy of Radical Honesty. He kept her completely informed of all his daily activities and plans for future activities. He even gave her a schedule of where he would be and a telephone number where he could be reached in an emergency.

But he still needed another rule to help her become an equal partner in their life together. That rule is one you should be very familiar with by now—the Policy of Joint Agreement: *Never do anything without an enthusiastic agreement between you and your spouse.*

The Policy of Joint Agreement

Never do anything without an enthusiastic agreement between you and your spouse.

The word "anything" in the Policy of Joint Agreement means that all rooms of a house and everything in each room are subject to scrutiny. So if Brian were to follow the policy, he had to think about Kay's reaction to *everything* he did, not just what went on in the "marriage" room, or even just a few of the other rooms. She had to be consulted about what goes on in every room.

But what about the requirement of Kay's "enthusiastic" agreement? Brian felt that a simple agreement would be a big step in the right direction—why insist on enthusiastic agreement?

I explained that marital agreements are often coerced or self-sacrificing. I didn't want Kay to think that she had to agree just to get along, and I didn't want her to sacrifice her own interests so that Brian could have what he wanted. She was not simply a guest in his rooms—she was an equal partner, with the right to rearrange them to make them comfortable for her, too.

Brian complained that if he were to let Kay have the kind of control I was advocating, she would dominate him completely, and he would lose all his peace and freedom. He felt that such a takeover would cause his identity to shrivel away, and he'd find himself a shadow of his former self. He'd become Kay's slave! His Taker was pulling out all the stops to convince him that this whole idea of an integrated lifestyle was a really bad move.

But the Policy of Joint Agreement does not turn anyone into a slave. In fact, it prevents slavery. It isn't just Kay's enthusiastic agreement that is required before a decision is made—it's Brian's enthusiastic agreement as well. There is to be no furniture or activities in any of his rooms that he does not also enthusiastically support.

The Policy of Joint Agreement encourages both husband and wife to be in enthusiastic agreement. Neither risks losing their identity or subjecting themselves to slavery when they themselves must be enthusiastic about each decision. The goal is to become united in purpose and spirit, not to overpower or control each other.

How Easy Is It?

Couples that already have an interdependent lifestyle have little or no trouble following the Policy of Joint Agreement because they have learned how to behave in sensitive and caring ways in each of their life's roles. But couples that have independent lifestyles have great difficulty with the policy—at first. They are accustomed to doing what they please regardless of its effect on each other, especially in certain roles. But if they follow the policy for even one day, they begin to see how their thoughtlessness has created the emotional distance they are experiencing.

As spouses try to apply the policy to each of their daily plans and activities, they begin to feel cared for by each other and are encouraged by each other's thoughtfulness. Over time, their emotional bonding becomes increasingly secure, and the policy

The Policy of Joint Agreement helps create understanding, emotional bonding, intimacy, and romantic love.

becomes easier and easier to follow as their thoughtful choices turn into habits.

Those who follow the Policy of Joint Agreement think about their spouse throughout the day, because as they make decisions they ask themselves how their spouse would feel. Phone calls are made whenever there is any doubt. As time passes, they become increasingly sensitive to their spouse's feelings.

If spouses consider each other's feelings in each decision they make, asking each other when there is any uncertainty, they eventually create a compatible lifestyle. The Policy of Joint Agreement helps create understanding, emotional bonding, intimacy, and romantic love in marriage. Over time, they experience what every couple hopes to create in marriage: a loving and compatible relationship.

By the time Brian had invited Kay into every room in his house and they had made adjustments that created a mutually comfortable lifestyle, she could no longer even imagine leaving him. That's because she wasn't standing in the hallways of his house feeling like a stranger. All his rooms were her rooms as well, and she was welcomed into his entire home as his cherished life partner.

Replacing Independent Behavior with Successful Negotiation

The Policy of Joint Agreement should be your goal in resolving every conflict in your marriage. But how do you get from the conflict to a mutually enthusiastic agreement? Whenever a conflict arises, I suggest that you use a certain procedure. I call it **Four Guidelines to Successful Negotiation.**

ACTION
STEP

Set ground rules for your discussion.

Step 1: Set ground rules for your discussion.

The first guideline is setting ground rules that your discussion must be **pleasant** and **safe**. It must be pleasant in that you should try to make sure that you and your spouse are enjoying the conversation. You should have a smile on your face as you're discussing the issue and some of the alternatives to resolving the conflict. And it must be safe in that you will not be engaged in selfish demands, disrespectful judgments, or angry outbursts. You are to both maintain zero tolerance for these three destructive instincts. If one of you cannot control yourself and the discussion becomes unpleasant or unsafe, end it immediately and begin again later when you've had a chance to gain control.

ACTION STEP

Introduce the conflict and try to understand each other's perspectives.

Step 2: Introduce the conflict and try to understand each other's perspectives.

After you've set these ground rules, that your discussion must be pleasant and safe, the second guideline is to introduce the conflict and try to understand each of your perspectives without being judgmental. What is the conflict and how do both of you feel about it? What would you like? And if you were to have it, how would it affect your spouse? Is there a way to have what you want with your spouse's enthusiastic agreement?

During this phase of problem solving, express your opinion without being critical of your spouse's opinions. And try to repeat your spouse's opinion in a way that accurately reflects it.

Step 3: Brainstorm.

For many conflicts, it isn't easy to find a resolution that accommodates the perspectives of both spouses so that you can arrive at an enthusiastic agreement. So you will need the third guideline, which is to brainstorm.

When the conflict is first introduced, a mutually agreeable resolution may not occur to either of you. So you may need time to think about possible solutions. Carry a pad around with you so that as solutions occur to you, you can write them

ACTION STEP

Brainstorm.

ACTION STEP

Find the solution that meets with your enthusiastic agreement.

down. It may take days before you have accumulated several possibilities. But remember, whatever you write down should take both you and your spouse's perspectives into account simultaneously.

Step 4: Find the solution that meets with your enthusiastic agreement.

You should check with each other daily to see what each of you wrote down on your lists until you find a solution that meets with your mutual and enthusiastic agreement. Of course, until there is something written on one of your lists that you can both enthusiastically agree to, you should continue to brainstorm.

In some cases you may not be able to find a solution. In those instances, I advise you to do nothing. I know of many happy marriages where some conflicts have never been resolved. "Resolving" a conflict in a way that hurts one of you is worse than not resolving it at all. In many sad marriages, spouses feel that one spouse must make the "final" decision when an agreement cannot be reached, but I encourage you not to do that.

Instead, I encourage you to continue to brainstorm until you find a solution that meets with your mutual enthusiastic agreement. And if you don't find that agreement, leave the problem unresolved. Otherwise, you'll be solving the problem in a way that hurts your love for each other.

The Choice Is Yours

Marriages usually go one of two ways: Nature takes its course and marital compatibility is eventually lost, or a couple can decide to build compatibility by eliminating independent behavior and replacing it with interdependent behavior. My years of marriage counseling have taught me a very important lesson: Unless couples create compatibility throughout their marriage, the compatibility they had at the time of their wedding will be destroyed.

When couples divorce or separate because they're "incompatible," does this mean they were doomed from the start? Is there some basic personality clash they just can't overcome? No, it just means they've been ineffective in *creating compatibility*. Very likely they developed interests and activities independently of each other. They weren't thoughtful enough to try to include each other in the most enjoyable moments of their lives.

What a shame! It didn't have to be that way. Their marriage, their family, and in many cases, their happiness could have been saved if only they had used a little thought and consideration.

That doesn't mean just giving your spouse a chance to join you in the lifestyle you've chosen. It means searching for a lifestyle full of *mutual* enjoyment until it's found and replacing activities that have come between you with ones that bring you together.

In the remainder of this book, I will introduce you to some of the most common conflicts in marriage. The first five can make marriage very unpleasant if not resolved with mutual enthusiasm—conflicts regarding friends and relatives, career choices, financial planning, child discipline, and sex. But the last two areas of conflict I'll discuss, infidelity and substance abuse, are absolutely devastating to marriage if they are allowed to run amok. They represent forms of independent behavior that are so incredibly thoughtless that they will set every marriage on a course of almost certain ruin. These illustrations will help me show you how important it is to avoid independent behavior, and how to create interdependent behavior to take their place.

Key Principles

- Independent behavior is the conduct of one spouse that is conceived and executed as if the other spouse did not even exist. Interdependent behavior is the conduct of both spouses that nurtures and protects each other.
- The most important reason independent behavior is tolerated in marriage is that it's instinctive.

- Whenever you ignore your spouse's interests and feelings, you are eroding the love he or she has for you, and you are destroying your emotional bond.

- Two policies help create interdependence: the Policy of Radical Honesty and the Policy of Joint Agreement.

- Unless couples create compatibility throughout their marriage, the compatibility they had at the time of their wedding will be destroyed.

Consider This...

1. What is independent behavior? Think of a few instances of independent behavior that have been a problem for you in the past, but that are no longer a problem for either of you. How did you go about ridding yourself of those Love Busters? Think of other examples that are still a problem for one of you. What are you presently doing to try to overcome them?

2. How has your Taker tried to justify your existing independent behavior? Has it tried to convince you that you have the right to make independent decisions, that those decisions will make you more attractive to your spouse, and that when your spouse challenges your decisions, he or she is being disrespectful? Are there other arguments your spouse has used? Regardless of your spouse's arguments that you should engage in independent behavior, what's the bottom line?

3. Describe each of your own imaginary houses. Which rooms are easy for you both to enter and which are more difficult to enter? Which are locked shut to the other spouse? What are the advantages and disadvantages of inviting each other into all of your rooms?

4. An invitation to enter a room is not enough to build compatibility in marriage. What must you do after you invite each other in?

5. What are the Four Guidelines to Successful Negotiation? How do they help eliminate existing independent behavior? How do they help prevent the creation of new independent behavior?

part three

RESOLVING MARITAL CONFLICTS

chapter nine

RESOLVING CONFLICTS OVER FRIENDS AND RELATIVES

Many of us value loyalty to our family and friends with almost religious fervor. Since our parents endured a great deal of sacrifice in raising us, we usually assume that we have a responsibility to care for them in their hour of need. The same kind of thinking applies to our siblings and possibly even extended family members.

Our loyalty often extends to lifelong friends as well. Those you've known since childhood may have helped you at a time of great personal need, so you may feel obligated to help them as well when they have a problem. After all, that's what friends are for.

Given our sense of responsibility to our family and friends—along with our enjoyment of their company, a question almost invariably comes up after marriage: *What do we do when our relationships with family and friends conflict with the interests of our spouse?*

If a member of your family or a friend needs your help, should you be there for them even if you don't have your spouse's enthusiastic agreement? If your mother cannot care for herself and wants you to care for her, possibly in your own home, should you

163

What do we do when our relationships with family and friends conflict with the interests of our spouse?

provide that care even if your spouse is unenthusiastic about the invasion of your privacy? If one of your friends is about to move and that friend had helped you move, should you help your friend even if your spouse would prefer that you spend the weekend at home with your family? Or, if you simply want to relax and have a good time with your best friends, should your spouse have the right to ruin it all by objecting?

Those are tough questions and in many cases, they are decisions that must be made almost instantaneously. You usually don't have the luxury of days or weeks of negotiation with your spouse.

In this book, I have discussed three approaches to marital problem solving. The first was to use control and abuse. This approach tries to force your spouse to do what you want to do when it's not in your spouse's best interest to do so. You tell your spouse that your parents will be coming over for dinner (selfish demands). If your spouse objects, you blame his or her reluctance on an uncaring attitude (disrespectful judgments). And finally, when all else fails, you raise your voice, stomp from room to room, and throw things around until you get your way (angry outbursts).

That's not the right way to resolve marital conflicts, and most people who have fights know it. So many spouses try a second approach that I introduced in the last chapter, independent behavior. *If you don't enjoy having dinner with my parents, I'll have dinner with them by myself.* It's not mutual agreement, but rather a unilateral choice that is sprung on a spouse with little or no notice. It's the "family-and-friends room" in the imaginary house, and the other spouse is locked out.

The third approach to marital problem solving is the only one of the three that actually resolves conflict the right way and builds love in marriage. It's inviting your spouse into the family-and-friends room by following the Policy of Radical Honesty (explaining your desires and describing your plans before they are implemented) and then giving your spouse equal rights in determining how the furniture is to be arranged by following the Policy of Joint Agreement.

164

This approach begins by telling your spouse that you would like to invite your parents over for dinner (without having discussed it with them first). Then you ask your spouse how he or she would feel about it, letting your spouse reveal any objections without countering with disrespect. Finally, you make a decision that is in the best interest of both you and your spouse. Your final decision may be to take your parents out to dinner so that your wife does not have to cook a meal and clean up after a busy day at work.

Many of the problems that I've witnessed between spouses and family or friends have been caused by the way family or friends treat the spouse—they may be disrespectful or downright cruel. Conflicts in these instances are due to the fact that a spouse feels obligated to be with these people regardless of how they are treated. But if the Policy of Joint Agreement is followed, there is no obligation for either spouse to spend time with people who make them unhappy. Family and friends come to realize early on that they must treat both spouses with utmost respect or risk losing their relationship with the couple entirely.

> **The Policy of Joint Agreement helps re-create your relationships.**

The Policy of Joint Agreement helps re-create your relationships with family and friends to satisfy both of you.

It Pays to Be Prepared

Because many of the decisions you make regarding the care of your parents or friends have to be made instantly, you and your spouse should discuss many of these issues before they actually arise. For example, if your parents or your spouse's parents were to require your care, what kind of care could you provide with an enthusiastic agreement? Now is the time for you to start thinking about what kind of care you can provide and for how long.

What would you do if a friend needed help moving? Or if a friend invited you both out to dinner? Or if a friend invited one of you out to dinner, but didn't invite the other?

You should also discuss possible relationships with friends of the opposite sex. How friendly do you really want these relationships to be? I have warned couples for years that opposite sex friendships are where most affairs begin.

By anticipating each type of problem you may face with family and friends and making some tentative decisions about how you would address it, if the problem actually arises you'll have a plan in place—a plan that you have both agreed to enthusiastically.

The genius behind the Policy of Joint Agreement is that it forces you and your spouse to negotiate with each other's best interests in mind. It forces you to make wise decisions when you are tempted to be foolish. Those decisions define your lifestyle. They determine the way you live and how others react to the way you live. If you follow the Policy of Joint Agreement, your family and friends will never have the opportunity to come between you.

If the problem arises you'll have a plan in place.

Get into the habit of discussing all invitations with your spouse before responding. When somebody invites you over, for example, say, "Let me get back to you after I've discussed it with my spouse." Your family and friends will get used to the idea that you make your decisions together.

But if my spouse doesn't even see or talk to my family or friends, how can they be disrespectful or cruel, you might be wondering. *What if I were to help my family by myself, while my spouse is doing something else?*

There's nothing wrong with that plan if your spouse enthusiastically agrees with it before you do it. But if you do it without your spouse's knowledge, or if it's done without your spouse's enthusiastic agreement, you risk losing your spouse's love for you. As I've already mentioned, what you do apart from each other affects each other, whether you intend it to or not. Arguing that your spouse shouldn't be affected by your independent behavior does not make it so. You may want your spouse to be immune from your thoughtlessness—what you do in private or in secret. But in an intimate relationship, it just cannot be done.

A Crusade for Religious Freedom

Shortly after their wedding, Sherrie told Dwight that to keep peace in her family he must join Trinity Church, where her parents attended. Having been a member of St. Paul's Church all his life, he preferred continuing to attend there. Besides, he and Sherrie had attended his church together before their wedding, and she loved it. But Sherrie insisted on the switch, so he agreed.

For about a year, Dwight attended Trinity with Sherrie but was never able to make the adjustment. He complained to her all year about how unfair it was that her parents determined what church they should attend.

One day he'd had it. "Sherrie, I just can't do it anymore. I will not attend a church just to make your parents happy."

"Well, then do it to make me happy."

"But I'm not comfortable at that church. Besides, you always enjoyed being at my church before we were married. What's so bad about it now?"

"Dwight, I enjoy the services at your church, but I can't disappoint my parents."

"You *can't* disappoint your parents but you *can* disappoint me?"

The following Sunday he announced that he was attending St. Paul's by himself. She could attend Trinity with her parents but he would attend the church of his choice alone.

When the couple saw me for counseling, I pointed out to Sherrie that she'd been making a selfish demand, gaining peace with her parents at the expense of her husband's feelings. She knew Dwight did not enjoy the church services at her parents' church, yet she forced him to attend so she would not have to deal with her parents' rejections.

Dwight had made the correct response to her selfish demand: He rejected it. He told her he would not continue to do something that made him uncomfortable. They needed to find a solution that would satisfy them both, and his attending Trinity was not it.

But when Dwight unilaterally chose to attend St. Paul's, he made the mistake of independent behavior, making a choice that failed to take Sherrie's feelings into account. I explained to them that neither selfish demands nor independent behavior would solve their problem. And both approaches to their problem were eroding their love for each other.

The concept of selfish demands was like a breath of fresh air for Sherrie. She had struggled with the issue of whom to please,

Dwight or her parents, ever since they'd married. Now she saw that whenever she tried to force Dwight to do something for her parents it was just as selfish as if it were for herself. I pointed out to her that in a sense it *was* for herself.

She felt as if she'd had a heavy burden lifted from her shoulders. They had already attended several other churches and discussed these alternatives. None of them would have pleased her parents, but with their new perspective they moved beyond that problem. Now they were simply looking for a church they would both enjoy.

If Sherrie had not enjoyed the services at St. Paul's, they would have visited other churches until they found one they both enjoyed. But after discussion, they agreed that they enjoyed and benefited most from the services at St. Paul's and should return to that church. Sherrie was very happy with the outcome.

When told of the couple's decision, Sherrie's parents announced that they would not speak to Sherrie and Dwight until they changed their minds. Sherrie had experienced this reaction in the past, because her family frequently used demands and intimidation. But this time she didn't buckle under the pressure. She and Dwight decided to honor her parents' request for silence. It took two full years, but her parents finally broke the silence and admitted they'd made a mistake.

In the end, Sherrie's parents adjusted to their decision. But even if they had not, the decision would still have been correct. As their counselor, I witnessed a noticeable improvement in the love Dwight and Sherrie felt for each other, and their entire family benefited.

Taking Generosity One Step Too Far

Judy's Giver worked overtime. Whenever someone was in need, Judy rushed to the rescue. Bill was attracted to that trait when they were dating, especially when he was on the receiving end of her generosity. But after marriage, it became a source of conflict when Judy's sister, Barbara, and Barbara's husband, Jack, moved in with them while Jack was "looking for work."

Bill didn't have any say in the matter. He came home one day to find his in-laws' possessions filling his house. That alone upset him, but it got worse as the weeks dragged on. Barbara and Jack seemed to be permanent fixtures.

"We cannot continue to support your sister and brother-in-law," Bill finally told Judy. "He'll just have to find a job like everyone else."

"But he's tried," Judy pleaded, "and if we don't help, who will? I can't just put my sister out on the street."

Our Giver can get us into a lot of trouble because it is willing to see us suffer for the sake of others. And when we're married, it's not just our Giver that we have to watch out for. Our spouse's Giver can also give us fits when it's generous at our expense. That's what Bill was up against. Judy's Giver wanted Bill to sacrifice along with Judy.

When is it wrong to be generous? It's wrong to be generous when your generosity takes advantage of your spouse. Granted, Judy willingly suffered to help her sister survive. But she made her husband suffer along with her.

As time went on, Bill became increasingly convinced that Judy cared more for her sister than for him. That belief was underscored by the fact that she was not able to meet his emotional needs the way she had in the past because they had lost much of their privacy. In addition, they were now supporting four and were having trouble paying their bills.

Again and again Bill tried to get Judy to ask them to leave, but she insisted on letting them stay until Jack found a job. "I just can't turn my sister away. You'll have to be patient," she told Bill.

But Bill's patience ran out. So many love units had drained out of Judy's account that eventually there was none left. He had lost his love for Judy and saw no purpose in being married to her, especially if it meant having to support his lazy in-laws as well. So he moved out.

Bill's decision brought them to my office for counseling. It didn't take long for Judy to realize that her generosity had been at Bill's expense, and she was willing to follow the Policy of Joint Agreement from that day on. She would never again make a decision without his enthusiastic agreement.

But Judy raised a very important issue. How should the Policy of Joint Agreement be applied to a decision that has already been made unilaterally? The damage is already done, so why not see it through to the bitter end? She wanted her sister and brother-in-law to stay until he could find a job, and from then on she would follow the Policy of Joint Agreement.

I explained to her that when the Policy of Joint Agreement has been violated, and a decision has been made without a joint agreement, a couple must correct the decision as quickly as possible. In this case, it meant going back to her decision to invite Jack and Barbara to live with them and making that decision again, this time with the Policy of Joint Agreement in mind. Since she now knew that Bill would not agree to that arrangement, she had no choice but to ask her sister and brother-in-law to find another place to live. As soon as Jack and Barbara moved out, Bill moved back in.

Now they could apply the Policy of Joint Agreement to their care of Judy's sister. And Bill was willing to help, as long as his interests were taken into account. Remarkably, he enthusiastically offered to loan Jack and Barbara enough money to pay rent for a few months, and he even agreed to let them use some of the furniture they had used while living with him. Bill and Judy were in enthusiastic agreement because they were not sacrificing anything they needed to be happy. And since they had enough privacy to meet each other's emotional needs, Bill's love for Judy returned within a few weeks.

From that one experience that almost ruined their marriage, they learned to apply the Policy of Joint Agreement to all their decisions, and as far as I know, Judy's generosity never again got them into such serious marital trouble.

There are many situations where you cannot please your friends and family and please your spouse at the same time. In those situations the Policy of Joint Agreement protects your marriage from the common yet tragic mistake of pleasing your friends and family at your spouse's expense. It demonstrates your care and preserves the love you have for each other.

The Former Lover

When Sue asked Jack, her new husband, to have dinner with Sam, her former lover, Jack was dumbfounded.

"Have dinner with Sam? Are you crazy? He's the last person in the world I'd ever want to see," Jack complained.

But Sue's persistence paid off—for her. Jack reluctantly agreed to dine with Sam and Sue. She simply wanted to maintain a friendship with Sam and didn't want it to be behind Jack's back. That made sense to her.

When it became apparent to Sue that Jack would never become Sam's friend, she decided to continue her friendship with Sam without Jack. Over the years, Sue would call Sam on the phone or even meet him somewhere, but she always told Jack about it. After all, she didn't want to be dishonest. Jack would become upset when she told him about these contacts, but it wasn't her honesty that withdrew love units, it was her persistence in a very thoughtless independent behavior.

It seems obvious to me that a former lover wouldn't be welcome in a marriage. But I guess if it were *my* former lover, it might not be so obvious to me. What should have been obvious was that Sue enjoyed her friendship with Sam at Jack's expense. Sue felt she had the right to see whomever she pleased. Marriage, she believed, should not restrain her basic personal freedoms.

Her indulgence in activities that benefited her at Jack's emotional expense eventually took its toll on him. Jack gradually lost his feeling of love for Sue. When that happened, he began to engage in disrespectful judgments by being critical and rude. Of course, that withdrew love units from her Love Bank, and by the time they came to see me, they both hated each other.

In my counseling, I first encouraged Jack to eliminate his critical and rude behavior. It was out of character for him to be that way, and he followed my recommendation without much difficulty.

Then Sue came to understand how her "freedom" had hurt Jack. She eventually apologized for what she had put Jack through and stopped seeing Sam.

The recovery of their romantic love was a long and difficult process, one they could have avoided if they had protected each other from Love Busters when they were first married. Their ability to meet each other's emotional needs had never been a problem, but their destructive habits prevented them from doing it. Once those habits were eliminated, slowly but surely they allowed each other to meet their emotional needs and restore their Love Bank balances.

Now they both understand and apply the Policy of Joint Agreement. Each time they have a conflict, they wait until they can both express enthusiasm for the solution. With each solution, they build romantic love.

"I Just Don't Like Her!"

Craig knew there was really nothing wrong with Joan's friend, Bev, but she annoyed him. In fact, he felt annoyed whenever Joan talked to Bev on the telephone. He believed Joan should be able to freely choose her friends, and she had known Bev long before she met him. He didn't want to break up that friendship, but he just didn't like Bev, and Joan's relationship with her was beginning to affect their marriage.

When they came to me for counseling, I helped them recognize that Joan's friendship with Bev was an independent behavior. It was innocent, as many independent behaviors are. Joan did not want her relationship with Bev to hurt Craig, but it was a Love Buster. Each time Joan saw Bev, love units were withdrawn from Craig's Love Bank.

Craig had no choice in the matter. His emotional reactions to Bev were strongly negative and consistent. He tried to like Bev, but it didn't work. Compromises had been attempted, but to no avail. In the end, it became apparent that Bev had to go.

Every one of us knows someone whom we dislike. It's normal to like some people and dislike others. Furthermore, just because you love your spouse there's no guarantee you'll like your spouse's friends.

Most of us who are married notice that the friends we had before marriage are not the same as those after marriage. Look at your wedding pictures. How many of those people do you still regard as close friends? For most of us, only those who were friends of *both* spouses before marriage remain friends after marriage.

Friendships are more difficult to develop than most people think. And they depend on individual taste. In general, there is nothing wrong with people I don't like, and there is nothing wonderful about people I do like. It seems that I'm programmed to like certain people and not others. Most people find this true.

After I convinced Joan that she needed to choose friends that she and Craig both liked, she ended her relationship with Bev. Then Joan and Craig formed new friendships they could both enjoy, and today Joan is just as happy with her new friends as she was with Bev. And her new friendships are helping her deposit love units into Craig's Love Bank.

"You Like Her Too Much!"

Sometimes a problem develops in marriage when you like your spouse's friend *too* much. If you find yourself infatuated with a mutual friend, you're headed for trouble.

Tom and his wife, Alice, bought a mobile home in a resort community when they retired. They liked the area so much they encouraged their best friends, George and Emma, to buy the home that was for sale next door to them. It turned out to be a great idea—until George died.

After his death, the three of them remained very good friends. Tom was more than willing to help Emma with repairs, and he often went over just to keep her company. Within a few months he had fallen in love with her. He didn't tell Alice about it, but he did tell Emma. She was also in love with him. Before long he was doing more than keeping her company!

This went on for more than a year before Alice caught them. They were both ashamed and begged her forgiveness, but she could not be consoled. She didn't know what to do. Should she forgive her friend's offenses and continue the friendship? Or should she abandon the relationship forever?

This problem affects married couples of all ages. But it is particularly troublesome among retired couples who have been lifelong friends. I know of more than twenty cases where the offending spouse was over seventy years of age. It's remarkable, yet predictable. Why *wouldn't* you fall in love with a lifelong friend?

Tom made his first mistake when he failed to tell Alice he was falling in love with Emma. If he had avoided the Love Buster dishonesty, the problem might have been nipped in the bud. Many affairs in the making can be safely sidetracked with honesty.

Tom had a million excuses why he kept the truth from Alice: He didn't want to hurt her feelings; he knew how important Emma's friendship was to Alice; it was a short-term fling that would end soon with no one the wiser.

Dishonesty always has its reasons. But it always brings the same result—solutions to marital problems become impossible because information critical to a solution is distorted.

Tom's second mistake was that he developed an independent behavior. He made decisions independently of Alice and her interests, and it inflicted unbearable pain on Alice once it was uncovered. He did not protect her from his own thoughtlessness.

When they came to see me for counseling, I taught Tom the importance of honesty. Over the next few weeks, he told Alice the details of the affair. She was terribly upset by his revelations, but she eventually recovered. He promised her he would never lie to her about anything again, even if it might hurt her feelings.

At the same time, we designed a plan so that Tom would never see or talk to Emma again. It's the first step in ending any affair. I recommended they sell their mobile home and move to another retirement community in another state. Years of experience have taught me that people cannot be trusted with former lovers, and the close proximity to Emma would have been extremely tempting to Tom and emotionally stressful to Alice. He was willing to make the move, even though he still loved Emma. He believed he could be trusted and thought the move was unnecessary, but he agreed because he wanted to put Alice's mind at ease.

Tom and Alice eventually restored their love for each other, and while it was a painful process, the positive outcome was something neither of them believed was possible. They had narrowly escaped marital and emotional disaster.

Don't Let Friends and Relatives Destroy Your Love for Each Other

Many conflicts regarding friends and relatives pit the interests of a spouse against those of the friends and relatives. In our first example, Sherrie had to decide who had the highest priority—her parents or her husband. When she chose her parents, she risked the loss of love in her marriage. But when she returned her husband's interests to its rightful place, her top priority, their love, was restored.

I could have related many other examples of parents' influence in marriage. One particularly difficult type of case is where the parents' judgment seems clearly superior to the couple's. But even in those cases, it's wiser in the long run for the couple to make the final decisions for themselves, taking each other's emotional reactions into account. Parental wisdom sometimes fails to take romantic love into account, and unless a couple applies the Policy of Joint Agreement to their conflict, the solution will sacrifice their love for each other.

Judy and Bill's case represented another common type of marital conflict regarding relatives—in this case, relatives with economic need. Under no circumstances should one spouse's generosity toward relatives be imposed on the other. All gifts and acts of kindness should be mutual decisions, and your relatives should give both of you credit.

The remaining three cases in this chapter dealt with friendships. Sue and Jack faced the issue of whether marriage should come between past lovers. It has always seemed reasonable for people to be upset when their spouses insist on remaining friends with former lovers. But in our age of "personal freedom of choice at all costs," it's often culturally incorrect to appear sensitive to such friendships. The Policy of Joint Agreement saves the day in these situations. It requires a mutually enthusiastic agreement that I rarely, if ever, find for such friendships.

The solution to Joan and Craig's problem was a little less clear. He simply didn't like her friend Bev. But again, the Policy of Joint Agreement led them to decide to pick friends they both enjoyed.

Many who see the wisdom of Sue dropping her friendship with a former lover can't see the wisdom of Joan ending her friendship with Bev. But the answer to both conflicts is the same. Don't have any relationships without the enthusiastic agreement of your spouse. Otherwise the relationships become Love Busters.

Likewise, even though Tom and Alice had a long mutual friendship with Emma, when Emma and Tom had an affair, she had to go. You are more likely to have an affair with a mutual friend than anyone else, and if you begin to have romantic feelings toward that friend, tell your spouse about it right away—and never tell the friend. Then ease out of the relationship entirely.

Your spouse is your most important friend and relative.

Your spouse is your most important friend and relative. No others should ever be allowed to come between you. Follow the Policy of Joint Agreement to make sure they don't.

Consider This . . .

1. What are three approaches to resolving conflicts over friends and relatives? Why should you always avoid two of them and learn to become experts at using the third?

2. Think of a conflict you have over relatives. If you used the first approach to resolving conflicts that I describe in this chapter, how would you try to resolve it? If you used the second approach, what would you do? Why would both of these approaches to marital problem solving diminish the love you have for each other?

3. Use the third approach I suggested to help you resolve your conflict over relatives (the Four Guidelines to Successful Negotiation, described more fully in chapter 9).

4. Use the Four Guidelines to Successful Negotiation to resolve a conflict you have over friends.

5. Why are commitments to please your friends or relatives of lesser importance than your commitment to please each other?

chapter ten

RESOLVING
CONFLICTS
OVER CAREER
CHOICES

Joyce was nineteen and I was twenty-one when we were married. And my career plans were anything but settled at the time. After graduating from college with a degree in philosophy, I attended graduate school for two years as a limited graduate student with no particular major in mind. But the birth of our daughter, Jennifer, hurried my career planning along. After Joyce rejected two of my career possibilities, we eventually agreed on my becoming a psychologist, and so I completed my education with a Ph.D. degree in that field.

Joyce and I decided together what career path I would take. But many couples today don't get married until they're in their late twenties, long after they've made decisions regarding careers. It was easy for me to reject a career that I hadn't gone to any trouble trying to prepare for, but if I had earned a professional degree and had ten years of experience, I might have thought twice about Joyce's reservations. Yet it's been proven to me time and time

A career choice can destroy a marriage.

177

again that unless a couple has enthusiastic agreement about each other's careers, a career choice can destroy a marriage.

When couples are dating, they may have enthusiasm for each other's careers, but when they marry and have children, their careers may make it almost impossible to have a mutually enjoyable lifestyle. That's because a career may support a couple in one phase of their relationship but destroy it in another.

Are you willing to change your career path out of consideration for your spouse?

Which brings up an important point. Career choices include more than the choice of the career itself—it also includes choices regarding the way the career is implemented. A career itself may not hurt a marriage if the work schedule or specific work assignments are decided with the interests of both spouses in mind.

If your spouse is unhappy with what your career is requiring you to do, you're making Love Bank withdrawals every time you go to work. You may think you don't have any choices and that your spouse simply has to adjust to your career. But it's more likely that your spouse will disconnect from you emotionally so that the effects of the career don't hurt him or her as much. In other words, your spouse will simply fall out of love with you.

It's easier for you to change your behavior than it is to change your spouse's reactions to your behavior. If your work schedule or career requirements make your spouse unhappy, change them. If necessary, create a new career that meets with your mutual enthusiastic agreement.

When I introduce this idea to couples many of them think I'm nuts. And yet when you consider the career paths of most people, careers usually change several times during a person's lifetime. One way or another, changes in your career are likely during your lifetime. Are you willing to change your career path out of consideration for your spouse, or will you let some of the random factors of life make those changes for you?

I'm a firm believer that your career should support your spouse and family and not the other way around. The purpose of a career is to earn a living so that you can have a satisfying lifestyle. But what if the career itself causes you or your spouse not to love each other anymore? Then the career is defeating its very purpose. Instead of creating a comfortable lifestyle for you at all, it's creating a miserable lifestyle.

Some people have tried to argue that their career choice is a personal decision. Since it's something that they will be doing most of their waking hours, the first and foremost consideration should be whether or not they like doing it. People who use this argument are usually afraid that their spouse will force them into a career that they really don't want. But the Policy of Joint Agreement handles that problem. It requires both of you to be enthusiastic about your final decision. It guides you to a career that you will enjoy because that's one of the conditions that must be met.

But your spouse must enjoy it too. If you follow the conditions of the Policy of Joint Agreement, when your negotiations are over you will have a career that you like just as much as the one you have now, if not more so. And your spouse will be just as enthusiastic about it as you are.

Once in a while a couple will ask me for guidance in selecting a career that's marriage friendly. In other words, are there certain careers that are easier on marriages than others? The answer to that question has to do with the requirements of the career and whether those requirements tend to prevent spouses from meeting each other's emotional needs.

Careers that are notoriously hard on marriages are those that separate spouses overnight. And the longer the separation, the more likely it is that the career will cause the loss of love, and possibly a divorce. Military marriages, for example, are notoriously bad because couples can be separated for months at a time.

Your spouse and family should not serve your career; your career should serve them.

But those who work on ships, pilots and flight attendants, over-the-road truckers, or train engineers also tend to have disappointing marriages because their jobs keep them away from their spouses for days or even weeks.

One of my cardinal rules in marriage is that couples should avoid being separated overnight. Joyce and I have followed that rule ever since we were first married, even though both of our careers require extensive travel. When either of us is called away, the other comes along. That way, we are not only more integrated into each other's careers, but we also continue to meet each other's emotional needs, even when on business trips. If your job does not allow your spouse to come along when you travel overnight, I strongly recommend that you change that condition of your job or change the job itself to keep your marriage from being at risk.

Other jobs that are hard on marriages are those that require a spouse to be on-call twenty-four hours a day, seven days a week. Physicians, for example, that are not in control of their own schedules can develop a lifestyle where the demands of their career control their day-to-day schedules. Scheduled time between the husband and wife is always at risk and can always be interrupted. To overcome this sad state of affairs I've encouraged many doctors to simply avoid being on call when they're with their spouse or family. They learn to leave their cell phones at the office.

Remember, the basic rule is this: Your spouse and family should not serve your career; your career should serve them. And if you're in a career where its demands are so great that your spouse's interests simply cannot be considered, you're in the wrong career.

The Unhappy Wanderer

Moving is never easy, but it's excruciatingly painful when you don't *want* to move. Jean was in tears all day as she packed.

"Brian, Duluth may be a wonderful city with wonderful opportunities, but I like it here in Sioux Falls. Please, don't do this to me," she begged.

"I'm sorry," he replied, shaking his head, "but we can't turn back now. I was fortunate to be offered this job, and I can't pass it up."

Jean moved to Duluth with Brian. Then she moved to Des Moines, Kansas City, and finally Minneapolis. Their children had not been in one school for any two-year period, and they were having trouble adjusting socially. Jean had experienced severe symptoms of anxiety, so she made an appointment with me to help her and her children.

During my first interview with her, she avoided the subject of her marriage and focused on her symptoms. But eventually she mentioned that her anxiety had threatened her marriage. Sometimes it's difficult to know if emotional symptoms cause a bad marriage or vice versa. I tentatively concluded it was probably the marriage that caused the symptoms and asked to see her husband.

Brian loved Jean dearly, tried to put her first in everything, valued his time with his family, and was intelligent and attractive besides. He seemed to be a perfect husband. But in my interview with him, he mentioned that Jean had been cold toward him ever since they moved from Sioux Falls. In further conversations with Jean, she admitted that the move had caused a change in her feelings toward Brian, and she wasn't even sure she loved him anymore. During the past year, they had made love infrequently.

The more we talked about Sioux Falls, the more visibly depressed Jean became, mentioning on several occasions having no hope of ever going back "home."

I explained to Brian that his wife could take drugs to relieve the anxiety symptoms that seemed to be caused by all their moving around, or he could move the family back to Sioux Falls. If they moved, I predicted that within two to five years, she'd be back to normal. Even if I was wrong, it was worth a try. She was becoming increasingly neurotic and soon her treatment would become prohibitively expensive and painful for the whole family.

Brian took my advice and was able to get an excellent job in Sioux Falls. The last I heard, Jean's love had been restored, she was no longer in therapy, and her anxiety symptoms had all but disappeared.

You usually know what you need better than anyone else. Jean knew she would suffer if she moved away from Sioux Falls. And she did suffer. But short of a divorce, she thought there was no way to return.

She experienced a conflict that commonly causes severe emotional symptoms: If she were to choose moving from one strange community to the next, she would suffer; and if she were to choose a divorce, she would suffer. This type of conflict is called an avoidance-avoidance conflict. In other words, regardless of what you do, you will experience pain. Conflicts like this tend to make people neurotic. In some cases, these conflicts lead to suicide.

Brian's insistence that the family move from one city to another was a selfish demand. If he had formulated his desire to move from Sioux Falls as a thoughtful request, they would not have moved, and none of this pain would have resulted. His mistake cost Jean years of unhappiness and caused his account in her Love Bank to become bankrupt.

When he finally withdrew his selfish demand and they returned to Sioux Falls, two things happened at the same time. First, Jean felt much better back home in Sioux Falls and eventually overcame her emotional disorder; second, the depletion of love units ended, and Brian began to rebuild his Love Bank account. Jean's romantic love for him was eventually restored.

Joyce and I experienced a similar situation, but we handled it differently at the outset. I was offered an attractive career opportunity in Chicago, but Joyce was not at all happy about moving from beautiful Santa Barbara. After discussing alternatives, we came to an agreement: She was willing to go to Chicago on the condition that we would move back if she found that she preferred living in Santa Barbara.

After a year in Chicago, I was offered another opportunity in Minneapolis. Again, we discussed the alternatives, and Joyce agreed to the move as long as a return to Santa Barbara was possible.

During that year, my daughter, Jennifer, was placed in four different schools, and Joyce's father died suddenly and unexpectedly. It was a time of unprecedented emotional upheaval. But through it all Joyce knew I'd be willing to return to Santa Barbara as soon as she said the word.

There were disadvantages to be sure, but there were also advantages to living in Minneapolis. Joyce was able to weigh them in her mind and each year chose to remain in the Twin Cities. We have lived here for thirty years now, and she could still decide to move back to Santa Barbara if it was what she wanted to do. But to this day she has never expressed a bit of resentment toward me regarding the move, because it was a *joint* decision.

Is He Ambitious or a Workaholic?

Renee didn't know exactly what she wanted in a husband, but she knew one thing: She didn't want to marry a lazy oaf! So when Jim came along, his tireless ability to work impressed her. He had not only put himself through college but had saved enough to pay cash for his car. It made her feel secure to know he was not the type to pile up debts.

While they were dating, he saw her or at least called her every day. Being with her was a part of his schedule. But after they married, his career took off, and his time with Renee gradually tapered off.

"Jim, you're working too hard," she would tell him. "Why don't you relax a little? Let's take a vacation together!"

He would just smile. "I am relaxed! Have you ever seen me on a vacation? I'm a bundle of nerves."

Jim didn't realize—and Renee didn't explain—that the problem was not his nerves but their relationship. They were not with each other often enough to sustain their love for each other. They couldn't possibly meet each other's emotional needs, and Renee had become very lonely.

Renee came to me to express her dissatisfaction with life. She lived in a beautiful home and had wonderful children and all the freedom a mother could ever dream of. But her emotional needs were not being met. In fact, she was seriously considering an affair, just to see if it would help.

She had indulged in the Love Buster dishonesty by failing to explain to Jim that she was unhappy with their relationship. She didn't want to appear unappreciative of all the material things he provided. And she didn't dare tell him she was thinking of having an affair. He might leave her, and then where would she be?

Arranging for an appointment with Jim was a Herculean task. He was scheduled for months ahead. I adjusted my schedule to fit his. Even then, he canceled at the last minute when a "business emergency" arose.

When I finally did see him, I asked if he felt his schedule was any of Renee's business.

He was puzzled by my question. "Of course it's her business," he responded.

Then I wanted to know if he had ever asked her how she felt about his schedule. He thought he had, but Renee was right there to tell him he had not.

Finally, I asked him if Renee's feelings would affect his schedule. If she were unhappy with something he planned, would he change his plans to accommodate her feelings?

By the end of the session, Jim had gotten the message. His work schedule had become his highest priority, and even though he said he was working to make Renee happy, he was actually doing it to make himself happy. He had imposed his work schedule on Renee, and his career fulfillment came at her expense.

They did not spend enough time with each other to meet their most important emotional needs. If Renee had expressed satisfaction with that arrangement, I would have concluded that she was in the emotional state of withdrawal. She would have wanted him gone so she wouldn't suffer from his inattentiveness. But, thankfully, she wasn't satisfied with his absence. She still wanted to be with him.

Over the next few weeks, Jim cooperated with Renee in creating a new schedule. It didn't include the independent behavior that peppered his old schedule. Instead, each event on his calendar met with her approval, and his career no longer withdrew love units from her Love Bank.

They fulfilled one of my counseling objectives, which was to set aside fifteen hours each week to meet each other's most important emotional needs (see chapter 17). During those hours Jim was able to make much-needed Love Bank deposits.

In the final analysis, Jim was still a workaholic in the sense that he enjoyed work more than most people do. But when Jim gave Renee's interests a higher priority than his career, he saved his marriage and possibly his career as well.

Renee's habit of dishonesty was part of their problem. Jim had always been willing to accommodate her feelings, but she needed to express them before he could make an adjustment.

I've counseled others, however, who were not as accommodating as Jim. They argue that unless they devote all their energy and effort to their career, their family will become homeless! These people have their priorities backward.

Your career should serve your marriage; your marriage should not serve your career. You and your spouse should work with each other to help develop each other's career, but the success of your careers should never be more important to you than the success of your marriage. To put it another way, the success of your career should never be at the expense of your spouse's interests and feelings.

I've spoken to many people who are close to death, and none of them have ever told me they should have spent more time at work. If people have regrets later in life, it's that they didn't spend more time with their spouse and children.

Flying into Clouds of Conflict

Any career that takes you away from your spouse overnight is dangerous to the health of your marriage. The more you're gone, the more dangerous it is.

I can thank the airline industry for giving me the opportunity to make a living as a marriage counselor. Their employees helped me become an expert on the subject of infidelity, because many of these folks were having affairs in almost every way possible. They also gave me confidence in my methods, since these couples provided such a difficult testing ground, and the methods proved successful even under those conditions.

Sarah absolutely loved her job as a flight attendant. She liked the work itself, earned a good salary, and could travel almost anywhere as an employee benefit. Her husband, Rich, didn't like her job at all. She had applied for it without consulting him, knowing he wouldn't like the idea and thinking she probably wouldn't get it anyway. But when they actually offered it to her, she was delirious with excitement.

When Rich came in the door from work, Sarah flung her arms around his neck. "I got it! I got it!"

He smiled and hugged her back. "Got what?"

"I got a job as a flight attendant. Isn't that great? Oh, I'm so happy!"

Rich's smile faded. But Sarah didn't notice. She ran all around their apartment, screaming, "I got it!"

"Hey, wait a minute, Sarah, you didn't tell me you were applying for a new job. Don't you like the one you already have?"

"It was okay, but I never thought I'd be able to work as a flight attendant. It's all right with you, isn't it?"

Rich didn't seem to have a choice. "Well, I guess we can try it for a while to see how it works, but I'm not too crazy about your being away so much."

Six months later the job was becoming a major issue in their marriage. Rich was not only being left alone for up to three nights at a time, but he was becoming jealous of the pilots and passengers who asked his wife out to dinner. Sarah would come home to find a beast in her apartment, and by the time he'd settle down, she'd be off on another trip.

When they came to me for counseling, Sarah was not sure she was in love with Rich anymore. And she was secretly meeting with a man she had met on a flight. A separation might be a good idea, she suggested, so she could decide how she felt about her marriage.

Rich didn't know about any of this and simply wanted me to tell her to quit her job.

Their marriage was hanging together by a thread. If I had followed Rich's advice, Sarah probably wouldn't have shown up for the next appointment.

So I had to begin therapy with Rich. He was guilty of selfish demands, disrespectful judgments, and angry outbursts. While it's true that they were in response to the pain he felt over Sarah's job, his abuse had done nothing to resolve the conflict and had punched a gaping hole into her Love Bank.

I explained that he would need to learn to control his abusive behavior before Sarah would be willing to negotiate with him regarding her independent behavior. It was in his best interests to stop making demands, start showing respect, and avoid losing his temper. In return for his commitment to avoid these Love Busters, Sarah agreed not to separate while in counseling.

Rich's success in avoiding angry outbursts was probably the most crucial step toward their recovery. Once Sarah felt he could control his temper, she could explain her feelings to him and even went so far as to tell him that she had been planning to move out, that she might be in love with someone else, and that she didn't love him.

Even after these revelations, Rich didn't become angry. Instead, he simply expressed his desire for reconciliation.

At that point in the counseling process, I had the opportunity to explain to Sarah that she had engaged in the Love Buster of independent behavior. She had been inconsiderate of Rich's feelings when she took her job. She had gained a career advantage at his expense.

Her face turned red. "Well, I suppose you want me to quit my job. That's what you really want, isn't it?"

I explained that I had no right to demand anything of her, and neither did Rich. But the truth was that her happiness led to his pain.

Sarah could have walked out of my office never to return. But Rich's proven ability to stop trying to control her with demands, disrespect, and anger encouraged her enough to begin a process of negotiation with the Policy of Joint Agreement. After they agreed that neither of them should gain at each other's expense, Sarah found another job with the same airline company, one Rich enthusiastically supported because it gave her many of the same benefits yet didn't require being away nights.

The happy ending did not take place immediately. There were many times that I thought their efforts might end in failure. But Sarah and Rich both used their intelligence to override their destructive instincts, and their combined wisdom trumped the foolishness of their Takers.

Sarah had lost her love for Rich but gave him an opportunity to redeposit all the love units he had squandered. His efforts clearly saved the day, and before they ended their sessions with me, her love for him had been restored.

What If God's Calling Is the Issue?

When he was nine, Al committed his life to the ministry. At a church service, when the preacher asked for a commitment from those willing to become full-time ministers, he responded and never forgot that decision. In college he majored in Bible to prepare for the ministry.

Toni was also a Bible major and had thought she would become a missionary. She and Al took many of the same classes and studied together. They dated and before long they were in love.

Before graduation Toni decided against becoming a missionary, changed her major to social work, and eventually completed that major. Al figured social work would be a great background for a minister's wife and encouraged her in her professional training.

They married immediately after college graduation. Al enrolled in seminary, and Toni found a job as a social worker. But after only one year of seminary, they both realized she would not be comfortable in the role of a minister's wife. She had come to know a few and didn't like what she saw. They all seemed to be complaining about the criticism they received from parishioners, and Toni hated criticism in any form.

"Toni, we're in this thing together. You have an important role to play," Al explained. When she expressed reluctance to accept that role, he trotted out Bible verses on the subject of a man's authority over his wife.

Toni became furious. "Don't you lecture me! I'll do what I please, and if I don't want to play Mrs. Reverend, I won't."

Then they broke into the biggest fight they'd ever had. When it was over, Toni agreed to support him in his ministry because he had made a commitment to God. But she didn't like it at all. It certainly wasn't "enthusiastic agreement." Al had made selfish demands and disrespectful judgments that would eventually come back to haunt him.

After graduating from seminary, Al took a position in a rural church of fifty members. He was happy with his career, but Toni suffered. She could not fit the role expected of her. There was little privacy in the church parsonage, and she hated living in a fishbowl. And even in a church of fifty, there were those who were critical of her. She put on a cheerful face when she met parishioners but when she was home alone, she cried.

Al felt her problems were spiritual and that Toni had not given herself to God's work. Her "rebellious spirit" was keeping her from enjoying the ministry as much as he enjoyed it. She believed him, and her depression became so bad that she could no longer hide it from others. Eventually Al felt she should see a psychologist.

It didn't take me long to discover the problem. Toni explained that she was not cut out for the role of pastor's wife. What's worse, she had come to hate her husband, a feeling she'd never felt toward anyone before. Because she couldn't tolerate the feeling of hatred toward anyone, she was on the brink of suicide. She even thought she might be possessed by an evil spirit.

Al had imposed his career on Toni, even though he knew she suffered as a result. He also demanded that she perform duties to further his ministry, even though they were painful to her.

The solution to their problem started with eliminating the mistakes that created it. I convinced Al that disrespectful judgments were not at all helpful. Pastors are in the habit of making moral judgments from the pulpit and often carry their preaching into their home. Al was no exception, and Toni had become a captive audience. He had to learn to talk to her without any reference to "shoulds" and "oughts."

He also came to understand the destructiveness of his selfish demands. He learned to avoid trying to force her into any particular role in the church, hoping that she would eventually find a comfortable way to help him.

Unfortunately, Toni had developed such an aversion to the entire scene that they both eventually came to the conclusion that he needed to make a career change to accommodate her.

As they discussed alternatives with each other, they settled on a career in counseling as mutually acceptable. Toni was able to find a full-time job as a social worker, which supported Al's retraining. The work was good for her, and I saw them long enough to see her recover completely from depression.

Al has now completed his retraining and has a job as a psychologist. He works closely with churches and supports ministers in their pastoral counseling. And last I heard Toni was in love with him again.

It's all a matter of priorities. In Al's case, he had to realize that once he was married, Toni had to be his highest priority. His marriage could not serve his career. His career had to serve his marriage, even though his career was the Christian ministry.

Al's choice was not between God and Toni—it was between his career and Toni. He had made a commitment to God to become a full-time minister. But he also made a commitment to God to be a caring husband. Al thought that his career was more important to God than his marriage. But the question I put to him was, *Which is really more important to God?*

I've counseled many pastors and their wives. In many cases, these men made a commitment to become a minister of the gospel. However, in the course of life, these men discovered that they'd married women who, for whatever reason, had failed to adjust to the role of pastor's wife. At that point each had a decision to make: *Does God want me to follow my commitment to Christian ministry and remain a pastor, or does He want me to reevaluate that commitment in light of the needs of my spouse?*

They struggle with the question. They think God might be disappointed with them if they choose to consider their wife's feelings in making career decisions. But I point out to them how silly that sounds. How could God be disappointed with thoughtfulness toward their spouse? He's in *favor* of thoughtfulness, not *opposed* to it! He wants us to treat our spouses with the utmost care and consideration, and that includes how we make career choices.

The Policy of Joint Agreement provides the wisest solution to this problem. When a wife realizes her husband is willing to consider a new career that she would enthusiastically agree to, she will usually take her husband's love for the ministry into account. The decision often keeps them in the ministry but provides an emotionally satisfying role for the wife.

Don't Let Your Career Destroy Your Love for Each Other

As I explained in the beginning of this chapter, I planned my career with my wife in mind. My first career choice was to become a minister and my second was medicine. Joyce didn't like either of them for various reasons. But by the time we had been married three years, we both agreed on the profession I have now, psychology.

It would have been pointless for me to start my career development without her support. After all, my career was to be a joint effort with joint compensation. If at some time she had second thoughts about the way it was turning out, I was prepared to abandon psychology to take up a new profession. Without her support, the career would not serve our mutual purposes in life. Her encouragement has made my choice particularly satisfying and undoubtedly accounts for much of its success.

Joyce's career choices were made with the same consideration for my feelings. I support her career as enthusiastically as she supports mine. I consider her work as a gospel singer and radio host/producer to be an effort we make jointly. I never resent the time she spends pursuing her career interests, because she is willing to accommodate my feelings with her schedule and choice of career activities.

Since we are both ambitious people, our career interests could have wrecked our marriage. But instead, our careers have strengthened our marriage, because we consider each other more important than our work. Our deep love for each other is the end result.

> **Make your career a Love Builder, not a Love Buster.**

I have counseled hundreds of couples whose marriages were threatened by foolish career choices. I gave you a few examples of these cases in this chapter. In every case one or both spouses felt that they should be able to make independent career decisions without adversely impacting their marriage. But their career gains were made at the expense of their spouse's love for them.

Don't lock your spouse out of your career room. It's one of the most important roles you play in marriage, and it should be chosen and carried out with your spouse in mind. Make your career a Love Builder, not a Love Buster.

Consider This...

1. How are selfish demands, disrespectful judgments, and angry outbursts used to force career choices? What are some common excuses spouses use to justify their selfish demands, disrespectful judgments, and angry outbursts? Have you used any of these forms of abuse to try to force your spouse to agree with your career choices? What is the likely outcome when a spouse is expected to adjust to a career that has not been enthusiastically accepted?

2. When is a career choice independent behavior? How is that different from trying to obtain agreement through demands, disrespect, or anger? Do either of you feel you have the right to make decisions about your career independently of the other's interests and feelings? Are you willing to give up that right for the sake of your love for each other?

3. Are you in agreement with each other's career choices, what you do while at work, and the way you schedule your time? Make a list of all aspects of each other's careers that bother one of you. Then, use the Policy of Joint Agreement and the Four Guidelines to Successful Negotiation (described in chapter 9) to try to resolve these conflicts by modifying your schedules and work assignments.

4. Why is commitment to your career of lesser importance than your commitment to please each other?

chapter eleven

RESOLVING
CONFLICTS
OVER FINANCIAL
PLANNING

A few years ago I read an article announcing that conflicts over finances had been shown to be the number one cause of divorce. That's not really true, but what is true is that if a couple doesn't know how to resolve their conflicts, they're likely to be arguing about money almost every day.

The reason most people divorce is because they've lost their love for each other. They stop depositing love units because they stop meeting each other's emotional needs. And they start withdrawing love units by not taking each other's feelings into account when they make decisions. Since so many decisions in marriage have to do with finances, it may seem that conflicts over money are actually what do them in. But it's actually a symptom of a much greater problem.

When a couple first comes to see me for counseling, I often ask them how they make their financial decisions. Do you have a joint checking account? Does the money that both of you earn go into that account? Do you make decisions together on how that money is to be spent?

For most of the couples I interview, that isn't the way it's done at all. For most couples with bad marriages, each spouse makes unilateral decisions about how money is to be spent. In many cases, the husband's salary goes into his checking account and the wife's salary goes into hers. They may have some sort of agreement on how the bills are to be split up so that he pays some of the bills and she pays others. Or they may decide that one of them takes full responsibility for all the bills. All the money may go into one account, but only one spouse has the right to make decisions about how that money is to be spent. The other spouse can only spend what they're given as an allowance.

> If a couple doesn't know how to resolve their conflicts, they're likely to be arguing about money almost every day.

Because I want couples that I counsel to become accustomed to using the Policy of Joint Agreement, I often use finances to teach them how to make decisions that take each other's feelings into account. We apply the Policy of Joint Agreement to literally every dime they spend. The money that both of them earn goes into a joint checking account, but no check is to be written unless both spouses are in enthusiastic agreement about it. In some cases I've actually set up a checking account, where both spouses have to sign each check in order for it to be valid. This exercise not only gets them used to making financial decisions with joint agreement, but it's also a good way to practice making joint decisions in general. As they learn to negotiate agreement on how each bill is to be paid, they develop good negotiating habits.

To show you how this works, the first step is that they deposit all of their income into a joint checking account. They agree that no check is to be written unless they both enthusiastically agree. A period of time is set aside each week for them to pay their bills and to write each other checks for pocket money.

Whenever there's a conflict about the purchase of a particular item or how much to pay toward a particular bill, both spouses follow my four-step procedure for negotiation. First, they set guidelines that guarantee each other that the conversation will be pleasant and safe. Then they discover each other's feelings about the issue in a nonjudgmental way in an effort to under-stand what kind of a solution would work for both of them. Next they brainstorm possible solutions, solutions that they think might make both of them happy. And finally, they find a solution to that conflict that they both enthusiastically agree to.

While they negotiate, the check is not written, regardless of how much one spouse senses urgency. If they cannot agree, noth-ing is spent. They must wait until they have enthusiastic agree-ment regardless of how long it takes.

For some couples this is a very difficult assignment. They feel that if they don't buy a particular item the earth will swallow them up and send them into oblivion. But I try to convince couples that their love for each other is far more important than a particular purchase.

What ruins marriages is not delaying a purchase—it's mak-ing a purchase where one spouse gains at the other's expense. You may feel that what you're doing is right, but if in the process of being right your spouse loses his or her love for you, what kind of victory does that turn out to be? Besides, it's been proven to me over and over again that a decision that can be made with mutual agreement is a far wiser decision than one made where one spouse agrees and the other disagrees. So joint agreement is not just a matter of insuring your love for each other, it also means that you're usually making a wiser choice.

Are your purchases more important than your love for each other?

If you and your spouse have not learned how to negotiate with each other and are not in the habit of using the Policy of Joint Agreement to make your decisions, you'll have a very difficult time coming to an agreement at first. You'll probably be very frus-trated, and you may feel that this procedure just isn't for you. But if you give the process a little bit of time and make sure that you don't use demands, disrespect, or anger as a shortcut to a solu-tion, you'll find that it gets easier and easier. You will also find that your agreements will set a standard for similar decisions in the future. Once they're made, you will know what to do when-ever the problem comes up. And as your negotiating skills improve, when new financial conflicts arise, you will be able to handle them much more quickly.

Married to a Tightwad

Frank didn't seem to worry about his finances. He earned enough to get by, and that was always good enough for him. But he never borrowed money.

After high school, he had moved from his home into a mortuary where he worked (while he slept) as night attendant. He earned free meals at his part-time job as waiter and took the bus whenever he needed transportation. Grants paid part of his college expenses, and he managed to complete his education without borrowing a dime.

Beth realized Frank couldn't afford much while he was attending college and admired his financial discipline and resourcefulness. While their dates and his gifts to her were inexpensive, they were thoughtful and reflected his deep love for her.

But after they married and both earned a good income, financial conflicts began to develop. Frank insisted from the beginning that all their income go into a bank account that he controlled. He was making a selfish demand, because he didn't ask how she felt about his plan.

Beth knew he was a good money manager and he wasn't squandering their income—but he wouldn't tell her how the money was being used. He was now engaging in the Love Busters of dishonesty and independent behavior—dishonesty, because he didn't tell her how the money was being spent, and independent behavior, because he was making financial decisions without her enthusiastic agreement.

One day Beth posed an important question. "Frank, do you think we're ready to raise children?"

"Not yet," he replied. "It'll be a while before we can afford them."

Beth bristled. "We can afford children now! We both earn good incomes and we've been saving most of it—haven't we?" Suddenly she felt uncomfortable. "By the way, how much have we saved?"

There was a long pause. "We just haven't saved enough. Take my word for it," Frank said.

His selfish demands, dishonesty, and independent behavior were beginning to catch up with him. The next day, when Beth was home alone, she started poking around Frank's papers. What she found blew her away. Frank had all their investments in *his* name. Savings accounts, money market accounts, and stocks— all in his name. The most remarkable part of it was that he had managed to save over forty thousand dollars in just two years!

That evening Beth confronted him with her discovery.

"Why are all our savings in your name? And how can you say we can't afford children when we've saved forty thousand dollars?"

Frank was furious. "I handle all the finances, and I do it the way I see fit. Besides, you wouldn't understand it even if I tried to explain it to you. So stay out of my desk!"

Frank may have been *saving* money but he was *losing* love units. Beth was terribly offended and ended the conversation.

The very next day she opened her own checking account. When she was paid, she deposited her check into it.

That evening, Frank said casually, "You haven't given me your check. Do you have it yet?"

"Yes, I do," she said flatly, "and you're not getting it!"

This time *she* lost love units in *his* Love Bank. In fact, for the next year, she lost love units each time she deposited her check into her own account. His independent behavior inspired her to carry out her own independent behavior. It seemed fair to her. After all, why should she deposit money into an account that she had no control over?

By the time Frank and Beth saw me for marriage counseling, their complaint was that they'd "grown apart." She had her life, and he had his. Their inability to resolve their financial conflict had implications in many other parts of their lives, and their separate checking accounts had begun the process of separating everything!

Their problems began with Frank's selfish demands, dishonesty, and independent behavior. He wanted to control the finances and didn't want her to interfere. With incomplete information, Beth gradually suspected that Frank was cheating her.

Frank's motives were pure: He was saving money for both of them and was not trying to cheat her, but his arrogant approach destroyed her trust in him.

Beth contributed to the problem when she set up her own checking account. Even though Frank had been secretive with her about their finances, she should not have made the same mistake. As an interim solution, she would have helped the situation by creating a joint checking account that required both of their signatures, and by depositing her check into that account. It would have set an example for Frank as to how all of their financial decisions should be made, without cutting him completely out of the loop.

It was Frank, however, who made the lion's share of the mistakes. When Beth explained that her discovery of their savings in Frank's name had upset her, he refused to transfer their investments into joint accounts. He knew his actions had been at her emotional expense but did nothing to protect her feelings. If he had simply added her name to all their investments and thoughtfully requested that she deposit her check into a joint account, she might have enthusiastically agreed. But his arrogance and thoughtlessness ruined that possibility.

Most of us would consider Beth's defensive reaction reasonable under the circumstances. But it is a good example of how defensiveness can be thoughtless. Her behavior deeply offended Frank, even though he'd done essentially the same thing to her. If she had not deposited her checks in any account, or into a joint account that required two signatures, until she'd reached an agreement with Frank, it would have been a thoughtful example to him.

The elimination of Love Busters and the application of the Policy of Joint Agreement solved their problem. Frank agreed to disclose his investment strategy to Beth and added her name to all their investments. At first, he felt offended that she had not trusted him, but he came to realize the mistake he made keeping financial information from her. She had a right to discuss all financial planning with him. Besides, it was essential in preserving her feelings of love for him.

They both agreed that from that point on, all financial decisions would be made together, all investments would be made in both of their names, and they would deposit their paychecks into a *joint* checking account. When it came time to pay the bills and decide how much would go to savings, they would both come to an agreement before any checks were written.

Their cooperation in financial matters encouraged a cooperative spirit in other areas of their marriage as well. As time went on, an increasing number of their habits and activities were changed to take each other's feelings into account. They no longer drifted apart, because they'd learned how to create compatibility.

They went on to have children, and as far as I know, conflicts in financial planning never again threatened their love for each other.

Married to a Spendthrift

For many of us, spending more money than we have seems to be instinctive. We usually know of at least one of our ancestors who was financially undisciplined. We probably inherited the trait from him!

Shirley had inherited the trait in its purest form. From early childhood she could not resist buying things she wanted. Her father had tried to help her control her spending, but she'd become so upset whenever she couldn't have something that he'd finally give in and hand her the money she needed.

While Joe dated her, he bought her things she wanted as gifts, because he enjoyed seeing her reaction: She seemed to live for her next gift from him. Shirley was an attractive woman, and Joe's generosity brought out the best in her and made her appear even more attractive to him. Within six months, they were head over heels in love with each other.

Since Joe was an executive in a growing company, he earned a good living. It never occurred to him that Shirley's buying habits could cost him more than he earned.

In the first few years of their marriage, he justified many of her purchases as necessary for their new home. But soon she wasn't satisfied with her initial purchases and had to buy replacement items. The closets in their home became so filled with her clothes that she gave away many items to make room for a new wardrobe.

Joe became alarmed. "Shirley, I think it's time we discuss something. You're spending more than we can afford."

She became genuinely concerned. "Oh, Joe, are you having financial problems?"

"*We* are having financial problems! My income is better than ever, but you're spending more than I earn," he complained. "We'll have to start a budget so we can keep our expenses under control."

"That's okay with me," she responded cheerfully. "Just give me an allowance each month, and I'll stick to it!"

Joe worked out a budget for Shirley, but in the first month she *didn't* stick to it. When Joe tried to talk to her about it, she shrugged it off as a bad month and promised to do better the next month. But the next month was no better.

Now Joe became upset. "Shirley, are you trying to ruin me? You're spending money I don't have."

Shirley's voice remained calm. "Take it easy, Joe. You must be upset about something that happened at work. I think you're overreacting."

He couldn't hold his anger in any longer. "Overreacting? My problem is that I haven't reacted soon enough. I've got to put an end to this immediately. I'm taking your name off our checking account and canceling all our credit cards. I'm sorry, but it's the only way I can get your irresponsible spending under control!"

Shirley was visibly hurt by Joe's words. She felt he had no right to treat her like a child. So his anger had the predictable effect—she ignored his demands. The next time she saw something she wanted to buy, she simply withdrew money from their savings account. Within six months, all their savings were gone.

By the time Joe and Shirley came to my office, Joe was threatening divorce. "How can she say she loves me—and rob me blind? I just can't go on like this."

"I admit I have a problem controlling my spending, but I love Joe and I think he still loves me. He knew I liked to shop before we were married. I'm no different now from how I was then," she said in her defense.

Shirley's excuse that she had a "problem controlling her spending" was nothing more than admitting her selfishness. She knew Joe would be furious when he discovered their savings gone but she cared more about buying that next item than protecting Joe's feelings.

It's important to realize that Shirley really loved Joe. She simply neglected to protect his feelings, and in the process Joe lost much of his love for Shirley.

Through counseling, I was able to convince Joe that Shirley was not doing all of this out of revenge for some unknown childhood experience. She had developed a very thoughtless habit. But that knowledge didn't restore any love units. Shirley had to overcome the habit if the marriage was to be saved.

Joe was on the right track when he tried to negotiate a solution, but when his initial effort failed to change Shirley's habit, he should have continued negotiation, perhaps with the help of a marriage counselor. His problem was that she would agree to anything he wanted, but not with enthusiasm. In other words, her Taker was never in on the deal. So when the time came to follow through on the agreement, her Taker would talk her out of it. But now that they both understood that their negotiation had to result in an enthusiastic agreement, they were on a track that would eventually lead to a solution.

Was Shirley's shopping an annoying habit, or was it an independent behavior? Sometimes a behavior, particularly an addictive behavior, like shopping, can be a little of both. But I approached Shirley's Love Buster as an annoying habit and used a procedure similar to the one I described in chapter 7 that deals with all annoying habits. She had already enthusiastically agreed to change her spending habits. Now she had to learn how to do it.

The issue was not shopping per se, but rather the amount of money she spent. So Shirley agreed to shop differently, at garage sales and discount stores, instead of the high-priced stores that emptied their bank account. At first, her every move had to be accounted for, and she did have a few slips along the way. By the time her habits had changed, she shopped as much as ever but didn't spend nearly as much money. The money she spent was well within the budget that had been set aside for shopping, and that change in her behavior stopped the leak in Joe's Love Bank.

What If You're Both Spendthrifts?

Financial problems trigger many divorces because of the way people treat each other when financial disaster looms before them.

Mel and Cindy were a happy-go-lucky couple who never missed an opportunity for a good time. Mel had a decent job but didn't earn nearly enough to support their standard of living. Cindy worked when she felt like it, which wasn't very often. Most of the time, they got along very well, but whenever they had a conflict over money, sparks would fly.

Mel had a terrible problem with his self-esteem, and once in a while Cindy would remind him that Nate, a former boyfriend, earned more money than he did. To prove to Cindy that she had made the right choice, Mel let her buy whatever she wanted—whether or not they could afford it. From time to time, he explained to Cindy how seriously indebted they were, but it would invariably start a fight, during which she blamed him for failing to earn more.

A point was finally reached where Mel could no longer pay the bills and, without telling Cindy, tried desperately to consolidate them one more time. He believed right up to the end that someone would lend him the necessary money. But one day the sheriff came to his home to serve his wife with a foreclosure notice.

Cindy had a few friends over the morning the sheriff arrived. She was embarrassed beyond words. When Mel came home that evening, he received the tongue-lashing of the century. Within a week, she had kicked him out of the house.

"When you have all this straightened out, you can return home. But until then I don't even want to look at you. You disgust me!"

"Listen to me for just one minute," Mel pleaded. "If it weren't for your reckless spending, we wouldn't be in this mess. I've done the best I can to keep us from bankruptcy, and you just keep spending money as if it's water."

"What about your motorcycle and your hunting and fishing equipment? You spend a lot more than I do!" she fired back. "The reason we are losing our house is that you can't control your spending. Get yourself in gear or say good-bye."

Mel came to my office to see if I could help him save his marriage. I arranged for an appointment with Cindy and discovered to my surprise that she was terrified at the prospect of trying to support herself. She was willing to take Mel back only because he was able to earn something, and something was better than nothing. Not a great motive to save a marriage, but I'll usually take anything at first!

Neither of them were taking responsibility for their financial woes, yet they were both to blame. In a way, they had conspired with each other to create the appearance of wealth. They both wanted more than they could afford, but they just weren't willing to accept the inevitable consequences.

Many of these situations end in divorce because both husband and wife become vicious in an effort to shift blame to the other. They punish each other so effectively that before long one or both of their Love Bank accounts become overdrawn, and the marriage comes to an end.

Whenever Mel tried to discuss finances with Cindy, she would throw in his face the last toy he bought for himself, and then they'd have a fight. Love units evaporated quickly whenever that happened, so they didn't discuss money very often. Because they couldn't control their anger, a thoughtful resolution never got off the ground.

So the first step toward reconciliation was learning to control their angry and defensive reactions. I helped them learn not to blame each other but rather assume their share of the responsibility for their problems. Once anger and defensiveness were gone, they could discuss problems intelligently and with consideration for each other's feelings.

Then they had to see their spending habits as a form of independent behavior, where they bought what they wanted for themselves without any consideration for each other. They had to learn to apply the Policy of Joint Agreement to every dime they spent. And they had to do it with a budget in mind.

Mel and Cindy did lose their house and had to file for bankruptcy. But because they both learned to avoid disrespectful judgments and angry outbursts, their marriage survived the ordeal. In a way, the bankruptcy gave their marriage a new start it couldn't have had without a clean financial slate.

With this new start, Mel learned to be radically honest with Cindy, partly because he understood how important it was to her. But it was much easier for him to be honest, because she stopped throwing a fit in response to disappointing information. They learned to share financial information with each other and to make decisions using the Policy of Joint Agreement. Before long they were in a rented home they could afford, and their standard of living kept pace with their income.

I'm almost certain Mel and Cindy will have financial problems again in the future. Almost all married couples do. But when these problems develop, they won't use the destructive methods of the past that withdrew love units. Instead, they'll use thoughtful solutions that help build romantic love.

Deciding between Two Worthy Causes

Both husband and wife often have legitimate positions in a disagreement, but they may be poles apart. Helping them decide on a common-ground compromise sometimes takes the wisdom of Solomon.

The issue that divided Kevin and Marcia was how to budget their income. Kevin had a good job, but he was always afraid he'd be laid off and the family would have nothing to fall back on, so he insisted on saving part of each paycheck. Marcia was more confident of Kevin's job security and felt that helping their children pay for college was more important than saving money. Setting aside part of each paycheck for unforeseen emergencies was a good idea. But helping their children through college was also a good idea. Which idea was better?

Kevin and Marcia came to my office in the hope that I would decide the issue for them. The solution to their problem, of course, was not mine. They had to decide for themselves.

To begin, I explained that whatever they decided had to take each other's feelings into account. They must both be enthusiastic about their final decision. I had each explain to the other why his or her position was important. Kevin told Marcia about his fear of losing his job and having difficulty finding another. Having savings that would carry them for a year would make him feel much more secure, since he felt he could be reemployed within that time. She felt the savings would be a waste, since he was already investing in a retirement plan, and the main purpose of a padded savings account would simply be to provide him with an added sense of comfort.

Then Marcia expressed her concern that without financial help their children might miss the opportunity to complete a college education. She considered it the obligation of parents to see their children through college. Since Kevin had never attended college, he wasn't sold on college as a necessary step toward adulthood.

I reminded them that they needed to resolve the conflict with a decision that would take both positions into account. The outcome could not bother either of them. One solution that would pass that test was to neither save their money nor help their children. (Remember, you have to *do* something thoughtless to be engaged in a Love Buster. Doing *nothing* may also be annoying but, technically, failure to act doesn't count.) They both objected to that solution and immediately set out to come to a compromise.

"How would you feel if . . . ?" took the place of "Stop being so stubborn!" Marcia suggested that she work more and that her salary go to their children's education. When she asked how Kevin felt about that idea, he pointed out that it would take her away from him and that if they gave the kids money for college, he wanted it to come from both of them.

Kevin suggested that he wouldn't object to cosigning student loans. If they had the money later on, they would pay off the loans for their children. When she was asked how she felt about that idea, Marcia explained that she didn't want her children to face life with debts, even if there was the possibility that they would be paid later.

Through their discussion of possibilities, they learned not to challenge each other's feelings. Even when they seemed unbelievable or unreasonable, their feelings were accepted as final. For both of them, this created a much greater willingness to cooperate. They became more and more creative in the discussion and finally arrived at a solution they both liked.

When their negotiations ended, they both agreed that the most important outcome of the discussion was the love they felt for each other. In fact it got to a point where both had reversed their original positions: He was willing to sacrifice his savings for the children's education, and she was willing to use the money for his savings. It was their Givers at work—encouraging them to sacrifice so that the other spouse could be happy. But I don't like the Giver's solution any more than the Taker's solution because in either case, someone gets hurt. I wanted them to negotiate until they both reached an enthusiastic agreement—one that would make them both happy.

Their ultimate compromise was a combination of taking some money from savings (but not enough to make Kevin uncomfortable), and cosigning a student loan that Marcia did not feel would be burdensome for their children. The compromise did not sacrifice love units, and that was the most important outcome.

Don't Let Financial Planning Destroy Your Love for Each Other

In each case I introduced to you, financial planning came between a husband and wife. What should have been to their mutual advantage ended up to their mutual disadvantage because the way they went about it caused Love Bank withdrawals.

When financial planning considers the feeling of both spouses, it's a wiser plan that also builds the feeling of love.

When budgets are created to benefit one spouse at the expense of the other, or when one spouse spends money without considering the interests of the other, love units are lost. It's that simple. But when financial planning considers the feelings of both spouses, it's a wiser plan that also builds the feeling of love.

In *His Needs, Her Needs,* the companion to this book, I explain in chapter 9 how to make realistic budgets and how to stick to them. If you need help with a budget, I encourage you to read that chapter.

Consider This...

1. How are selfish demands, disrespectful judgments, and angry outbursts used to force financial decisions? What are some common excuses spouses use to justify their selfish demands, disrespectful judgments, and angry outbursts when making decisions about money? Have you used any of these forms of abuse to try to force your spouse to agree with your financial decisions? What is the likely outcome when a spouse is expected to adjust to a financial decision that has not been enthusiastically accepted?

2. When is a financial decision independent behavior? How is that different from trying to obtain agreement through demands, disrespect, or anger? Do either of you feel you have the right to make decisions about your finances independently of the other's interests and feelings? Are you willing to give up that right for the sake of your love for each other?

3. Do you and your spouse have a conflict over financial planning? Is your situation at all similar to any of the examples I used? Describe your conflict as clearly as possible, with respect for each other's interests and opinions. Then, use the Policy of Joint Agreement and the Four Guidelines to Successful Negotiation (described in chapter 9) to try to resolve these conflicts by creating a budget that you both accept enthusiastically and are both willing to follow.

4. Explain why some would choose money over love as a higher priority in marriage. Is it done intentionally after love is already lost? Do your actions make money seem like a higher priority to you when in fact it is not? Why should commitment to your finances be of lesser importance than your commitment to please each other?

chapter twelve

RESOLVING
C O N F L I C T S
O V E R   C H I L D R E N

It's been known for some time now that children are hard on marriages. Research on the subject has consistently shown that the divorce rate increases with the number of children born to a couple. The more children you have, the more likely it is you'll be divorced.

We also know that the divorce rate in blended families is astronomically high. A family is *blended* when a husband and/or wife have children from previous marriages. I read a recent report that claimed only about 20 percent of these marriages survive. The report viewed blending families as the single most important cause for divorce.

Why is it that the divorce rate increases with the number of children, and that blending families is so devastating to marriages? One answer to that question is that the care of children often takes the place of spouses' care for each other. With more children to raise, there is less time and energy to meet the most important emotional needs in marriage. And when those needs go unmet, spouses lose their love for each other. Parents can be so committed to the care of their children that they forget about the care of each other.

The way to overcome this first reason for the adverse effect of children on marriage is to set aside time in the week to give each other undivided attention—without the kids present! It's during that time that you'll meet some of the most important emotional needs in marriage, the need for affection, conversation, recreational companionship, and sexual fulfillment. Don't neglect this time together, because what your children need most from you is parents who love each other.

At the end of this book, I have included two "bonus" chapters, "Building Romantic Love with Care," and "Building Romantic Love with Time." If care for your children is preventing you from meeting each other's important emotional needs, be sure to read those two chapters.

There is also a second reason the addition of children adds stress to marriages: In most marriages, conflicts over children are extremely difficult to resolve. And the way most spouses go about trying to resolve those conflicts destroys their love for each other. So in this chapter I will show you how to resolve conflicts over children in a way that will sustain your love for each other, regardless of how many children you have. And if

> **What your children need most from you is parents who love each other.**

you're in a blended family, I'll show you how to beat the odds, how to make your marriage the exception by making decisions about your children that meet with your mutual enthusiastic agreement.

The single biggest mistake made in child rearing is that parents make unilateral decisions regarding their children. Decisions about discipline, for example, are often made independently, without a joint agreement. One spouse takes it upon him or herself to discipline the children in a way that is offensive to the other spouse. When they don't agree regarding discipline, one becomes the disciplinarian and the other becomes the protector of the children. When that happens, the spouse doing the protecting often feels the pain of the discipline more acutely than the children do. And the one doing the disciplining feels totally unsupported.

It's a Love Buster to discipline your children when your spouse is not in agreement with you. You're sure to withdraw love units whenever that happens. And it's likely that if your spouse does not support your discipline, your children will not learn much from it.

Love units can also be withdrawn when favors are given to a child without enthusiastic agreement. When one spouse gives something to a child that's not approved by the other spouse, the disapproving spouse can sometimes look like the evil parent who doesn't care enough about his children to give them what they really want. Unilateral giving of favors by a parent can sometimes cause as much resentment as unilateral discipline.

In blended families, these mistakes usually have a greater effect on Love Bank balances than they do in nuclear families (where children are offspring of both parents), because spouses have a natural instinct to protect their own. And when any bias is detected, a very strong negative reaction results.

So if you want plenty of children without it interfering with your love for each other, or if you're part of a blended family and you don't want to end up the way most blended families do, you simply must make all of your decisions regarding your children with mutual and enthusiastic agreement. All disciplinary action should be made bilaterally, where both you and your spouse agree to the disciplinary action before it's implemented. And whenever you want to reward your children, it should also be done bilaterally. You and your spouse should reward and punish them together, as a couple. Then both of you become heroes—neither one of you become the evil parent.

> **You must make all of your decisions regarding your children with mutual and enthusiastic agreement.**

This approach to parenting will make both of you much better parents. The perspectives that each of you brings to child rearing are both valuable. If you come to an agreement about the way you raise your children, your children will benefit through your joint wisdom. On the other hand, if one of you makes a unilateral decision, your child will be frustrated and confused. When one spouse disciplines a child without the other spouse's support, the child rarely learns a lesson from the experience. Instead the child feels that one parent seems to love him more than the other.

And even when a child is rewarded by only one spouse, he or she receives a mixed message. What he did was valuable from one parent's perspective, but not valuable from the other parent's perspective. Was it or wasn't it valuable? The child doesn't know for sure. But if you come to your children with a united front, with consistency and with agreement, you deliver to your children a powerful message, lessons that are sure to impress them.

Your Daughter's a Thief and a Liar!

Greg was a single parent of two teenagers, Allan (age 13) and Vivian (age 15). The three of them had a comfortable lifestyle, and Greg tended to spoil his children. Since the death of his wife eight years earlier, he had dated only two women, Bobbi and Janet. He liked them both very much, but Janet enjoyed being with his children, and Bobbi didn't. That single factor caused him to break up with Bobbi and eventually marry Janet.

As soon as they were married, however, conflict developed between Janet and Vivian. Once Janet had moved into their home, Vivian started "borrowing" her clothes without asking. Janet didn't say anything at first, but after her favorite sweater disappeared, she'd had it!

"Vi, have you seen my pink sweater?" she asked.

Vivian didn't miss a beat. "Nope."

"Are you sure?" Janet pressed. "You may have taken it to school and left it there."

"I've never taken any of your sweaters to school! Why would you think I took it?"

"Well, you've taken some of my other clothes, and I thought maybe you'd taken the sweater, too."

"I can't believe this! Look, I haven't taken your sweater. *Okay?*"

There was no way to prove Vivian had worn the sweater, but Janet knew her clothes hadn't sprouted legs. When Greg came home that night, she explained her problem to him. Greg asked Vivian about the sweater. She denied ever wearing it and became angry that they were ganging up on her over something she had nothing to do with.

After that incident, more of Janet's clothes disappeared. One day while Vivian was in school, Janet searched Vivian's room and found almost all her missing clothes. When Greg came home, she told him what she'd found. He confronted Vivian with the evidence. His daughter burst into tears and denied having had any of those clothes in her room. It was her word against Janet's, and she accused Janet of putting them there just to get her into trouble. In an effort to calm everyone down, Greg said they'd discuss the matter some other time.

Janet was furious.

Vivian put a lock on her door.

As the months passed, the relationship between Janet and Vivian worsened. When her father was gone, Vivian made rude remarks to Janet and openly challenged her right to live there. Greg tried to stay out of the growing conflict. But one day Janet could take no more.

"Greg, it's either me or Vivian. The two of us can't live in this house together."

Greg was stunned. "What do you want me to do? I can't kick out my own daughter. Besides, she'll only be with us for another three or four years. Can't you hold out that much longer?"

"Yes, Greg, I could. But I won't. It's perfectly clear to me that she comes first in this house—and I'm not living in a home run by a spoiled brat!"

Greg lost control with that remark. "I think we have *two* spoiled brats living in this house. But Vivian's only fifteen! What's your excuse?"

Janet moved out.

In my office, Greg and Janet reviewed their disastrous first year of marriage. Each of them thought it had been a mistake to get married.

But I reminded them that prior to marriage, they were highly compatible and loved each other as much as they had loved anyone. Their loss of love was a direct result of the way they had handled Vivian. She had come between them. They needed to discover a way to complete the job of raising her without further destroying their love for each other.

Greg laid his cards on the table. He told Janet he had never punished Vivian for anything. When he knew she had taken Janet's clothes, he didn't know how to respond. So he tried to avoid the issue. He recognized now how much Janet needed him to help her resolve the problem, and he apologized for his failure.

I encouraged Greg and Janet to decide how they would handle the situation when Vivian verbally abused Janet or took her clothes. Simply telling Vivian to stop wouldn't work.

Throughout their discussions, they made no demands on each other and agreed they would not settle on a plan that was unacceptable to either of them. The discussion itself was hard on Janet because Greg kept coming up with ideas that favored Vivian. She was hurt by each suggestion. But I explained to her that Greg did not intend to hurt her and that the negotiation itself was an opportunity to help him understand her reactions to these alternatives.

I suggested that Janet remain separated from Greg until the solution regarding Vivian's behavior was decided and then implemented. For several weeks, they worked out this problem together and eventually agreed on a strategy to overcome it.

Janet admitted that the loss of her sweater was not as painful as the feeling of being abandoned by Greg. He admitted he was in the habit of defending his daughter unconditionally, and it was clearly at Janet's expense. He agreed to consider Janet's feelings first in family decisions, the same way he'd treated his first wife.

This was a significant turning point in their crisis. When Greg agreed that protecting Janet's feelings would be his highest priority, the crisis was essentially ended. That was all Janet wanted from him. She knew teenage girls can be hard to handle, but she wanted reassurance that she would come first in his life.

With Janet gone for several weeks, Vivian started feeling guilty about the whole thing. On her own initiative, she invited Janet back to the home but never did admit stealing the sweater. While she didn't take any more clothes from Janet, she was still rude and insulting once in a while.

The next time she offended Janet—and it was within a week of her homecoming—Greg and Janet discussed the problem with

Vivian as if it affected them both. He explained to her that whenever she hurt Janet's feelings, she was hurting him too. She had to learn that her dad was now a part of Janet; if she loved him, she needed to care for his new wife.

Each time she offended Janet, Vivian could expect to engage in a discussion with Janet and her dad. And she could expect him to believe Janet's version of the incident. Within a year, her rude remarks had all but disappeared.

By teaching his children to be considerate of Janet's feelings, Greg implemented a good childrearing objective that helped both children learn to become less self-centered. But something else was far more important: Greg and Janet learned that once they were married, not even his children should come between them.

This example shows how Love Busters can interfere with the solution of a marital problem. Selfish demands, disrespectful judgments, angry outbursts, annoying habits, and independent behavior all made it impossible for Greg and Janet to achieve a wise solution.

Some of the most frustrating and difficult marital problems are found in blended families, where at least one spouse brings children from another marriage into the new marriage. The rate of divorce in these families is extraordinarily high because couples in blended families are less likely to apply the Policy of Joint Agreement. But when they are forced to be thoughtful by following the Policy of Joint Agreement, reasonable solutions begin to emerge, and the risk of divorce is greatly reduced.

From Perfect Lover to Perfect Mother

Wayne had dated many women and was even engaged once, but no one seemed to meet his high standards well enough to make him want to tie the knot—that is, until he met Kris. She was everything he'd always hoped for, and she loved him too. She was absolutely perfect as far as he was concerned.

Those who knew Kris well were not surprised by the good job she did as Wayne's new wife. She had a history of doing things well. Ever since early childhood, she was able to focus her attention on personal objectives and achieve them with excellence, one by one. When she fell in love with Wayne, she wanted nothing more than to be everything he needed in a wife, and she was able to achieve it.

Kris became the perfect lover, meeting all Wayne's known emotional needs and some he never knew he had. She was his lover, friend, recreational companion, greatest admirer, and kept herself extraordinarily attractive.

When Rachel, their first child, was born, Kris's focus of attention changed. Now she had a new personal objective: to be the perfect *mother*. At first, Wayne was delighted with the care and attention she gave their daughter. After all, he wanted the very best for Rachel and knew that Kris could provide it.

But after a while it became apparent that Rachel's gain was his loss. Kris couldn't leave Rachel for a moment, and when they were together as a family, Rachel had her mom's undivided attention. Wayne knew that he had to find time alone with Kris.

Walking in the front door one evening, he said, "Hey, hon, let's go to the hockey game tomorrow night. A guy at work has tickets he'll give me."

"No, thanks, not this time," she said pleasantly. "But you go ahead, if you'd like, dear."

"What's gotten into you?" he teased. "You used to *love* hockey!"

Kris was not smiling. "We can't go out and have fun and forget about Rachel. She needs as much attention as we can give her. What we do for her now will affect the rest of her life."

"Now wait a minute! I'm talking about one evening out. Surely her whole life won't be ruined if she spends an evening with your parents."

"I *said* I won't go. That's it!" Kris turned and walked out of the room.

Wayne wondered what had happened to his perfect lover. She apparently left one day, and her twin sister, the perfect mother, showed up in her place. He did go to the hockey game with a friend at the office. It started a pattern in which he worked late or went out with friends most evenings.

Even though their marriage had started to show signs of decay, Kris wanted more children. Over the next seven years, they had three more, and she dedicated herself to their care. They loved her dearly because she not only took responsibility for their training but was cheerful and fun-loving in the way she went about it.

She wished Wayne would take a more active role in raising their children, but when she tried to discuss it with him, he explained that with four children he had to keep his nose to the grindstone to keep up with the bills.

In my last example, Greg had let his daughter from another marriage come between him and Janet. But even when the children are your own, they can easily come between you and your spouse. Kris's effort to give their children the best opportunities in life came at Wayne's expense.

People usually enter marriage with the best intentions to be loving and caring partners in life. But when children arrive, a new ideal—to be loving and caring parents—sometimes conflicts with the ideal of partnership. When that happens, the Policy of Joint Agreement becomes particularly important to follow.

Wayne showed up in my office one day to try to gain perspective on his life. He was falling in love with a woman at work but didn't want to start an affair. Marrying Kris, he thought, had been the biggest mistake of his life. He couldn't go on living this way but didn't know how to change things without filing for divorce.

"All she really wanted was children. I don't think she ever really did want a husband," he told me. "I'm not even sure she loved me. How could I have been so stupid?"

I tried to assure him that Kris had loved him and probably still did. She had simply made a choice between two ideals—being a good lover and being a good mother—and chose one at the expense of the other. She had not grasped the consequences of her shift in emphasis. At the end of our conversation, he was willing to let me speak with her about their marriage.

Kris was upset about the marriage, too. She felt Wayne had abandoned her as soon as their children arrived. When he left her alone so much of the time, it encouraged her to focus on the children even more.

I explained to her that it was in the children's best interest for their parents to be in love. To achieve that objective, their schedules had to take each other's needs and feelings into account. Her schedule took the children's feelings into account, but not Wayne's. His schedule didn't take her feelings into account, either.

I recommended a plan designed to flush out all the cobwebs: a vacation for just the two of them.

It worked like a miracle. During their vacation together the old Kris returned. Wayne couldn't believe it. He became the center of her attention again, and it brought the best out in him.

When they returned home, I saw them immediately. Habits are often conditioned by environment, and I knew Kris was likely to revert to old habits on her arrival home. Sure enough, as soon as she got home with the children, her twin sister, the perfect mother, arrived!

But they were prepared. They had already agreed on a schedule that would allow them to be together without the children fifteen hours each week. As part of the overall agreement, Wayne scheduled an additional fifteen hours to be with Kris and the children.

At first Wayne didn't think he could find thirty hours to spend alone with Kris and their children. As they discussed his schedule together, he realized that he engaged in numerous activities and interests that did not have Kris's enthusiastic support. Since they'd agreed to apply the Policy of Joint Agreement to all their behavior, he abandoned these activities in favor of those he could share with Kris, and in the end everything fell into place.

They'd made the mistake of failing to take each other's feelings into account. Unilaterally, they created independent behaviors that bothered each other terribly. But they couldn't seem to escape from them because these activities were based on important ideals. Their story illustrates well how ideals can help create Love Busters and how the Policy of Joint Agreement can protect you from them.

If you know that your spouse is uncomfortable with something you're doing, you should be on notice that a change of behavior is due, regardless of how right that behavior might seem to you. The Policy of Joint Agreement will help you identify a change that takes your ideals and your spouse's ideals into account. And it will also protect your love for each other.

Three in Bed Is One Too Many

Andre and Patti had a great marriage, and when the kids came along it was still great. But they had one fly in the ointment: Susan, their three-year-old, insisted on sleeping with them at night. At first Andre thought it was cute. But after a while, when Susan became a nightly resident in their bed, he didn't think it was so cute anymore.

"Patti, we've got to do something about Susan sleeping with us," Andre suggested one morning over coffee. "Don't you think we need more privacy?"

"Oh, she'll outgrow it. It's just a phase she's going through," Patti responded.

"Well, it's starting to bother me, and it sure has affected our love life!"

Patti shook her head. "If we tell her she can't sleep with us, she may think we don't love her. We can't do that. Just be patient."

Every once in a while, Andre would raise the issue with Patti. Her response was always the same: She felt it was wrong to create anxiety in Susan by forcing her to sleep in her own room. Besides, whenever they encouraged her to try it, Susan threw a fit.

The problem didn't improve for a solid year, and Andre became increasingly upset. Before he asked Patti to help him solve the problem, she hadn't lost too many love units in his Love Bank. But after she told him to just put up with it, he started to blame her for the problem—and love units were withdrawn at a rapid rate.

It never occurred to either of them that Andre's love would be affected by the situation. He only knew his interest in Patti had taken a nosedive. When they came to see me for counseling, he blamed his loss of passion for Patti on his work, his personality flaws, and possible unconscious negative attitudes toward women. Patti couldn't imagine what his problem was, since she still loved him very much.

An analysis of their marriage identified Susan as the unwitting culprit. In most cases I encourage a husband and wife to come to a joint agreement without my interference. But in this case, Patti wanted my professional opinion regarding Susan's emotional welfare. I suggested that Susan be taught to sleep in her own bed, not only for the sake of the marriage but also because it was healthier for Susan. I suggested that if this habit continued, Susan might grow up emotionally handicapped by an unhealthy dependence.

An even more important consideration was that Patti had given the feelings of her daughter a higher priority than the feelings of her husband. Letting her daughter sleep with them annoyed Andre, yet Patti did nothing to protect him from that annoyance.

The plan for getting Susan back into her own bed using rewards worked. And Andre's love for Patti was eventually restored. To me, that outcome was a foregone conclusion. As soon as they removed the burr in the saddle, all the great things they'd learned to do for each other prior to Susan's intrusion would take over, and romantic love would be restored.

When Discipline Becomes a Love Buster

Alex had a short fuse. His friends and family all knew it. But when he fell in love with Christine, he cared so much for her that he managed to keep his temper under control whenever he was with her. Christine became his bride because of his victory over this ugly Love Buster.

Their marriage went well because he kept his vow never to subject her to his angry outbursts. He never punished her either verbally or physically.

However, he had been brought up in a tradition where heavy-handed discipline was considered the father's duty. As a child, his father had beaten him on many occasions—if he disobeyed, he could expect disastrous consequences. And Alex had learned firsthand all about those disastrous consequences.

When Alex and Christine had their first child, Alex expected the same unwavering obedience that his parents had expected of him. Whenever little David misbehaved, Alex disciplined him the way *he* had been disciplined as a child.

The first time this happened, Christine became very upset and begged Alex to stop. When his violent methods continued, she went to her pastor for help. He recommended that she leave the discipline up to her husband and gave her examples of children who grew up to be criminals because women raised them without a father's punishment.

But the pastor's advice made matters much worse. Alex had actually been holding back his temper somewhat because he realized how it affected Christine. But now that he had his pastor's permission to do whatever he felt was right regarding discipline, he released all his pent-up fury on young David. Whenever he felt irritated about something, he punished his son even more severely than before, and it seemed David would grow up in considerable fear of his dad.

All the while, Alex was careful never to treat Christine abusively. In fact he went out of his way to be sure she understood that his punishment of David was a father's responsibility, something that their pastor had encouraged him to do.

But still she suffered every time he punished the child, crying as if he were punishing her. Even though Alex had shown her exceptional care in other ways, this punishment caused a huge withdrawal from her Love Bank.

What should Alex do? How would you try to solve this problem?

The answer should be obvious to you by now. If Alex and Christine were to agree to the Policy of Joint Agreement, he would never beat David again. Every act of discipline would have to be with Christine's enthusiastic agreement, and Alex would have to radically change his approach to discipline in order to obtain that agreement.

In my experience counseling families, I have found that every couple's **joint** methods of discipline are superior to their **independent** methods. In other words, couples are wiser in the way they train their children when they agree on a training method. By discussing options and agreeing on a particular approach, they eliminate many of the foolish and impulsive acts of discipline that either one of them might try individually. Furthermore, children take parents more seriously when they both agree on an approach.

Christine wanted Alex to focus more attention on David's good behavior than on his bad behavior. She wanted him to reward his son far more often than he was punished. And she wanted the punishment to be nonviolent—taking away privileges rather than physical beatings or verbal assaults.

Deep down Alex knew she was right. He knew how resentful he was about the way he was treated as a child, yet he had always assumed that it was somehow a father's responsibility to physically punish his children. But when he came to realize how much he had been hurting Christine whenever he punished David, he enthusiastically agreed to her plan. And the more he thought about it, the more he knew that it was the way he should have been raised.

Only when spouses make each other's feeling their highest priority can children be successfully integrated into a family.

It took some effort on his part to break his abusive habits, but in the end he broke the chain of violence that had been following his family for generations. Under the Policy of Joint Agreement, not only was David spared a traumatic childhood that Alex had suffered, but Christine's love for him was restored.

Don't Let Your Children Destroy Your Love for Each Other

Joint decisions of child rearing are wise and effective. Children clearly gain when both parents can agree on how they're to be raised. This eliminates confusion from mixed messages and stupid, emotional, and impulsive decisions made by one spouse in the heat of anger. If one spouse makes child-rearing decisions independently, without enthusiastic joint agreement, they are almost certain to fail.

But even more important, independent child-rearing decisions are Love Busters. Each time you reward or punish your children without your spouse's enthusiastic agreement, you lose some of your spouse's love for you.

Children can come between a husband and wife, destroying their love for each other. In most cases, it isn't the children's fault, but rather one or both parents, who assign a higher priority to the care of their children than they do to the care of each other. Only when spouses make each other's feelings their highest priority can children be successfully integrated into a family without the loss of love. For further information on this very important subject, I suggest that you read chapter 11 ("Family Commitment") in *His Needs, Her Needs*.

Consider This . . .

1. How are selfish demands, disrespectful judgments, and angry outbursts used to force child-rearing decisions? What are some common excuses spouses use to justify their selfish demands, disrespectful judgments, and angry outbursts when making decisions about children? Have you used any of these forms of abuse to try to force your spouse to agree with your child-rearing decisions? What is the likely outcome when a spouse is expected to adjust to a child-rearing decision that has not been enthusiastically accepted?

2. When is a child-rearing decision independent behavior? How is that different from trying to obtain agreement through demands, disrespect, or anger? Do either of you feel you have the right to make decisions about your children independently of the other's interests and feelings? Are you willing to give up that right for the sake of your love for each other?

3. Do you and your spouse have a conflict over child rearing? Is your situation at all similar to any of the examples I used? Describe your conflict as clearly as possible, with respect for each other's interests and opinions. Then use the Policy of Joint Agreement and the Four Guidelines to Successful Negotiation (described in chapter 9) to try to resolve these conflicts by creating an approach to child rearing that you both accept enthusiastically and are both willing to follow.

4. Explain why you would choose caring for your children over your love for each other as a higher priority in marriage. Is it done intentionally after love is already lost? Do your actions make children seem like a higher priority to you when in fact they are not? Why should commitment to your children be of lesser importance than your commitment to please each other?

chapter thirteen

RESOLVING
CONFLICTS
OVER SEX

About 5,000 years ago, as part of Sumerian culture, a man and woman who planned to marry would write on a clay tablet what they expected of each other during the marriage. If either person was unwilling to sign the list of expectations drawn up by the other, the marriage was off.

I wish that custom could be resurrected today. Today our marriage agreements say almost nothing about what a husband and wife are to expect of each other. And as a result, after marriage, disappointment is almost a certainty.

In an attempt to remedy this problem, I've created three promises for couples to make when they exchange rings. These promises embody what a husband and wife should expect of each other—very much like the marriage contracts that the ancient Sumerians created.

These promises embody what a husband and wife should expect of each other.

The first is the **promise of care: *I promise to meet your most important emotional needs.*** They would try to identify their own needs prior to marriage and then promise to meet each other's needs after they were married.

223

The second is the **promise of time:** *I promise to give you my undivided attention at least 15 hours each week.* They would understand that time should be set aside to meet each other's important emotional needs of affection, sexual fulfillment, conversation, and recreational companionship.

The third is the **promise of protection:** *I promise to avoid being the cause of your unhappiness.* They are to avoid all six of the Love Busters that I've been discussing in this book—selfish demands, disrespectful judgments, angry outbursts, dishonesty, annoying habits, and independent behavior. And by following the Policy of Joint Agreement, they are to avoid making decisions that would be good for one spouse and bad for the other.

By agreeing to these expectations up front, it would be much easier for a couple to get into the habits that would build a loving and fulfilling relationship with each other. They would deposit love units by meeting each other's most important emotional needs, and they would avoid their withdrawal by being considerate of each other's feelings.

I share this with you because as far as I'm concerned, failure to understand these three important promises ultimately creates the sexual problems found in most marriages.

Let's start with the promises of care and time: if your spouse has an important emotional need, sex for example, you're obligated to devote time to meeting it.

The Sumerian custom was to record an engaged couple's expectations in the form of a contract. Three thousand years later, certain marital expectations were recorded in the Bible. In 1 Corinthians 7:5, the apostle Paul writes, "Do not deprive each other except by mutual consent." He's writing about sex, and it's interesting how he puts it. He doesn't say you should have sex with mutual consent; he says you should only deprive each other of sex by mutual consent. In other words, he's arguing that if a spouse has a need for sex, the other spouse should meet it unless there's mutual consent not to meet it.

This basic principle is true not only for sex, but for all other important emotional needs as well—if your spouse has an important emotional need it's up to you to meet it. Unfortunately, in most marriages spouses don't understand how incredibly crucial it is to meet each other's important emotional needs. And as a result, these needs go unmet, causing a great deal of disappointment and frustration, to say nothing about the loss of romantic love.

> **Promise to avoid being the cause of your spouse's unhappiness.**

But even those who understand the importance of meeting emotional needs, especially the need for sexual fulfillment, often find themselves incapable of meeting that need because of a violation of the third promise, the promise of protection: to avoid being the cause of your spouse's unhappiness.

Violations of the promise of protection make fulfilling a sexual need difficult, if not impossible, for most people. If the Love Busters we discussed earlier—demands, disrespect, or anger—are ever used to force lovemaking, it makes the experience so unpleasant that sex is avoided rather than encouraged.

I know of many spouses who have **selfishly demanded** sex instead of thoughtfully requesting it. They give their spouse no choice about whether or not to make love or in what way they should do it. Instead of applying the Policy of Joint Agreement to their lovemaking, where they would both enjoy the experience simultaneously, they force their spouse into unpleasant or even painful sexual experiences to obtain sexual gratification. If a conscientious spouse tries to meet the need for sex under those conditions, a sexual aversion is likely to form, where no matter how committed they might be to fulfilling the other's sexual need, the aversion becomes so intense that they simply can't do it anymore.

Spouses are also known to use **disrespectful judgments** to get their sexual needs met. Instead of encouraging a reluctant spouse, they belittle, they criticize, and they make him or her feel totally inadequate. The outcome is less sex, or no sex at all!

And then there's the Love Buster, **angry outbursts,** that often ruins what could have been a fulfilling sexual relationship. When a spouse doesn't find the sexual fulfillment that he or she is looking for, instead of negotiating for improvement, he or she flies into a rage. I know of many spouses that have lost their tempers while in the act of lovemaking simply because they were disappointed with some aspect of it.

The Love Buster, **dishonesty**, should also be avoided. You and your spouse should honestly express your sexual desires and your sexual reactions to each other. But remember not to confuse honesty with demands, or disrespect, or anger. Honesty is simply reporting what you like and what you don't like about what the other person does sexually. You communicate to each other the conditions that help you desire a sexual relationship and then, while you're making love, the conditions that make the experience most enjoyable for you.

Honest communication about your reactions to each other is not criticism. It's simply the expression of positive and negative feelings. And from that honesty you can make adjustments to each other that will make your lovemaking great for both of you.

Finally, **independent sexual behavior** can make sexual adjustment in marriage seem almost impossible. By independent behavior, I mean ways of having your sexual needs met outside of your marital relationship. Masturbation, pornography, sex chat rooms on the Internet, and infidelity are all forms of sexual gratification that are usually very offensive in marriage—it's a major cause of Love Bank withdrawals. But if you do not have an exclusive sexual relationship with your spouse, where he or she is your only source of sexual gratification, you will do more than offend your spouse—you will also find that your own sexual experiences in marriage will tend to be very shallow and unfulfilling.

Ask yourself if Love Busters may be at the root of your problem.

When a couple has a conflict over sex, the underlying problem can sometimes be due to a failure to understand the importance of meeting that need. In other words, the promise to care has not been kept. But in most cases, the problem can be traced to one or more Love Busters. So before you tackle some of the conflicts you may have over sex, ask yourself if Love Busters may be at the root of your problem. If so, by overcoming those Love Busters, you will not only be able to resolve conflicts over sex, but you will be able to resolve most of your other conflicts as well.

All He Needed Was Practice

Kathleen was a very attractive woman. To be more precise, she was an absolute knockout!

Jeffrey was one of the only men Kathleen had dated who seemed more interested in conversation than sex. In fact they spent their first date discussing how to help the handicapped, one of her greatest concerns. Since they both majored in social work, they shared many of the same values. They would discuss the problems of society with each other for hours on end, and they expressed to each other their deep compassion for the under-privileged. Jeffrey also had a profound respect for women, which Kathleen appreciated.

Even though she had made love to some of her past boyfriends and usually enjoyed it, Kathleen had felt guilty and sometimes used. When she explained these feelings to Jeffrey, he suggested they wait until marriage to make love. At first, she thought his suggestion was too impractical—but it got her attention and impressed her! She interpreted his patience as respect for her and a willingness to place her feelings above his selfish desires. He earned hundreds of love units for that "selfless" attitude.

After graduating from college, they were married, and on their wedding night Kathleen looked forward to making love, having waited for two years. But Jeffrey was too tired! Kathleen was crushed and cried most of the night.

The next morning, however, they did make love for the first time. But Kathleen was visibly disappointed. Jeffrey ejaculated after less than a minute of intercourse.

Kathleen wanted to try again that afternoon, but again Jeffrey was too tired. And that evening he was still too tired. From the beginning to the end of their two-week honeymoon, they made love only five times, and each time it lasted only a few minutes. Kathleen must have tried to get him interested fifty times! It was a frustrating way to start her marriage, and she lost her temper. In fact she threatened to get an annulment if he couldn't get his act together.

But Jeffrey did everything else right. He was affectionate and considerate, made her the center of his life, and was a great conversationalist. She couldn't have asked for anything more—except sex!

"What's the matter with you?" she blurted out shortly after they arrived home.

"What do you mean?" he asked.

"Do you realize that when a woman is sexually rejected by her husband it makes her feel unattractive? Maybe I'm not your type!"

"Oh, no, Kathleen, you're the most beautiful woman I've ever seen."

With that he gave her a big hug and tried to make love to her. He made a real effort to improve his sexual responsiveness, but within three months he found he could no longer have an erection when they tried to have intercourse.

"What does this mean, Jeffrey? You really don't find me attractive, do you? All the time I thought you were treating me with respect, you were simply uninterested! Why did you marry me, if you didn't find me sexually attractive?"

"You are sexually attractive, believe me. I simply have a problem expressing it. I want to make love to you, but my body doesn't cooperate!"

"You're not telling me the truth," she pressed. "If I were attractive to you, your body would work just fine."

At our first interview I discovered that Jeffrey was more sexually frustrated than Kathleen. He needed a good sexual relationship more than she did, but the pressure she put on him to perform had made him afraid to have sex with her, and it had eroded her account in his Love Bank.

He sat bewildered, telling me how preposterous his situation was. She was, indeed, very attractive, and most men would consider her the sexual fantasy of all time. But here he was, unable to respond the way she wanted, and now he was finding himself unwilling to respond.

In almost all marriages one spouse is more ignorant of sex than the other. Usually it's the wife, but in Jeffrey and Kathleen's marriage, it was Jeffrey. He had postponed sex until marriage, a commendable goal. But that decision left him sexually inexperienced. Since his sexually experienced wife knew considerably more about it than he, he felt intimidated by her.

When they made love for the first time, all his worst fears were realized! He completely lost confidence in himself. After their first month of marriage, he had been raked over the coals so many times that he had started to develop a strong aversion to having sex with Kathleen. From there, it was a short trip to impotence.

Kathleen was deeply offended by Jeffrey's poor sexual performance because she thought he didn't find her attractive. She even wondered if he might have homosexual tendencies and had lied to her about his attraction to her. It made her feel very angry, and she felt a little better after she let him have it!

After my interview with Jeffrey, I was thoroughly convinced that he really did find Kathleen to be sexually attractive, and his problem was inexperience. I explained to Kathleen that no marital conflict is resolved through punishment or ridicule. Angry outbursts and disrespectful judgments don't bring solutions closer; they drive them away. So she made a commitment to provide him with the experience he needed to become a good lover—and that meant no more ridicule or anger. That crucial first step provided the opportunity for a solution to be implemented.

The assignment I gave them—a common approach to impotence—was for Jeffrey to take sexual initiative on a prearranged schedule. Whenever they made love, he was to explain to Kathleen what she did to make sex enjoyable for him, and what made it unpleasant. She made a few changes in her approach to lovemaking, but the most important change was to avoid disrespect and anger. That helped him achieve an erection whenever he wanted.

Then he learned how to hold an erection without ejaculating while having intercourse. We used a technique that is described in most self-help books that help men overcome premature ejaculation. It involves thrusting fast enough to keep his erection, but not so fast as to have an orgasm. Whenever he felt an orgasm coming on, he would stop his thrusting movement entirely. At first, Kathleen would lay motionless, so he could completely control all movement. During this phase of the training, she felt very little sexual pleasure, because her motion was crucial to her sexual responsiveness. But eventually, as he developed the ability to hold his erection longer and longer, with increasing stimulation, she was able to become an active participant.

When the wife has problems with sexual responsiveness, the solution is essentially the same with reversed roles: She learns how to become sexually aroused by taking initiative and training her husband to do what it takes to create her arousal. Then she learns how to come to a climax during intercourse by voluntarily tightening her vagina, and thrusting rapidly. Her husband follows her instructions, and he learns from her how to make love to her in a way that gives her the greatest sexual pleasure.

Kathleen had sexual techniques in mind that she had abandoned when they discussed the effects they had on Jeffrey. She also wanted him to engage in sexual marathons from time to time, and for Jeffrey these were worse than Chinese water torture. By the time they got it all sorted out, though, they not only made love several times each week, they also both found it very fulfilling.

If Kathleen had used her experience to help train Jeffrey to become a good lover and had never been disrespectful or angry toward him, he would have been a quick learner. He was eager to make love to her. But Love Busters almost prevented her from having great sex with her very best friend. It taught her an important lesson about marital conflicts in general, and from their rough start, they would apply that lesson to all the other conflicts they would have throughout life.

An individual's sex drive is usually related to the ease with which he or she engages in sex. The more one enjoys it, the greater the drive becomes.

Think about that the next time you make love to your spouse. If your spouse enjoys the experience, it will contribute to his or her willingness to make love the next time. But if you do something to make the sexual experience unpleasant, it will lower your partner's sexual interest.

Does Sin Make Sex Painful?

Nicole was born out of wedlock, and her mother never married. In fact her mother had sex only once in her lifetime—when

Nicole was conceived. That single sexual encounter had been extremely painful, and she felt certain it was God's punishment for her indiscretion.

She told her daughter that God often punishes women by making sex painful and that if she ever married she should expect pain while having intercourse.

Nicole married Doug, a quiet, hardworking farmer. They didn't make love prior to marriage, but on their honeymoon her first sexual experience was as painful as she had ever imagined. In fact, it brought her to tears. Doug didn't know what to make of it and figured that whatever it was, it would go away. He tried making love to her several times on their honeymoon, and each time she ended up crying.

Remembering her mother's prediction, Nicole simply expected to experience pain every time she made love. Over the next few weeks the pain not only remained intense, but the opening to the vagina eventually closed each time they attempted intercourse. It became impossible for Doug to penetrate. Nicole thought it was God's punishment for her mother's sin, carried over to her. Doug thought it was her way of keeping him from having sex with her.

A year later, they attempted intercourse again, but to no avail. It was just as painful as before. Shortly thereafter, Doug informed Nicole that he was considering a divorce. That brought them to me for counseling.

They were both incredibly naive about sex. Nicole had been warned by her mother that God punishes sexual impropriety, so she had never engaged in any sexual experimentation. Doug had learned to masturbate but had no other sexual experiences prior to marriage. He felt that reading books on sex was a form of perversion. Coming to a counselor was clearly an act of desperation for both of them.

I assured them that if they followed my instructions completely, their problems would be over within three months. It actually took less than six weeks.

Nicole had a condition called vaginismus, in which a muscle spasm closes the opening to the vagina. It's usually caused by tears in muscle tissue somewhere in the reproductive tract or a vaginal infection. It has nothing to do with sin.

231

I explained to her that her mother probably had the same condition when she made love her first and only time. Not knowing what to make of it, she passed it off as punishment.

I asked Nicole to see a gynecologist first to be certain she was free of infection and had a normal-sized vagina. Sometimes an abnormally small vagina can cause the same symptoms and can be corrected with surgery. The report came back showing that all was normal.

Then she and her husband completed a series of exercises designed to desensitize the vaginal opening so that the muscle spasm would be eliminated. The exercises were carried out daily (a very important part of the assignment), and within three weeks they were gingerly having intercourse. She was completely cured of vaginismus within six weeks and experienced a climax for the first time in her life.

This opened up a whole new world to Nicole, and she couldn't understand why Doug didn't want to make love at every opportunity—at least twice a day! Doug had to explain to her that he didn't enjoy making love twice a day, and she'd have to settle for three to four times a week. By their last appointment, they had made an outstanding sexual adjustment to each other.

This case is a good example of how failing to take feelings into account can cause physical problems as well as the loss of love units. When Doug tried to make love to Nicole, knowing she was experiencing pain, he made her physical problem worse. He tried to force his penis into her vagina, and then once inside he used quick strokes that were not only extremely painful but also strengthened the painful reflex.

The solution to the problem of vaginismus was a procedure that simply required a very slow and painless penetration of the vagina, enough stimulation to be felt but not enough to cause pain. Over time the speed of penetration was increased, but slowly enough to be painless. The reflex eventually disappears entirely when that method is used.

If Doug had simply insisted on painless penetration when he made love to Nicole using plenty of lubrication and going very slowly, he would have followed the correct procedure on his own. Thoughtfulness makes marital problems much easier to solve.

If you ever do something sexually that causes your spouse to experience physical or emotional pain, you may lose more than love units. You may contribute to physical and emotional problems that your spouse may find very difficult to overcome.

Solutions to sexual problems should follow the Policy of Joint Agreement. The procedure leading to a resolution of the problem should be mutually agreeable and enjoyable. When you're both happy making love, your sexual conflicts have been resolved.

Don't Wait until It's Almost Too Late

Throughout their long marriage, Grace and Ben had been known for the affection and consideration they showed each other. No one, including Grace, imagined the seriousness of their marital problem.

From their first anniversary on, Ben had expressed his deepest love for his beautiful and charming wife. But on their fiftieth wedding anniversary, an occasion for special appreciation for a long and happy marriage, he gave her a card that said, "Thanks for ruining my life!"

Grace thought she was having a nightmare. It was totally unexpected, and she cried for days. Ben felt ashamed and begged her forgiveness. But the cat was out of the bag.

When she finally gained enough composure to discuss the matter with him, Grace wanted him to explain himself. "Ben, I expect an answer. What did I do that ruined your life?"

"Please believe me," he pleaded. "I don't know what got into me. You haven't done anything. It's all my fault."

"What's all your fault?"

"Oh, it's nothing. Please forgive me for wrecking our anniversary." He insisted, "I'm just an old fool."

"What is this all about? I will not let you sleep until you tell me, so you may as well tell me now and get it over with."

"Okay," he agreed, "but remember, it's not your fault! I know you've never experienced a climax, and sometimes I feel I've missed out on something that's very important to me. That's all."

"Ben, I don't know how."

233

"Don't worry about it." He shrugged. "We're too old to do anything about it now anyway."

Throughout their marriage, Grace had not put much effort into sex. At first she didn't think it was all that important. But when it became apparent that Ben enjoyed it, she went through the motions just to make him happy. She always thought that someday she'd learn what it was all about.

It never occurred to her that *her* pleasure was an essential part of making love and that Ben couldn't be sexually fulfilled unless she experienced arousal and climax with him.

But she took a very important step that day. She decided to get help and made her first appointment with me that week.

I suggested she bring her husband with her next time and had them read the book *Woman's Orgasm: A Guide to Sexual Satisfaction* by Georgia Kline-Graber, R.N., and Benjamin Graber, M.D. (New York: Warner Books, 1975). The book not only showed her how to climax but also how to climax during intercourse, a difficult achievement for most women. They worked daily on the prescribed exercises and had never had so much fun with each other.

Grace learned how to climax and was happy that Ben had brought the problem to her attention. Her regret and his was that Ben had waited so long to tell her how much it bothered him. If he had told her early in their marriage, she would have done something about the problem. The solution would not only have helped Ben, it would have revealed to her how enjoyable sex can be.

The Love Buster that prevented their sexual fulfillment was dishonesty. Ben failed to communicate his frustration until it was almost too late. Although he used an angry outburst to communicate his problem, the revealed truth was more constructive than the anger was destructive. Grace recovered from the pain quickly because it was so out of character for Ben. In other words, his angry message was not a habit but rather a single act for which he later apologized.

When Grace discovered the problem, she eagerly set out to solve it. To a large extent, her love for Ben made it rather simple to learn to climax. She trusted him completely and felt safe and relaxed in his company. The quality of their relationship made the solution easy.

We're all wired right; it's just a matter of learning where the controls are. If you're a woman who isn't sure you've ever experienced a climax or if you climax very seldom, get a copy of the book I mentioned above (call 1-800-343-9204, the Little Brown order department, to order a copy) or some other book explaining how women can experience a climax. If you go through the recommended exercises and still can't quite get it, consider the help of an experienced sex therapist.

An effective sex therapist won't mind if your husband is part of each counseling session, and all exercises should be done in the privacy of your own home, either alone or with your husband. A therapist should never touch you or have you experience any form of sexual arousal in the office. Therapy for most sex-related marital problems is completed within three months and is sometimes covered by health insurance.

If you're at all uncomfortable with one therapist, go to another. Your gynecologist should be able to recommend several, and you may wish to consult with two or three before you settle on one.

Sex Should Always Be Shared

Whenever a client tells me her husband is impotent, I'm a little suspicious. While I've treated many men who were truly impotent, more often than not the problem turns out not to be impotence at all, but rather excessive masturbation.

I once counseled a man who brought himself to ten climaxes each day. By the time his wife wanted to make love, he was sexually exhausted! When he stopped masturbating, he had absolutely no problem at all making love to her.

But that wasn't Jerry's problem. He could do both. If Jane, his wife, ever wanted to make love, he was ready and able. He initiated lovemaking on a regular basis himself. But every once in a while she would discover evidence that he'd been masturbating. It offended her deeply—so much so that she made an appointment for marriage counseling.

When Jerry discussed the problem with me, he couldn't understand why she was upset. "Why should she care if I masturbate?

We make love whenever she wants, don't we? And I'm an excellent lover besides. What's her problem?"

Jane had explained to him that she wanted all of his sexual feelings to be shared with her. She felt that his masturbation was like a mistress, and she didn't want to share his sexual feelings with anyone else—even a fantasy.

I explained to Jerry that whenever he masturbated, he was doing something that he enjoyed but that Jane hated. Her alternative suggestion wasn't unreasonable either: She was willing to make love to him anytime he wanted.

Then came the real dilemma. Jerry confessed that he enjoyed masturbation more than he enjoyed sex with his wife. He wasn't sure if he could stop doing it.

Masturbation had become such a pleasurable experience for him that sex with his wife was sometimes boring in contrast. He made love to her out of duty and did a good job of it, but he looked forward to masturbating more than anything else. He felt that since no other woman was involved, it was okay for him to develop a sexual habit that brought him so much pleasure.

But he actually *had* another lover: himself! Jane had good reason to feel jealous. Some of the effects of an affair were developing in his marriage: He was robbing his wife of some of the very best feelings he could have toward her, sexual feelings. All those love units that could have been deposited in her account were squandered.

Besides, many married men I've counseled with sexual perversions—such as making obscene telephone calls and exposing oneself in public—were addicted to masturbation. Their embarrassing and illegal perversions could have been avoided if they had limited their sexual experiences to those they could enjoy with their wife. In fact, some of the most remarkable cures I've witnessed for deviant sexual conduct was with men who made their wife a permanent fixture in the sex room of their imaginary house. I recommended to Jerry that if at all possible, sexual feelings be reserved for marital lovemaking. He should avoid sexual fantasies if they didn't involve his wife, he should avoid sexual arousal if his wife were not present, and he should never experience a climax unless it was while making love to his wife.

In this case my recommendations were followed, and Jerry was able to overcome his habit of masturbating. He knew this Love Buster offended Jane, but he had done it anyway because he enjoyed it so much. In other words, he gained pleasure at her expense. When he decided to protect her feelings, he stopped masturbating. It also may have prevented him from developing an embarrassing sexual perversion. But most important, it helped build romantic love for both of them.

Don't Let Sex Destroy Your Love for Each Other

We've seen in this chapter how sex can come between a husband and wife. Anything, including sex, can drive spouses apart when it has a higher priority than the marriage itself.

Years ago, as I was trying to improve my marriage counseling technique, I abandoned emphasis on "communication" and focused attention on teaching couples the importance of meeting each other's emotional needs. The one emotional need that was identified as important by almost every couple was the need for sexual fulfillment. So I focused most of my attention on helping couples learn to have mutually enjoyable sex. I was an instant success. The couples I counseled not only restored their love for each other, but they referred many other couples who were also having problems with sexual adjustment.

Today, I balance my emphasis across many other emotional needs, but I haven't forgotten that, without a mutually fulfilling sexual relationship, a marriage is usually in serious trouble. If a marriage counselor succeeds in helping a couple create a fulfilling lovemaking experience, the couple feels that what they spent for counseling was well worth it.

The trick to solving sexual problems is to be certain that sexual desires and behavior do not come between a husband and wife. It's easy to see how in-laws, children, or a career can come between spouses, but sex can also be a very important agent of marital destruction, particularly when it is self-serving and not in the interest of both spouses.

One of the most important marital skills is the ability to make love with sexual arousal and climax. All married couples should develop that skill so they can provide sexual fulfillment for each other. I've written more on this subject in chapter 4 ("Sexual Fulfillment") of the companion book, *His Needs, Her Needs.*

Sex is a tool that helps bring a man and a woman together in marriage but can actually drive them apart when it is given a status higher than that of the marriage itself or when it is overlooked and ignored. Without a good sexual relationship, a marriage is usually in serious trouble. All married couples need to develop the skills that will help them provide sexual fulfillment for each other.

What's Next?

I've come to the end of describing common marital conflicts that are relatively easy to resolve once Love Busters are overcome. But in the next two chapters, I will describe two examples of the Love Buster of independent behavior that represent the marital conflict itself. The first is drug and alcohol addiction and the second is infidelity. These two incredibly thoughtless behaviors create a conflict that is extremely difficult to resolve, because the behavior itself is so difficult to eliminate. And even when the behaviors of substance addiction and infidelity finally are eliminated, they've often done so much damage that marriages seem doomed.

It's important to include these two chapters because substance addiction and infidelity are so pervasive in our society and lead to unending and intolerable pain. Their elimination ranks in importance among the cures of our worst and most painful diseases.

But in these two chapters, I will not emphasize how these Love Busters are overcome. A description of successful treatment methods requires much more space than is available. Instead, I'll show you how to restore your love for each other once these Love Busters have been eliminated. In most cases, they've had such a destructive effect that couples give up hope of ever being in love with each other again. But my experience demonstrates that, even in these cases, when the Love Busters are gone, romantic love can be restored.

Consider This...

1. How are selfish demands, disrespectful judgments, and angry outbursts used to force sex in marriage? What are some common excuses spouses use to justify their selfish demands, disrespectful judgments, and angry outbursts when trying to make love? Have you used any of these forms of abuse to try to force your spouse to make love to you? What is the likely outcome when a spouse is expected to adjust to lovemaking when it has not been enthusiastically agreed to?

2. When is sex independent behavior? How is that different from trying to obtain agreement through demands, disrespect, or anger? Do either of you feel you have the right to have sex independently of each other? Are you willing to give up that right for the sake of your love for each other?

3. Do you and your spouse have a conflict over sex? Is your situation at all similar to any of the examples I used? Describe your conflict as clearly as possible, with respect for each other's interests and opinions. Then use the Policy of Joint Agreement and the Four Guidelines to Successful Negotiation (described in chapter 8) to try to resolve these conflicts by creating an approach to sex that you both accept enthusiastically, and you both are willing to follow.

4. Explain why you would choose sex over your love for each other as a higher priority in marriage. Is it done intentionally after love is already lost? Do your actions make sex seem like a higher priority to you when in fact it is not?

chapter fourteen

R E S T O R I N G
L O V E
A F T E R D R U G O R
ALCOHOL ADDICTION

In marriage, as in our society as a whole, drug and alcohol addiction has played an incredibly destructive role. Besides being physically and emotionally harmful to those using addicting substances, drugs and alcohol also harm those whose lives addicts touch. Addiction makes people insensitive to the feelings of those who care for them, since they will stop at nothing to feed it—their highest priority in life is using the addicting substance. Even though they know that their use of drugs or alcohol causes their spouse intolerable pain, they continue to use—at the emotional and physical expense of their spouse.

Addiction to drugs or alcohol is a clear example of a Love Buster. Remember, a Love Buster is any habit of one spouse that causes the other to be unhappy—and there are many ways that alcoholics and drug addicts make their spouses miserable.

First, when a spouse is under the influence of drugs or alcohol, it's not a pretty sight. Intoxication undermines confidence and respect, two very important ingredients to a fulfilling marriage.

Second, addiction helps create other painful habits that make the addict a miserable marriage partner. The following are but a few of the tragic examples of behavior that characterizes addicts:

Infidelity—Infidelity is common among alcoholics and drug addicts. But the fact that a man is drunk at the time is no consolation to his grief-stricken wife who finds him in bed with another woman.

Abuse—Spouses often suffer cruel physical and emotional abuse from their addicted partners. Most instances of domestic homicide and physically disabling abuse are committed while under the influence.

Emotional Turmoil—Children of alcoholics, particularly girls, suffer greatly from the emotional turmoil of their childhood. Mental health clinics throughout America have noticed that a very high percentage of adult clients have alcoholic parents.

Molestation— An Iowa survey once found that about 70 percent of the daughters of alcoholic fathers had been sexually molested while their fathers were intoxicated. Wives of alcoholics usually know about their husbands' sexually abusive behavior toward their children and offer themselves as "bait" to prevent their abuse. The pain suffered by these women during these frightening sexual encounters is commonly reported in the safety of a therapist's office.

As tragic as they are, these examples of an addict's typical behavior are only the tip of the iceberg. If you were raised by a parent or parents who were addicts, I'm sure you can testify to the nightmare that drugs or alcohol brought to your family.

Much has been written on codependency, where an addict's spouse tries to "save" him or her but ends up making matters worse by enabling the addiction. Codependent spouses find themselves feeding a black hole, where

> **Intoxication undermines confidence and respect.**

their care is sucked in and not returned. Eventually they become exhausted and disillusioned, finding that their care does nothing but increase the strength of their spouse's addiction.

In most cases, the spouse of an addict must separate entirely, providing no care at all until the addiction is overcome. Separation not only protects the spouse of an addict from destructive behavior, but it also provides the addict with the best hope for recovery. The only one who can overcome an addiction is the addict—the spouse cannot do it for him or her.

> **The only one who can overcome an addiction is the addict.**

One of the first things I do when couples come to me for marriage counseling is to evaluate them for drug and alcohol addiction. If either is addicted at the time, I usually refer the addicted spouse to a treatment program. That's because the Love Buster of drug or alcohol addiction prevents them from overcoming any of the other Love Busters that it creates. As long as they have any contact at all with the addictive substance, hope of marital recovery is very slim.

Marriage counselors usually make a big mistake when they try to treat addiction while conducting marital therapy. Even though I've been trained to treat those with drug and alcohol addiction and have operated ten different treatment centers, I do not begin marriage counseling when a spouse is still using an addictive substance. That's because the addict simply will not follow the plan that leads to marital recovery. Besides, the treatment of drug and alcohol addiction usually requires specialized facilities and resources that most marriage counselors do not have readily available.

My job as a marriage counselor begins when an addict has been treated successfully and is sober—when he or she is no longer using the addictive substance. If the former addict slips and returns to drugs or alcohol again, therapy is suspended and he or she returns to treatment.

The spouses of addicts are usually so relieved when treatment is successful that they often think their marital troubles are over. But while addiction makes it impossible to resolve marital conflicts, sobriety itself doesn't resolve them—it simply makes them *resolvable*. Once addiction is overcome, a couple is faced with the legions of other Love Busters that were ignored in the shadow of addiction or that were created by addiction. In marital therapy, these Love Busters must be overcome one by one.

In this chapter I will describe a few of the cases I've witnessed where couples came to love each other after the addiction was overcome. They did it by meeting the emotional

> **While addiction makes it impossible to resolve marital conflicts, sobriety itself doesn't resolve them.**

needs and overcoming the Love Busters that the addiction had made impossible to achieve.

Windshield Washer Fluid to the Rescue

Herb and Char were raised in a religious setting, where the use of alcohol was strictly forbidden. The idea that Herb could become an alcoholic seemed preposterous.

It all started in high school. At a party one evening, Herb had his first taste of alcohol. He drank too much but was able to get home and in bed without his parents knowing he'd been intoxicated. The same thing happened at a few other parties, and while his closest school friends knew what was going on, none of them went to his church.

When he married Char, she never knew about his drinking in high school. And since she was opposed to the use of all alcoholic beverages, he didn't dare drink in her presence.

As an attorney with his own practice, it wasn't too difficult for Herb to figure out ways to slip gin, his favorite drink, into his office. There he would drink enough to satisfy his addiction but not enough to cause him embarrassment in the performance of his duties.

He and Char attended church regularly. He even served as a trustee. But none of his friends at church suspected his addiction.

Over a period of years, their marriage suffered. Herb spent little time at home, and when he was there, he had a low tolerance for conflict. Char walked on eggshells and wasn't able to understand what bothered him. She knew he was under constant pressure at work and thought his emotional distance was caused by a preoccupation with his cases.

Since she had never tasted alcohol herself or known anyone who drank, she never knew when he'd been drinking. He'd always been quiet at home, and his silence was a great way to avoid being discovered when he had too much to drink.

After a few years, Herb discovered a way to drink at home. He took a bottle of windshield washer fluid, emptied it, and put in a gallon of gin with blue food coloring. He kept the bottle in the closet near his garage.

It worked like a charm. Each time he felt like a drink, he stepped into the closet and took a swig.

Both at work and at home he was falling farther and farther into the pit of addiction. Char found him increasingly distant and unempathetic. He seemed to have lost his personality somewhere along the line. She spent many days in tears, reflecting on the nightmare her marriage had become. Yet she couldn't understand why it was turning out so badly.

One day it all became clear.

Herb's brother, Rob, came over to the house during the morning to borrow a baseball and bat. While he was there, he put what he thought was windshield washer fluid into his car. When he returned the ball and bat that afternoon, he also returned with some real windshield washer fluid to replace what he had taken. Herb came home that night and took a swig of the windshield washer fluid, swallowing it before he realized it wasn't gin.

Herb went into a blind panic. He thought he was about to die! Char came running, to find him more talkative than he'd been in years. "I drank this windshield cleaner! Quick, get me to the hospital!" he shouted.

She was bewildered. "Why'd you do that? Were you trying to kill yourself?"

"No, I thought it was gin! Quick, get me to the hospital!"

"You thought it was gin? I don't understand. . . ."

"*Never mind!* Just get me to the hospital, quick!"

At the hospital his stomach was pumped, and he was sent home. But Herb believed God had put him through the ordeal to teach him a lesson. He knew he was an alcoholic, so he admitted himself to a treatment program the next day. Char was overwhelmed.

While he was in treatment, Char asked me to help her sort it all out.

I explained to her how this sort of thing can happen if you create a secret second life, and I also explained how Herb's alcohol addiction affected their marriage. His unwillingness to face conflict, his emotional distance, his lack of empathy, and his apparent disinterest in her and the family were all symptoms of alcoholism. Some people have those characteristics when they're sober, but for Herb they were out of character.

Alcohol withdrawal was very difficult for Herb, and following treatment he was often tempted to sneak gin again. So he joined Alcoholics Anonymous and met three times a week for support. At the same time, he joined Char for marriage counseling.

She explained to him that she had missed intimacy and a sense of closeness in their marriage. He had been distant and difficult to reach because of his addiction. But the addiction itself had created Love Busters that prevented them from meeting each other's marital needs. The most serious of these was dishonesty. So they spent several weeks catching up on a lifetime of misinformation.

Herb went back to his high school days and explained how he'd fooled everyone, including Char. He went on to tell her about his deepest feelings—how important she and their family really were to him now that alcohol was not coming between them. He also admitted how lonely he had felt and that his dishonesty had kept him from being emotionally close to her.

When Herb learned to overcome dishonesty, everything else fell into place. He spent considerably more time with Char and was able to express his feelings openly. He had nothing to hide. It created emotional bonding that they had both been lacking for years. Within a few months, their love for each other had been restored.

The case of Herb and Char was particularly easy to treat. The Love Busters to overcome were dishonesty and independent behavior. And the worst of the independent behavior was already overcome when Herb's addiction was treated. But in most cases the list of Love Busters that remain in the marriage seems overwhelming.

The remaining cases in this chapter are more characteristic of these difficult cases. But it should be encouraging to know that even when marital conflicts seem impossible to resolve, the power of the Policy of Joint Agreement can come through to help restore romantic love.

Addiction Made Them Feel Compatible

Norm and Ruth had grown up together in the same neighborhood and fell in love while still in their early teens. He introduced her to alcohol and cigarettes, and she introduced him to marijuana while they were still in grammar school. In junior high, whenever one came across a new drug, he or she would share it with the other.

They were raised by alcoholic parents and were taught at an early age that drugs and alcohol are what life's all about. Their home lives were wretched, but they didn't realize that their parents' addiction was primarily responsible for all the sadness.

In the eleventh grade, they dropped out of school and found low-paying jobs. They made enough money to support their drug habits. Selling drugs on the side and living with his divorced mother also helped.

After a year of relative irresponsibility, Norm was kicked out of his mother's home and told to support himself. He invited Ruth to move into an apartment with him, to help cover expenses, and for a while life was rosy. That is, until Ruth became pregnant.

They married, and Ruth gave birth to Linda. Those two events wrecked everything. Drugs had always been their highest priority, and they had learned to respect each other's idol. But marriage and Linda interfered with all that.

It started with arguments over who would take care of Linda. Neither had learned much about responsibility, and parenthood came much too fast. Norm's first solution to the problem was to stay away from home. But Ruth chased him all over creation until she found him, so that strategy didn't work.

Then they tried fighting with each other. Ruth was the first to start swinging, but she was also the first to be thrown across the room. She explained to the doctor that she had fallen on the ice.

Norm was sorry he'd lost his temper but warned her not to mess with him again.

She didn't take his advice, and this time she landed in the hospital. There was no way to conceal the abuse she'd suffered, so she did the right thing: She filed a criminal complaint for assault.

Norm was arrested, and the judge convicted him but gave him a suspended sentence on the condition that he receive therapy. During the evaluation, his addiction was identified, and the counselor convinced him he needed treatment.

While in treatment, he became sober for the first time since grade school. He woke up to the world around him, saw his life for what it really was, and made an astonishing recovery. Once out of treatment, he never used drugs again, as far as I know.

Ruth, however, was still addicted. While at first she felt encouraged by his recovery, before long he wanted her to go into treatment, too. That wasn't what she had in mind. Norm was becoming a real nuisance.

While he was learning how to be more responsible, she looked less responsible in contrast. Her favorite drinking buddy was sober. Now she had to get drunk alone, and that wasn't nearly as much fun.

One night she left him with Linda, went to a bar, and met someone. By the end of the evening, she had had sex with four different men. It was the first time she'd ever cheated on Norm, and the next morning she was on the verge of suicide.

Her escapade at the bar was enough of a crisis to convince Ruth that she, too, needed treatment. The program was as successful for her as it had been for Norm, and they were ready to begin their lives together—sober!

I saw them for marriage therapy for the first time three years after her sobriety began. Their marriage was in shambles. Apart from drugs and alcohol, they had little in common. Now that they had achieved sobriety, the only thing keeping them together was their love for Linda.

The first point I made to Norm and Ruth was that marital compatibility is *created*. Because of their addiction, drugs had retarded their ability and motivation to create it in their marriage. During their years of courting and early years of marriage, conflicts were never resolved—they were simply medicated with drugs and alcohol. They hadn't rooted out Love Busters and never bothered to learn to meet each other's marital needs. Drugs seemed to be all they needed.

I explained to them that when they woke up out of their drug-induced stupor, they discovered something that should have been no surprise: they had absolutely no marital skills. Without these skills, the love units that had been artificially created by drugs quickly disappeared. Norm and Ruth didn't know how to replace them.

Second, I told them they had come to the right place! I was trained in teaching couples how to *create* compatibility in their marriages. Since they didn't love each other, they would have to commit themselves to my program for three months. After that time had passed, they could decide if they wanted to continue marriage counseling for another three months. I wasn't certain how long it would take them to build a strong marriage, and I explained that it might take up to two years.

We began with a commitment to time (see chapter 17). I explained that they needed to set aside fifteen hours each week to work on their assignments with undivided attention and without interruption.

The next step was to apply the Policy of Joint Agreement to the way they resolved conflicts. Unless they *both* felt good about a solution to a problem, they were to negotiate until they were in enthusiastic agreement.

They had problems with every Love Buster: selfish demands, disrespectful judgments, angry outbursts, dishonesty, annoying habits, and independent behavior. Systematically, each time a Love Buster would appear, it would become the target of elimination. My job was to keep them both on course and encourage them to continue until the enemy was defeated.

Eventually they could identify and overcome Love Busters without my help. No arguing or defensiveness remained. If one of them felt bad about the other's behavior, it was a Love Buster—it had to be eliminated!

Those with a history of addiction usually have a difficult time learning to be thoughtful. The self-centeredness they perfect as addicts stays with them even when they've overcome the addiction. What looks like thoughtfulness often turns out to be manipulation—they appear to be thoughtful to get their way.

True thoughtfulness accommodates the feelings of others *for their sake*. It is a willingness to *give up* behavior that is offensive to others and create new and appealing behavior. You create romantic love when you do something that is deeply appreciated. It's preserved when you avoid behavior that is deeply resented.

Over time, Norm and Ruth learned to be thoughtful. They not only eliminated the Love Busters in their marriage, they also identified and learned to meet each other's most important emotional needs. By the time marital therapy ended, about nine months later, they were in love with each other again. But this time the love units were not deposited by drugs and alcohol—they were deposited by their care for each other.

Daughters of Alcoholism

How would you like to fall in love with a person who leaves you for other women, is chronically unemployed, beats you, and molests your children? If your father had those characteristics, you would undoubtedly hate that behavior—but you would probably fail to see it in men you date.

Laura was the daughter of an alcoholic. She'd been divorced five times before she made her first appointment with me, and she was only thirty-seven. The longest any marriage lasted was three years—the shortest was three months, the time it took to get the divorce. Fortunately, she had no children.

Laura was in love again, and this time she wanted her marriage to work. She had met her fiancé, Matt, two months earlier. He'd also been divorced several times. He had five children from an assortment of wives and lovers but didn't have custody.

He was living with Laura because he was "temporarily" out of work and had also borrowed about $1,000 from her. At forty-six, he was broke and a recovering alcoholic.

When I asked them why they thought this marriage would work when the others had failed, Laura explained that this time she hoped a counselor would help them correct their past mistakes.

I told Laura I could help them correct past mistakes if they'd commit themselves to a supervised courtship of at least one year. They could not live together during that time, and Matt had to repay the money he borrowed.

Matt was furious.

We all make a living somehow. Some work for their pay, and other don't. Matt was one of those who didn't work. He made his money living with vulnerable women. But this woman was different from some of the others: He was in love with Laura, at least at the moment.

I told them to make another appointment when they were living in separate apartments. I didn't really expect to see them again, but three months later, there they were. Matt had found a job and moved into a rooming house. He had even paid back part of the money he owed Laura.

Apparently my blunt observations about Matt made sense to Laura, and she'd kicked him out. But they had enough love for each other to try my courtship plan.

Matt's marriages had failed because he was self-centered and inconsiderate. He had learned many of his inconsiderate habits while he was addicted to alcohol but never learned to overcome them after he became sober.

Laura had seen those characteristics in her father, but because she loved him, she overlooked them in the men she dated. While most women are warned by self-centered behavior, she was blinded to those signs. When men said the right words, that's all she heard.

The men Laura married were more concerned with what they'd *get* than with what they had to *give*. Their marital *needs* motivated them to marry, but their inability and unwillingness to *meet* marital needs guaranteed divorce.

The first step I took in helping to create compatibility was to overcome dishonesty. I asked Matt to reveal to Laura any part of his past that could be a threat to her. I explained that good marriages are based on trust, and if he was hiding something that could later hurt her, he should come clean now.

At the risk of losing Laura, Matt admitted he had served time in prison for assaulting one of his former wives and that he had initially been interested in Laura so she'd support him financially. He also mentioned that one of his children would not see him because he had beaten him two years earlier.

He was willing to answer any and all questions she had for him and allowed her to speak to any of his former wives, old girl-friends, children, relatives, or friends. I encouraged her to take him up on his offer and gather as much information as she could from the people who knew him at various times in his life.

I explained to them that all his irresponsible behavior, much of it done while he was using drugs, reflected a basic self-centered-ness he had not yet overcome. The fact that he'd been sober for two years was only the first step toward preparing for marriage. The destructive behavior of his past was a present threat to Laura.

Matt was encouraged to do a background check on Laura, too. Each man he spoke to told him she was great to be with until they were married, then she turned mean. Even her brother and sisters told him she was incredibly hard to get along with.

I kept reminding them that the best prediction of the future is found in the past. Unless tremendous effort is made, we all tend to make the same mistakes over and over again.

After they had both made progress in overcoming dishonesty, it became apparent that they needed to overcome all the other Love Busters as well.

With the Policy of Joint Agreement as their guide, they completed assignments that helped them gain awareness of destructive independent behavior, and then eliminated them.

Then they were ready to negotiate a fair exchange of care toward each other (see chapter 16). First, they explained what they needed from each other in marriage and then looked at what they had to offer. It became clear that they needed quite a bit but had little to offer.

I explained that care was not just a willingness but an ability to make someone happy. The only way they could actually care for each other was to learn the skills that met each other's needs.

The most obvious skill Matt needed was learning to provide consistent financial support. He also needed to learn to share all financial decisions with Laura. He'd been accustomed to putting money he earned into his own pocket. Now he put his paycheck into a joint checking account that required *both* their signatures.

Laura needed to learn to be less critical and to provide Matt with admiration. The men who had been in her life had so many serious problems that she didn't believe men *could* be admired. Even though she loved Matt, it took her quite a while to learn to compliment him. They worked on other skills as well and within a year had done a good job preparing for their marriage.

Agreements made *before* marriage are much easier to keep than those made *after* it. Since his employment was a *condition* to their marriage, Matt kept it. Laura learned to meet his needs as well, by pre-agreement. None of her former husbands would have believed the changes she made. Demands were out—admiration was in!

So far, the marriage has worked for Matt and Laura. She married a man who was very much like her father, but he was able to overcome her father's most destructive habits.

Don't Let Drug or Alcohol Addiction Destroy Your Love for Each Other

Clearly, drug or alcohol addiction comes between a husband and wife. The addiction itself is a higher priority than marriage, and as a result, the Policy of Joint Agreement cannot be followed and Love Busters prevail. But even after sobriety is achieved, Love Busters acquired during addiction persist.

In marriages where at least one spouse has been addicted, learning to overcome Love Busters is essential for marital success. But in most cases, even after sobriety, they are not overcome, and these marriages usually end in divorce.

In this chapter, I selected cases where marriages were saved because the couples learned to overcome Love Busters. In the course of counseling, they learned to overcome self-centered and inconsiderate habits. They also learned to develop skills that each of them expected of the other in marriage. The application of the Policy of Joint Agreement helped them beat the odds and build successful marriages.

Whenever I counsel a formerly addicted couple and witness their complete marital recovery, it seems like a miracle. When they first see me, their future together seems utterly hopeless. But their recovery is not a miracle at all—it is the result of steady progress toward a goal of depositing as many love units as possible and avoiding withdrawals. Anyone can do it, but it takes perseverance, and I give those who succeed a great deal of credit for ending in their generation the suffering that drug and alcohol addiction creates.

> Recovery is the result of steady progress toward a goal of depositing as many love units as possible and avoiding withdrawals.

Consider This...

1. How does addiction to drugs or alcohol help create Love Busters? How does it prevent their removal?

2. Why is it almost impossible to be addicted to drugs or alcohol if the Policy of Joint Agreement is followed in marriage?

3. Are you or have you ever been addicted to drugs or alcohol? Has the addiction contributed to the creation of Love Busters? If so, are you willing to eliminate these habits so that love can be restored to your marriage?

4. Have you ever been arrested for driving while intoxicated? Has your spouse ever suggested that your use of drugs or alcohol has interfered with your relationship? If you completely eliminated all future use of drugs or alcohol today, would you feel resentful or depressed? If the answer to any of those questions is yes, for the sake of yourself and your spouse, see a qualified chemical dependency specialist for an evaluation. If the results indicate addiction, it means drugs or alcohol is your highest priority and marital conflicts will be impossible for you to resolve until the addiction has been overcome. Follow the advice of the specialist and complete a treatment program that will help you eliminate the barriers to a fulfilling marriage.

chapter fifteen

RESTORING LOVE
AFTER INFIDELITY

Infidelity tops the list as the most destructive, cruel, and perverse example of independent behavior. As a marriage counselor, I cannot think of a more effective way to hurt your spouse than to have an affair. Yet infidelity is rampant in our society.

The vast majority of those I've counseled who have experienced both rape by a stranger and an affair by a husband have told me that the affair was much more painful. How can so many people inflict that kind of pain on the ones they promised to cherish?

There's no good excuse for infidelity.

There's no good excuse for infidelity. If a man's wife is not meeting his sexual need, finding another sex partner is the cruelest solution of all. If a woman's husband is uncommunicative or lacks the skills of affection, what right does she have to develop a romantic relationship with another man?

It's no surprise that almost all wedding vows promise to "forsake all others." Most couples tying the knot may not know much about how to have a great marriage, but they know enough to demand assurance that they will not have to go through the worst experience of their lives—their spouse's unfaithfulness.

Infidelity is an addiction to a lover. The highest priority of an unfaithful spouse is being with the lover. He or she thinks about the lover almost constantly and needs reassurance that the lover is still available. The need to be with the lover overrides the interests of their betrayed spouse, and an affair usually persists with full knowledge of the suffering it causes.

As a marriage counselor, my first reaction to infidelity was to consider reconciliation hopeless. I wanted to encourage betrayed spouses to file for divorce. But in case after case, that's not what they wanted to do—and neither did the unfaithful spouse. In spite of the affair, they wanted to reconcile. So I developed a plan that would restore love and trust to a marriage, in spite of the devastating experience of infidelity.

My plan for marital recovery after an affair cannot begin until there is no further contact with the source of addiction—the lover. As long as a lover is seen or spoken to by the unfaithful spouse, hope for marital recovery is almost zero. When a betrayed spouse asks what to do while the affair is still active, I give the same advice as I give to spouses of alcoholics—express willingness to create a fulfilling marriage after the addiction has ended, then separate with as little contact as possible.

The unfaithful spouse will either end the affair the right way by making a decision never to see or talk to the lover again, or the affair will end the wrong way—by dying a natural death. Affairs almost always die because they are nurtured by dishonesty and thoughtlessness, characteristics that eventually destroy any relationship. The passion that keeps an affair alive cannot be sustained without honesty and thoughtfulness. And once the passion has ended, the foolishness of the affair becomes apparent to the unfaithful spouse. In most cases, he or she wants to be given another chance to restore what was lost in the marriage. I prepare the betrayed spouse for that moment, and if both spouses agree, their plan for recovery can begin.

The first part of my plan is to guarantee no contact with the lover. Extraordinary precautions are agreed to and followed by the unfaithful spouse to guarantee that outcome. If contact is made with these precautions in place, the bar must be raised with even more precautions. Many of my clients have had to find new jobs and move to other states to avoid the temptation of seeing or talking to a former lover.

Next, both spouses agree to radical honesty. An affair is almost impossible without a secret second life, so all secrets are exposed. Privacy is not permitted.

If you're having an affair or if you've ever had one, don't think you're protecting your spouse by keeping it from him or her. Reveal it, even if you think the problems that helped create the affair have been resolved. It represents the first step toward protection: giving your spouse information regarding your destructive habits. You may lose some love units at first, but without honesty you'll be unable to explain your feelings completely in the future. How can your spouse ever understand your feelings if there's a part of your life you can never expose?

> **Thousands of couples have restored love and trust to their marriage, in spite of infidelity.**

The final step to my plan for recovery is to teach the couple to make Love Bank deposits and avoid their withdrawal—something every couple should do.

My complete guide to recovery after an affair is described in the book I wrote with my daughter, Dr. Jennifer Chalmers. The book is titled *Surviving an Affair*. In it, we explain each phase of the recovery process and how love and trust can eventually be completely restored.

As in the case of drug and alcohol addiction, separation from the source of addiction—the lover—is only the first step toward marital reconciliation. When an affair ends, there's a lot of rebuilding to do. Love Busters must be overcome, and marital needs must be fulfilled. In the cases that I present in this chapter, I will give you a glimpse of how this has worked for a few of the couples I've counseled.

But don't get the impression that a fulfilling marriage after an affair is a rare outcome. In spite of my initial misgivings, I've been a witness to literally thousands of couples who have restored love and trust to their marriage, in spite of the most destructive Love Buster—infidelity.

All He Wanted Was a Friend

Dean's first marriage was great until children arrived. Then he had an affair with his secretary, whom he later married.

When his second wife had a child, he had an affair with another secretary, divorced his second wife, and came to see me for counseling. He couldn't understand what made his marriages so fragile and his secretaries so appealing!

Upon examination the answer was clear.

His first wife, Sandy, had been a constant companion and devoted friend while they were dating. They'd grown up together and fully expected to be married for life. But he expected her to give him undivided attention, which she willingly did right up to the time she had their first child. Then her attention was turned from him to the child. Two more children made matters worse.

Dean wasn't happy with her shift of interest, but he loved his children and wanted them to have ther mother's attention. So he devoted his time and energy to becoming a successful businessman.

Dean's private secretary, Kim, was paid to give him attention. So she became his closest friend—and eventually his lover.

Sandy never did discover his affair with Kim. During the divorce, he told her that they'd "grown apart," and he no longer loved her. She could do nothing to stop him. But after their divorce and his eventual marriage to Kim, she suspected he might have had an affair with her.

Kim didn't continue as Dean's secretary after their marriage. Instead, she wanted to raise children, which he encouraged. But after her child arrived, Dean struck up a deep friendship with his new private secretary, Joan. Needless to say, after Kim's second child arrived, Dean was in love with Joan and divorced Kim—who was totally surprised. She didn't suspect Joan, because Dean had always told her she wasn't his type. But after their divorce, she knew he'd lied.

Before he married a third time, Dean thought it would be helpful to consult a marriage counselor. He'd already seen the pattern, and he wanted Joan to be his third and *final* wife. What could he do to avoid a third divorce?

In most cases, I do not help an unfaithful spouse and the lover create a lasting relationship. Instead, I try to help restore the broken marriage after the affair dies a natural death. But in Dean's case, both of his former wives wanted nothing to do with him, and without their cooperation, reconciliation was impossible. So I helped Dean make his next marriage his last.

As with most cases of infidelity, Dean's marital needs had not been met. His wives had shifted their attention from caring for him to caring for their children. When the change took place, Dean willingly took a backseat to children whom he loved, too. Since he wanted them to have the best care, instead of complaining, he simply had his needs met by someone else.

But to make his plan work, he had to engage in the Love Buster of dishonesty. He lied so effectively that neither of his first two wives ever suspected him of infidelity until it was too late.

He thought, *what they don't know won't hurt them.* I explained to him that what they didn't know *did* hurt them. His dishonesty was thoughtless, because it enabled him to please himself at their expense. If he had been honest about his feelings *and* his activities, the affairs would have been almost impossible to engineer.

I asked him to let Joan join the counseling sessions. I wanted Dean to describe his past marriages and subsequent affairs to her while I listened, to be sure he didn't leave anything out.

He told her that he'd lied to both of his former wives and had already lied to her about a few things. It would be difficult for him to be truthful with her, since he had established the habit of lying to all the women in his life, including his mother.

Over the next few counseling sessions, Dean explained to Joan how he felt toward his wives while having affairs with his secretaries. He cared about them and never thought the affairs would lead to divorce. He even thought they were good for his marriage, since they helped him overcome resentment from his wives' failure to meet his needs.

Romantic love was something Dean never quite understood until then. He didn't realize his feeling of love could be sustained only if his wife were meeting his emotional needs. To allow someone else to meet those needs assured the loss of his love for his wife and the creation of love toward the new woman. He began to understand that love is created and destroyed and that he had quite a bit of control over what direction it took.

His practice of dishonesty made it impossible for his former wives to adjust to his needs. He would tell them he was satisfied with their behavior, when he was not. No wonder they were shocked when he left them for someone else. They couldn't see it coming.

Another mistake was to let someone else meet his most important emotional needs. By making another woman his best friend, he was setting up a Love Bank account that was sure to eventually trigger his feeling of love. In his marriage to Joan, he had to "forsake all others," which meant he could not even have friends of the opposite sex. Joan had to be his best, and only, female friend.

I taught him to express his feelings about the way Joan treated him and encourage changes in her habits when he felt the relationship was suffering. I also recommended that they continue to spend the same amount of time together after marriage as they did while they were having an affair.

They've been married for about ten years now, and the last I heard, it has been very successful. Joan had no children, and she still plays an active role in his business as his secretary and lover . . . and best friend.

Every Woman's Dream

Cheryl wasn't getting any younger and was starting to worry if she'd ever find a man who could meet her standards. Then she discovered Nate. He was the most incredibly helpful and thoughtful person she'd ever known. He fixed her car and washing machine; he mowed her lawn; and he painted one of her rooms. He did anything she'd ask him to do. What a man!

Within a year, they were married, and two years later they had their first child. Cheryl had no idea what a mess children could make, and she was thrilled to have a husband who'd help her make dinner and clean up the house after he came home from work. Every evening she'd make a list of things for him to do that would keep him busy until bedtime. Weekends were also filled with projects. She was delighted to see so many things accomplished, but she rarely told him how much she appreciated his work. If he ever complained about all the work, she'd become angry. What had started out as thoughtful requests had become selfish demands.

Over a period of time, however, Cheryl found Nate helping the neighbors more with their household projects and helping her less. In fact, he became a legend in their neighborhood because he was such a skilled repairman and was always willing to help. The neighbors praised Nate for his helpfulness and Cheryl for her willingness to put off her own projects so that he could help others. Cheryl wasn't exactly thrilled with his being gone from home so much, but since she got some of the credit, she tolerated it.

One day, Norma, a neighbor whose husband had died three years earlier, called Cheryl to ask a favor. "I hate to bother you, but something's wrong with my water heater. I haven't been able to find a repairman to fix it this weekend, and I was wondering if Nate would be willing to look at it for me."

Now that was the right approach! "Oh, certainly," said Cheryl. "I'll send him right over."

Within an hour, Nate had fixed Norma's water heater. He also fixed the garbage disposal unit and her garage door opener. By the time he was ready to leave, she was in tears.

"I can't tell you how much this has meant to me. Since Roger died, I've had one problem after another, with no one to help me. And I've been so lonely. You've made me happier than I've been in years." She gave him a big bear hug.

Nate was speechless, but hugged her back. As he left, he told her to call him if she ever needed help.

The next Saturday Norma didn't call Cheryl for permission to use Nate. She called him instead, and he was right over. He helped her clean up a pile of leaves that had been rotting in a corner of the front yard for two years.

When he was ready to go, she invited him inside for coffee, and they spent three hours talking to each other. She shared many of the struggles a widow faces, among them, her loneliness and sexual frustration. He shared some of his problems, which included

Cheryl's constant demands and lack of appreciation. By the end of the conversation, they were making love.

Slowly but surely, Cheryl's love units had been withdrawn from Nate's Love Bank. Every time she demanded work from him, he felt offended. Once in a while he would tell her how he felt. When he did, she'd remind him that he didn't mind helping all the neighbors, why wouldn't he help his own wife? A compliment would have meant so much to him. But she took his help for granted.

Norma, on the other hand, showered him with praise, cooked for him when he came over, and made love to him besides.

While Nate's excuse for visiting Norma was that he helped her with projects, he eventually spent very little of his time working. Instead they talked and made love. When he did fix something, she was with him, saying how much she appreciated his effort.

Cheryl didn't suspect a thing at first. When Nate came home, he got right to work on her projects and didn't go to bed until he completed them. Their sexual relationship didn't suffer either.

Over the next six months, however, Nate began to neglect his own home. Cheryl's lists of projects began to gather dust, and Nate visited with Norma several times a week. She praised every effort he made on her behalf, and he just loved all the attention he was getting from her. They made love two or three times a week but were very careful so that they wouldn't be discovered. Love units poured into both of their Love Bank accounts.

Cheryl eventually became suspicious, particularly when their own sexual relationship started to fall apart. Nate claimed to have lost interest in sex. She finally confronted him, but he lied about his relationship with Norma.

Over the next two years, Cheryl tried very hard to determine if Nate was having an affair. She never caught them making love, but she appeared at Norma's house unannounced on several occasions. Nate finally became alarmed with her increasingly suspicious behavior. He told her if it would make her happy, he simply wouldn't see Norma any longer. She replied that it would certainly help and that apparent concession made her much more relaxed—at least until Norma's neighbor called several weeks later.

Nate and Norma were seen driving into Norma's garage, her neighbor reported. She thought Cheryl should know about it.

Cheryl walked right over and found them together. Now she *knew* Nate was having an affair and insisted that they see a counselor. He agreed to go with her but continued to deny the affair.

My first conversation with Nate was typical for those having an affair. He simply couldn't be pinned down. He told me that his wife was perfect; he was happily married, and he merely had compassion for a widow in the neighborhood. But the evidence was so overwhelming that I knew he was lying to me.

I told Cheryl I wanted to counsel Nate alone for a few weeks before I could begin marriage counseling, and they agreed to that plan. The next time I saw Nate, he told me about his relationship with Norma but made me promise I wouldn't tell Cheryl about it. We discussed the pros and cons of marital reconciliation, and within three weeks Nate decided to save his marriage.

His primary motive for reconciliation was his children—by then they had three. He realized he had a lot to lose in a divorce. Besides, Cheryl was more attractive to him than Norma, and they had more interests in common. He knew he wouldn't marry Norma, even if he divorced.

The first assignment I gave Nate was to overcome the Love Buster of dishonesty. So he admitted to Cheryl that she'd been right about his affair but that he'd decided to end his relationship with Norma and rebuild his marriage. Even though she had suspected it all along, she did what most spouses do when they first discover an affair—she became very angry and depressed. At first, she wasn't even sure she wanted to save their marriage, or that she could ever trust Nate again. But eventually she agreed to give their marriage a chance to succeed.

Since affairs are incredibly difficult to end, Nate had to create extraordinary precautions to avoid ever seeing or talking to Norma again. Since she lived in their neighborhood, I recommended they move away.

Nate and Cheryl had invested thousands of dollars and hours into their home, and it was hard for either of them to even think of selling it. But I felt that the home represented a way of life that had enslaved him, and a new home would give them a fresh start.

I also mentioned that I didn't feel he could be trusted living so close to Norma, and Cheryl would be constantly suspicious.

They eventually sold their home and moved about thirty-five miles away, far enough so that he could avoid seeing Norma but close enough to his job so he wouldn't need to find another.

We began marriage counseling with an emphasis on honesty. Nate never had shared his deepest feelings with Cheryl, and he used work to help him remain superficial. I taught him how to talk to her about what he thought and felt and recommended that, for the next few weeks, he spend all his leisure time at home talking rather than working.

In his conversations with Cheryl, he told her how unhappy he'd been with her lack of appreciation. She explained that she had the greatest admiration for him but had simply neglected to tell him how she felt.

Cheryl's list of projects for him to complete had become a selfish demand. She had to learn to ask how he felt about doing them, and Nate needed to tell the truth about his emotional reactions. To her surprise, she discovered that when he came home from work, he wanted her to have his dinner ready and the house cleaned. He preferred watching television to doing one of her projects.

When he did agree to do something for her, she saw it as an act of care on his part, and she learned to compliment him for it.

Instead of spending all his time on projects around the house, Nate used some of it to be alone with Cheryl, where they could meet each other's most important marital needs. They already had countless interests in common and had little difficulty enjoying recreational activities together. Their sexual relationship had never been a problem until Norma came along. By limiting home projects to those he really felt like doing and receiving appreciation from Cheryl whenever he did them, Nate's love for her was quickly restored.

Two years later Cheryl told me that her marriage was better than it had ever been and that her mistrust of Nate had disappeared. She didn't get quite as many projects done, but she was much happier than she had been when every task had been completed—and so was Nate.

Don't Let Infidelity Destroy Your Love

Dishonesty is the primary agent of infidelity. Without it, it's extremely difficult to get an affair off the ground. But infidelity itself is another Love Buster. As in the case of drug and alcohol addiction, it's a destructive independent behavior.

Infidelity is the result of allowing important marital needs to be met outside marriage. It's often motivated by the fact that those needs are not being met inside marriage. But whatever the reason, it creates untold pain and sorrow for an entire family.

In this chapter, I do not explain how couples learn to end infidelity (I do that in my book *Surviving an Affair*). Instead, I selected three cases to illustrate the process of restoring romantic love once infidelity has ended. As long as infidelity is still in process, I don't begin marriage counseling. Infidelity is such a powerful barrier to the resolution of marital conflicts that there is no way to resolve them while it persists. But once an affair is over, marriage can be restored to a level of satisfaction never before achieved.

Consider This...

1. Which Love Buster provides the opportunity for infidelity? Which Love Buster *is* infidelity? What other Love Busters can it create?

2. How does the Policy of Joint Agreement prevent infidelity?

3. Have you ever engaged in infidelity? Have you ever discussed it with anyone? Have they encouraged you to keep it a secret or confess it to your spouse? If you've kept it a secret until now, are you willing to eliminate the Love Buster of dishonesty in your marriage?

4. Have you ever had fantasies about having an affair? Have you ever fallen in love with someone else? Have you ever been infatuated with someone else? Have you ever been tempted to have an affair? If you fail to tell your spouse about these "close calls," you're engaging in dishonesty. Are you willing to restore honesty to your marriage?

BONUS
CHAPTERS

chapter sixteen

BUILDING
ROMANTIC LOVE
WITH CARE

When Jo and Pete married, the most clearly understood part of their wedding vows was that they would care for each other throughout their lifetime. They understood that care means more than a feeling; it's a commitment to make every reasonable effort to meet each other's needs.

While they were still dating, Pete told Jo that if she married him he'd make her the happiest woman in history. She would be the center of his life, and his world would revolve around her. Jo knew that if the marriage was to work she had to treat him the same way. She had to make him happy as well and make every effort to meet his needs.

While they each had the right intentions and the correct understanding of care as a marital commitment, they did not understand how difficult it would be to *learn* to care for each other. They both thought care was something you could decide to do, and that once the decision was made, acts of care would be spontaneous.

But because their care for each other was not carefully planned, it fell far short of their expectations. Both Jo and Pete felt neglected.

Care is the *willingness* to change your own personal habits to meet the emotional needs of the person you have chosen to marry and then *making sure* that those habits are effective. Jo and Pete had the willingness part of care right—but they failed to *deliver* the care they had promised.

> **Care**
>
> The willingness to change your personal habits to meet the emotional needs of your spouse and to make sure those habits are effective.

There are some people who object to the quality of care I recommend in marriage. They think that by changing personal habits rather than doing what comes naturally, they sacrifice their true identity—they become robots. But care does not cause anyone to lose identity or become a robot. Our habits are very often developed through chance and are not necessarily a reflection of our character or our values in life. When we change them to accommodate our spouse's needs, we are actually controlling our behavior to fit our character.

But the process of discarding old habits and developing new ones can be difficult and stressful. This is one reason well-intentioned couples often fail in their efforts to learn more accommodating habits. It's not only difficult for us to change for our spouse, but it is also difficult to put our spouse through the stress of making changes to accommodate us.

Jo and Pete were very compatible when they were married. They got along with each other extremely well and felt that they were made for each other. It did not occur to them that after marriage their prior acts of care would fade away if they were not deliberately nurtured. Their marriage gave them the illusion that their care was somehow on autopilot and that the marriage itself would guarantee that care.

> **The process of discarding old habits and developing new ones can be difficult and stressful.**

But life can get very complicated after marriage, especially when children arrive. It's easy to understand why spouses become distracted and focus their attention away from each other. And yet, failure to meet each other's emotional needs with consistency and effectiveness will ruin any marriage.

But care is much more than just learning to meet another's needs at one point in time and then sustaining those particular habits for a lifetime; it also requires the willingness and ability to meet changing needs—adjusting to a moving target. Jo's emotional needs changed after their first child arrived—she needed a husband who would be committed to the development and education of little Jessica. She had always assumed that

Growing apart simply means that a couple has not grown together.

when the time was right, he would be a good father. But it turned out to be something that he had to learn to do—it wasn't as natural as she thought it would be.

One of the more popular reasons cited for divorce today is that a husband and wife have "grown apart from each other." One of them may have completed an education, while the other did not. One may have developed a new career interest, and the other did not join in that interest. Children can also impact a couple's interests and send them in different directions.

At the time of our marriage, my wife, Joyce, dropped out of college after completing her second year while I went on to earn a Ph.D. degree. Did that make us incompatible? Not a bit, because we were able to make adjustments in our care for each other. But most couples do not make those adjustments. Instead of learning how to meet each other's needs under new circumstances, couples assume that their instincts will carry them. Then when instinct seems to fail, they conclude that they must be incompatible.

Growing apart simply means that a couple has not grown together. They have let nature take its course, and new circumstances and new needs that are inevitable in marriage are left unmet, because no effort has been made to create new habits to meet them.

Extramarital affairs and multiple marriages represent one strategy in adjusting to the failure to meet important emotional needs. Over a period of time, as needs change and a relationship falls apart, a new relationship is developed with another individual who happens to be prepared to meet those new needs.

If we were unable to adjust to each other's changes in life, then I suppose multiple marriages would be about the only solution to satisfying relationships. But we have an enormous capacity for adjustment. Learning to meet each other's marital needs is far less destructive and complicated than going through the agonizing ritual of divorce and remarriage.

In this book, I have shown you how to avoid making Love Bank withdrawals. But there is another side to the coin—Love Bank deposits. Without deposits, you have no hope of ever being in love with each other.

In a companion book, *His Needs, Her Needs: Building an Affair-proof Marriage*, I focus attention on making those Love Bank deposits. In this bonus chapter and the next, I will summarize some of the main points I make in *His Needs, Her Needs*.

How do you learn to care for your spouse so effectively that he or she will be in love and stay in love with you? There are two essential steps you must take.

Discover Your Spouse's Most Important Needs

The first step in learning to care for your spouse is discovering his or her emotional needs and identifying the most important ones.

Men and women usually have the same basic emotional needs, but their priorities are often very different. What is most important to men is usually much less important to women and vice-versa. That makes this first step more complex and difficult than you might first think.

When men and women don't understand each other's most important emotional needs, they tend to meet those that are most important to them—husbands try to meet needs most important to men, and wives try to meet needs most important to women. In most cases, that strategy completely misses the mark.

ACTION STEP

Discover your spouse's most important emotional needs.

When the best efforts of a husband and wife go unappreciated and needs are not met besides, they often give up trying. If they had only directed their efforts in the right places, they would have been effective *and* appreciated.

270

My experience as a marriage counselor has helped me identify ten of the most important emotional needs that can be met in marriage. While all ten are important, five are of critical importance to most men, and the other five are of critical importance to most women. All these categories may not apply to your marriage, but they can help you begin a discussion with your spouse to identify each other's most important emotional needs—the ones that when met will deposit so many love units that it will cause you to be in love with each other.

His Needs

A man's five most important needs in marriage tend to be:

1. *Sexual fulfillment.* His wife meets this need by becoming a terrific sexual partner. She studies her own sexual response to recognize and understand what brings out the best in her; then she shares this information with him, and together they learn to have a sexual relationship that both find enjoyable.
2. *Recreational companionship.* She develops an interest in the recreational activities he enjoys most and tries to become proficient at them. If she finds she cannot enjoy them, she encourages him to consider other activities that they can enjoy together. She becomes his favorite recreational companion, and he associates her with his most enjoyable moments of relaxation.
3. *Physical attractiveness.* She keeps herself physically fit with diet and exercise, and she wears her hair, makeup, and clothes in a way that he finds attractive and tasteful. He is attracted to her in private and proud of her in public.
4. *Domestic support.* She creates a home that offers him a refuge from the stresses of life. She manages household responsibilities in a way that encourages him to spend time at home enjoying his family.
5. *Admiration.* She understands and appreciates him more than anyone else. She reminds him of his value and achieve-

ments and helps him maintain self-confidence. She avoids criticizing him. She is proud of him, not out of duty, but from a profound respect for the man she chose to marry.

When a man is married to a woman who has learned to meet his most important needs, he'll find her irresistible. Love units are deposited into his Love Bank in such great numbers that he finds himself helplessly in love. That's because the fulfillment of these needs is essential to his happiness.

Her Needs

A woman's five most important needs in marriage tend to be:

1. *Affection.* Her husband tells her that he loves her with words, cards, flowers, gifts, and common courtesies. His hugs and kisses are symbols of his willingness to be there for her when she needs him and that he is deeply concerned about her welfare. His acts of affection are repeated daily, creating an environment that clearly and repeatedly expresses his love for her.
2. *Conversation.* He sets aside time every day to talk to her. They may talk about events in their lives, their children, their feelings, or their plans. But whatever the topic, she enjoys the conversation because it is never judgmental and always informative and constructive. She talks to him as much as she would like, and he responds with interest.
3. *Honesty and openness.* He tells her everything about himself, leaving nothing out that might later surprise her. He describes his positive and negative feelings, events of his past, his daily schedule, and his plans for the future. He never leaves her with a false impression and is truthful about his thoughts, feelings, intentions, and behavior.
4. *Financial support.* He assumes the responsibility to house, feed, and clothe his family. If his income is insufficient to provide essential support, he resolves the problem by upgrading his skills to increase his salary. He does not work

long hours, keeping himself from his wife and family, but he is able to provide necessary support by working a forty- to forty-five-hour week. While he encourages his wife to pursue a career, he does not depend on her salary for family living expenses.

5. *Family commitment.* He commits sufficient time and energy to the moral and educational development of the children. He reads to them, engages in sports with them, and takes them on frequent outings. He reads books and attends lectures with his wife on the subject of child development so that they will do a good job training their children. He and his wife discuss training methods and objectives until they agree. He does not proceed with any plan of training or discipline without her approval. He recognizes that his care of the children is critically important to her.

When a woman is married to a man who has learned to meet her most important emotional needs, she'll find him irresistible. Love units are deposited in her Love Bank in such great numbers that she finds herself helplessly in love. That's because the fulfillment of these needs is essential to her happiness.

Identify Your Needs

Of course, *these categories do not apply to everyone.* Some men look at my "man's needs" list and throw out two of them to make room for two from my "woman's needs" list. Some women do the same. Believing that these categories are right for everyone is a big mistake!

I simply suggest these needs to help you start the process of identifying what you need most in marriage. It is simply a way of helping you think through what makes you the happiest and most fulfilled. I also want you to realize that what a man needs in marriage is usually quite different from what a woman needs. That makes the whole process of discovering your needs very personal; it's something you must do for yourself. Then you should reveal your discovery to your spouse.

Prioritizing Needs

To make this process more accurate and reliable, I suggest that you first select the need you think is the most important for you. Pretend that, in your marriage, it's the only need you'll have met. The other nine needs will *not* be met. What need would you select if you knew you would never get the rest? That's probably your most important emotional need. When it's met, the most love units are deposited.

Then do the same for need number two. If you will *not* get the other eight needs met, what two would you pick? Continue this process until you've picked five. Those are the needs you want your spouse to be particularly proficient in meeting.

Take a hard look at the needs you left behind. For example, if you did not include financial support, you should not expect your spouse to earn a dime! Are the needs you chose more important to you than that one? How about physical attractiveness? If your spouse neglects her appearance, gains weight, or dresses carelessly, what would your emotional reaction be?

Some of my clients tell me that all ten are of critical importance. They could not survive a marriage that neglected any of them. But my experience has shown me that if you can learn to do an outstanding job meeting only the *five* most important needs, you build more romantic love than if you do a mediocre job on all ten.

Most of us cannot be outstanding at everything; we must pick what is most important and concentrate on that. If you want to build romantic love with your spouse, be proficient at meeting only the *most important* emotional needs.

Once you and your spouse have communicated your five most important emotional needs to each other, you're ready for the second step in learning to care for each other.

ACTION STEP

Learn to meet your spouse's most important emotional needs.

Learn to Meet Your Spouse's Most Important Needs

Learning to meet your spouse's five most important marital needs usually requires hundreds, maybe thousands of new habits. But the habits all eventually come together to form a whole. It's like learning a part in a play: You begin by learning each line, each motion, each cue, but eventually it comes together. It's naturally whole; it doesn't seem like hundreds of little pieces.

To build the myriad of habits necessary to meet your spouse's needs, you must have a carefully planned strategy. *His Needs, Her Needs* provides a few strategies for you to consider for each of the ten needs. And you may benefit from professional help as well. The need for financial support, for example, may require you to consult a vocational counselor. The need for sexual fulfillment may require help from a sex therapist.

However you develop it, a strategy—a plan—should be created that has a good chance of improving your ability to meet the needs your spouse identified as most important.

Once you implement your plan, you may need someone to report to for accountability. Your spouse is not a good choice, because your mentor may need to criticize your effort, and your spouse should not be forced into that role. A pastor or professional counselor may be better suited.

If you are successful, you will see it in his or her eyes and in the way your spouse talks to you and responds to you. The "look of love" is unmistakable.

I view marriage as a profession. The skills I learn are designed to meet my spouse's most important emotional needs, and if I'm successful, she'll be in love with me. If she's not in love with me, I'm probably at fault and need to develop new skills. Of course, if I'm not in love with her and I've been honest about my feelings, it's her problem to solve.

As I've said earlier, *compatibility is created.* As a couple increases the number of habits that meet each other's marital needs, it improves their compatibility and their romantic love for each other.

Compatibility is created.

We have such an opportunity in marriage to give each other exactly what we need. Many couples squander that. Don't let it happen to you!

chapter seventeen

BUILDING
ROMANTIC LOVE
WITH TIME

Before Jo and Pete were married, they spent the majority of their free time together. Her girlfriends knew that spending time with him was one of her highest priorities. Whenever they invited her somewhere, she would first check to see if she'd be missing an opportunity to be with Pete. Her girlfriends thought it was silly. On some occasions, she even broke dates with her girlfriends if he had time to be with her.

Pete did the same. Soon he found that many of the things he enjoyed doing were abandoned because he was spending so much time with Jo.

They tried to see each other on a daily basis. On days when they couldn't get together, they called each other and sometimes talked for hours. When they were together, they gave each other lots of attention.

The total amount of time spent with each other in an average week was fifteen to twenty-five hours. This included time on the telephone. But they weren't counting. They just took advantage of every opportunity.

After they were married Jo and Pete were with each other more often, but a change took place in the quality of their time together—they spent much less time giving each other attention. Pete came home and watched television all evening. Sometimes he barely said a word to Jo.

> **Policy of Undivided Attention**
> Give undivided attention to your spouse a minimum of fifteen hours each week, meeting his or her most important emotional needs.

Before they were married, they scheduled time to be with each other. But after marriage, they felt that "dates" were not as important, so their time together was incidental to other priorities.

Courtship is a custom that gives people a chance to prove they can meet each other's marital needs. If enough love units are deposited, love is the result and marriage usually follows. Without time together, the test would fail because it takes time to deposit enough love units to create the feeling of love.

As a reminder to couples who tend to neglect spending time together, I've suggested the Policy of Undivided Attention: *Give undivided attention to your spouse a minimum of fifteen hours each week, meeting his or her most important emotional needs.*

One difficult aspect of marriage counseling is scheduling time for it. The counselor must work evenings and weekends because most couples will not give up work to make their appointments. Then the counselor must schedule around a host of evening and weekend activities that take the husband and wife in opposite directions.

> **It takes time to deposit enough love units to create the feeling of love.**

Another difficult aspect of marriage counseling is arranging time for the couple to be together to carry out their first assignment. Many couples think that a counselor will solve their problems with a weekly conversation in his or her office. It doesn't occur to them that it's what they do after they leave the office that saves their marriage. To accomplish anything, they must reserve time to be together. This may be painful, but eventually they get the point and little by little they rearrange their lives to include each other.

ACTION STEP

Establish privacy so you can give each other undivided attention.

It's incredible how many couples have tried to talk me out of the Policy of Undivided Attention. They begin by trying to convince me that it's impossible. Then they go on to the argument that it's impractical. Then they try to show me that it's impractical for *them*. But in the end, they usually agree that without scheduling at least fifteen hours for undivided attention, they cannot possibly achieve romantic love.

To help me explain how the Policy of Undivided Attention is to be applied in marriage, I've broken it down into three parts: privacy, objectives, and amount.

Privacy

The time you plan to be together should not include children (who are awake), relatives, or friends. Establish privacy so that you are able to give each other undivided attention.

It is essential for you as a couple to spend time alone. When you have time alone, you have a much greater opportunity to meet each other's emotional needs and make Love Bank deposits. Without privacy, undivided attention is almost impossible, and without undivided attention, you are unable to meet the emotional needs of affection, conversation, and sexual fulfillment.

First, I recommend that you learn to be together without your children present. I'm amazed at how difficult this is for couples, especially when the children are very young. Many couples don't think that children interfere with their privacy. To them, an evening with their children is privacy. And, technically, when they are with their children they are meeting at least one emotional need—the need for family commitment. The problem is that if they are never together without their children, they are not able to meet other needs that usually have a higher priority.

Of course, they know they can't make love with children around. But I believe that the presence of children prevents much more than lovemaking. When children are present, they interfere with affection and intimate conversation that are crucial needs in marriage. Besides, affection and intimate conversation usually

278

lead to lovemaking, and without them, you will find that your lovemaking suffers. And if your recreational companionship always includes your children, you will be so restricted in what you find mutually enjoyable that you will be tempted to make one of the biggest mistakes in marriage—spending your most enjoyable leisure time apart from each other.

Second, I recommend that friends and relatives not be with you in your time together. This may mean that after everything has been scheduled, there is little time left for friends and relatives. If that's the case, you're too busy, but at least you will not be sacrificing your love for each other to have time with friends and relatives.

Third, I recommend that you understand what giving undivided attention means. It's what you did when you were dating. You probably would not have married if you had ignored each other on dates. You may have parked your car somewhere just to be completely alone and to rid yourselves of all distractions. That's the quality of undivided attention I'm referring to here.

When you see a movie together, the time you spend watching it would not usually count toward your time for undivided attention—unless you behave like the couple who sat in front of my wife and me last week. It's the same with television and sporting events. You should engage in these recreational activities together, but the time I want you to commit yourselves to is very clearly defined—it's the time you pay close attention to each other.

Now that you're alone with each other, what should you do with this time? The second part of the Policy of Undivided Attention deals with objectives.

Objectives

During this time, create activities that will meet your most important emotional needs: affection, sexual fulfillment, conversation, and recreational companionship.

Romance for most men is sex and recreation; for most women it's affection and conversation. When all four come together, men and women

ACTION STEP

Create activities that will meet your most important emotional needs.

279

alike call it romance, and they deposit the most love units possible. That makes these categories somewhat inseparable whenever you spend time together. My advice is to try to combine them all.

After marriage, women often try to get their husband to meet their emotional needs for conversation and affection without meeting their husband's needs for sex and recreational companionship. Men, on the other hand, want their wife to meet their needs for sexual fulfillment and recreational companionship without meeting her needs for affection and conversation. Neither strategy works very well. Women often resent having sex without affection and conversation first, and men resent being conversant and affectionate with no hope for sex or recreation. By combining the fulfillment of all four needs into a single event, however, both spouses have their needs met and enjoy the entire time together.

> Your time for undivided attention should be the best time of the week for both of you.

A man should never assume that, just because he is in bed with his wife, sex is there for the taking. In many marriages, that mistake creates resentment and confusion. Most men eventually learn that if they spend the evening giving their wife their undivided attention, with conversation and affection, sex becomes a very natural and mutually enjoyable way to end the evening.

But there are some women who don't see the connection either. They want their husbands to give them the most attention when there is no possibility for sex. In fact, knowing that affection and intimate conversation often lead a man to wanting sex, they try hardest to be affectionate when they are out in a crowd. That tactic can lead to just as much resentment in a man as nightly sexual "ambushes" create in a woman. Take my word for it, the fulfillment of the four needs of affection, conversation, recreational companionship, and sexual fulfillment is best when they are met together.

Your time for undivided attention should be the best time of the week for both of you. But if you have not been "dating" lately, it may not begin that way. If you do not yet know how to meet each other's emotional needs, you may find your time together boring or even unpleasant. This is particularly true if your conversation includes demands, disrespect, and angry outbursts. If you want to meet the need for conversation, you must learn to avoid hurting each other with what you say.

But if you do not schedule this time to be together now, you will never have the opportunity to learn how to make it enjoyable for both of you and how to avoid making it unpleasant. The time that you schedule for each other will eventually become the best time of the week, when you have finally learned to meet each other's needs and avoid hurting each other.

Don't waste precious weeks, months, and years hoping that somehow your relationship will improve. Take the first step toward insuring your success by actually putting each other in your schedules. And once you are there, do whatever it takes to make it the best fifteen hours of your week.

But why do I suggest fifteen hours each week for undivided attention? Won't five hours work just as well? The next part of the Policy of Undivided Attention helps explain why I am so adamant in encouraging couples to spend that amount of time alone with each other.

Amount

Choose a number of hours that reflects the quality of your marriage. If your marriage is satisfying to you and your spouse, plan fifteen hours. But if you suffer marital dissatisfaction, plan thirty hours each week or more, until marital satisfaction is achieved. Keep a permanent record of your time together.

How much time do you need to sustain the feeling of love for each other? Believe it or not, there really is an answer to this question, and it depends on the health of a marriage. If a couple is deeply in love with each other and find that their marital needs are being met, I have found that about fifteen hours each week of undivided attention is usually enough to sustain their love, as long as they use the time to meet each other's emotional needs.

ACTION STEP

Choose a number of hours that reflects the quality of your marriage.

When a marriage is this healthy, either it's a new marriage or the couple has already been spending that amount of time with each other throughout their marriage. Without fifteen hours of undivided attention each week, a couple simply can't do what it takes to sustain their feeling of love for each other.

When I apply the fifteen-hour principle to marriages, I usually recommend that the time be evenly distributed throughout the week, two to three hours each day. When time is bunched up—all hours only on the weekend—good results are not as predictable. Spouses need to be emotionally reconnected almost on a daily basis to meet each other's most important emotional needs.

How can a workaholic businessman find time to have an affair? The man who couldn't be home for dinner because of his busy schedule is suddenly able to fit in a midafternoon rendezvous three times a week! How does he get his work done?

Fifteen hours a week is often not enough time for couples that are not yet in love.

The answer, of course, is that he had the time all along. It's simply a matter of priorities. He could just as easily have spent the time with his wife. Then they would have been in love with each other. Instead, he's in love with someone else, all because of a shortsighted schedule.

The reason I have so much difficulty getting couples to spend time with each other is that when I first see them for counseling, they have forgotten how to have a good time. Their relationship does not do anything for them, and the time spent with each other seems like a total waste at first. But if I can motivate them to schedule the time together every week, they use that time to learn to re-create the romantic experiences that first nurtured their love relationship. Without scheduling that time, they have little hope of restoring the love they once had for each other.

But fifteen hours a week is often not enough time for couples that are not yet in love. To help them jump-start their relationship, I usually suggest increasing the number of hours spent alone with each other so that they can learn more quickly the skills that will meet each other's emotional needs. I sometimes suggest abandoning most other responsibilities so that they can spend twenty-five or thirty hours a week of undivided attention until they can meet each other's emotional needs almost effortlessly. By the time that happens, they are both in love with each other again. In some cases I have even recommended a two- or three-week vacation together so they can give each other undivided attention around the clock.

Your time together is too important to the security of your marriage to neglect. It's more important than time spent doing anything else during the week, including time with your children and your job. Remember that the fifteen hours you should set aside is only equivalent to a part-time job. It isn't time you don't have; it's time you will use for something much less important, if you don't use it for each other.

If you have not been in the habit of spending fifteen hours a week for undivided attention, it will mean that something else that takes fifteen hours will have to go. But you have about 110 total waking hours each week that are spent doing something, and if you schedule your time productively, you will find that the fifteen hours you lose will have been spent on your least important goals. And you will put in its place fifteen hours for your most important goal. Think of it—your highest priority will take the place of your lowest priority. It will radically change your life for the better, because in exchange for something that really isn't that important to you, you will be investing in the single most important factor in your life—your relationship with your spouse.

It should be obvious to you that it will take time to meet most of each other's emotional needs, and unless you schedule that time, you simply won't get the job done. Time has a way of slipping away if you don't set it aside for important objectives. And what objective is more important than you and your spouse being in love with each other?

To help you plan your week with each other's emotional needs in mind, I encourage you to meet with your spouse at 3:30 Sunday afternoon to look over each other's schedule for the coming week. That's the time for you to be sure that you have provided for each other. And while you're at it, try to plan a little extra time just in case an emergency arises that prevents you from being together the full fifteen hours you originally plan.

You and your spouse fell in love with each other because you met some of each other's most important emotional needs, and the only way to stay in love is to keep meeting those needs. Even when the feeling of love begins to fade, or when it's gone entirely, it's not necessarily gone for good. It can be recovered whenever you both go back to being an expert at making Love Bank deposits.

As you've seen in this book, though, meeting important emotional needs is only half of the story. While that's how couples make the most Love Bank deposits, they must be sure that they're not depositing into a sieve. They must also avoid making Love Bank withdrawals.

Learn to become experts at making Love Bank deposits, and then keep your balances secure by avoiding Love Busters.

In this book, I have introduced to you some of the most common ways that spouses hurt each other. Unless you protect each other from your destructive habits and instincts, you will hurt each other so much that eventually your Love Bank accounts will be in the red. Instead of loving each other, you will hate each other. Don't let that happen to you. Instead, learn to become experts at making Love Bank deposits and then keep your balances secure by avoiding Love Busters.

What does it take to make your marriage *sizzle*?

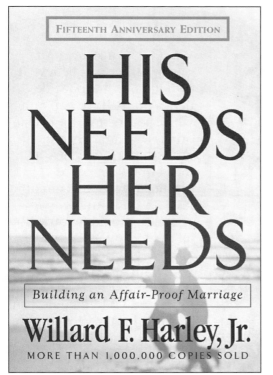

In this classic book, Dr. Willard F. Harley, Jr. identifies the ten most vital needs of men and women and shows husbands and wives how to satisfy those needs in their spouses. He provides guidance for becoming irresistible to your spouse and for loving more creatively and sensitively, thereby eliminating the problems that often lead to extramarital affairs.

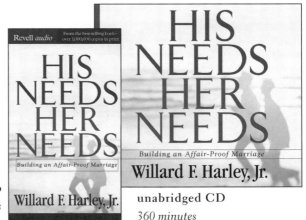

unabridged audio
360 minutes

unabridged CD
360 minutes

Fall in Love, Stay in Love

A comprehensive look at Dr. Harley's total program for building and sustaining a good marriage.

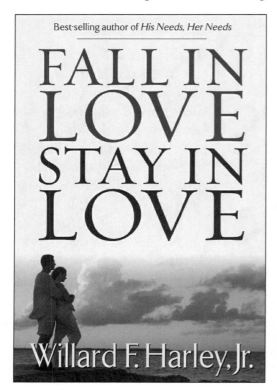

Whether you know it or not, whether you believe it or not, your marriage depends on the love you and your spouse have for each other. Dr. Harley has spent more than thirty years helping couples create, re-create, and sustain romantic love. In this foundational book, he provides you with all the tools you'll need to fall in love and stay in love with your spouse.

Step into Dr. Harley's office and let him guide you through his proven steps to building a marriage that lasts a lifetime.

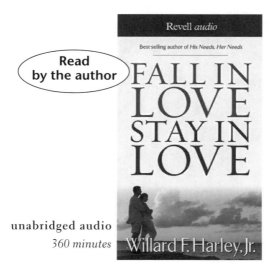

Read by the author

unabridged audio

360 minutes

More books *by* Dr. Willard F. Harley Jr.

Five Steps to Romantic Love
A Workbook for Readers of Love Busters *and* His Needs, Her Needs

A helpful workbook containing all the contracts, questionnaires, inventories, and worksheets Dr. Harley recommends in *Love Busters* and *His Needs, Her Needs*.

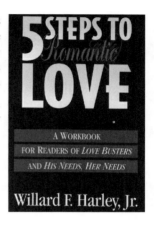

I Cherish You
Words of Wisdom from His Needs, Her Needs

Give others the knowledge to build a lifelong, romantic love! *I Cherish You* highlights the concepts of *His Needs, Her Needs* in a beautiful gift format—perfect for celebrating a wedding or anniversary, or just to say "I love you."

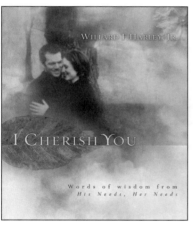

Surviving an Affair

A guide to understanding and surviving every aspect of infidelity—from the beginning of an affair through the restoration of the marriage.

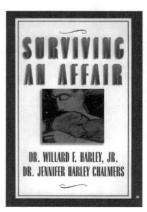

Visit Dr. Harley's Web Site—
http://www.marriagebuilders.com

"Building Marriages to Last a Lifetime"

Dr. Harley has saved thousands of marriages from the pain of unresolved conflict and the disaster of divorce. His successful approach to building marriages can help you too.

Why do people fall in love? Why do they fall out of love? What do they want most in marriage? What drives them out of marriage? How can a bad marriage become a great marriage? Dr. Harley's basic concepts address these and other important aspects of marriage building.

At www.marriagebuilders.com Dr. Harley introduces visitors to some of the best ways to overcome marital conflicts and some of the quickest ways to restore love. From the pages of "Basic Concepts" and articles by Dr. Harley to the archives for his weekly Q&A columns and information about upcoming seminars, this site is packed with useful material.

Let Marriage Builders help you build a marriage to last a lifetime!